COMMON CORE MATHEMATICS

NEW YORK EDITION

Grade 3, Module 3: Multiplication and Division with Units of 0, 1, 6-9, and Multiples of 10

COMMON CORE™ *consider the source*

JB JOSSEY-BASS™
A Wiley Brand

Cover design by Chris Clary

Published by Jossey-Bass
A Wiley Brand
One Montgomery Street, Suite 1200, San Francisco, CA 94104-4594—www.josseybass.com

ISBN: 978-1-118-79342-8

Printed in the United States of America
FIRST EDITION
PB Printing   10 9 8 7 6 5 4 3 2 1

WELCOME

Dear Teacher,

Thank you for your interest in Common Core's curriculum in mathematics. Common Core is a non-profit organization based in Washington, DC dedicated to helping K-12 public schoolteachers use the power of high-quality content to improve instruction.[1] We are led by a board of master teachers, scholars, and current and former school, district, and state education leaders. Common Core has responded to the Common Core State Standards' (CCSS) call for "content-rich curriculum"[2] by creating new, CCSS-based curriculum materials in mathematics, English Language Arts, history, and (soon) the arts. All of our materials are written by teachers who are among the nation's foremost experts on the new standards.

In 2012 Common Core won three contracts from the New York State Education Department to create a PreKindergarten–12th grade mathematics curriculum for the teachers of that state, and to conduct associated professional development. The book you hold contains a portion of that work. In order to respond to demand in New York and elsewhere, modules of the curriculum will continue to be published, on a rolling basis, as they are completed. This curriculum is based on New York's version of the CCSS (the CCLS, or Common Core Learning Standards). Common Core will be releasing an enhanced version of the curriculum this summer on our website, commoncore.org. That version also will be published by Jossey-Bass, a Wiley brand.

Common Core's curriculum materials are not merely aligned to the new standards, they take the CCSS as their very foundation. Our work in math takes its shape from the expectations embedded in the new standards— including the instructional shifts and mathematical progressions, and the new expectations for student fluency, deep conceptual understanding, and application to real-life context. Similarly, our ELA and history curricula are deeply informed by the CCSS's new emphasis on close reading, increased use of informational text, and evidence-based writing.

Our curriculum is distinguished not only by its adherence to the CCSS. The math curriculum is based on a theory of teaching math that is proven to work. That theory posits that mathematical knowledge is most coherently and

---

1. Despite the coincidence of name, Common Core and the Common Core State Standards are not affiliated. Common Core was established in 2007, prior to the start of the Common Core State Standards Initiative, which was led by the National Governors Association and the Council for Chief State School Officers.

2. *Common Core State Standards for English Language Arts & Literacy in History/Social Studies, Science, and Technical Subjects* (Washington, DC: Common Core State Standards Initiative), 6.

effectively conveyed when it is taught in a sequence that follows the "story" of mathematics itself. This is why we call the elementary portion of this curriculum "The Story of Units," to be followed by "The Story of Ratios" in middle school, and "The Story of Functions" in high school. Mathematical concepts flow logically, from one to the next, in this curriculum. The sequencing has been joined with methods of instruction that have been proven to work, in this nation and abroad. These methods drive student understanding beyond process, to deep mastery of mathematical concepts. The goal of the curriculum is to produce students who are not merely literate, but fluent, in mathematics.

It is important to note that, as extensive as these curriculum materials are, they are not meant to be prescriptive. Rather, they are intended to provide a basis for teachers to hone their own craft through study, collaboration, training, and the application of their own expertise as professionals. At Common Core we believe deeply in the ability of teachers and in their central and irreplaceable role in shaping the classroom experience. We strive only to support and facilitate their important work.

The teachers and scholars who wrote these materials are listed beginning on the next page. Their deep knowledge of mathematics, of the CCSS, and of what works in classrooms defined this work in every respect. I would like to thank Louisiana State University professor of mathematics Scott Baldridge for the intellectual leadership he provides to this project. Teacher, trainer, and writer Robin Ramos is the most inspired math educator I've ever encountered. It is Robin and Scott's aspirations for what mathematics education in America *should* look like that is spelled out in these pages.

Finally, this work owes a debt to project director Nell McAnelly that is so deep I'm confident it never can be repaid. Nell, who leads LSU's Gordon A. Cain Center for STEM Literacy, oversees all aspects of our work for NYSED. She has spent days, nights, weekends, and many cancelled vacations toiling in her efforts to make it possible for this talented group of teacher-writers to produce their best work against impossible deadlines. I'm confident that in the years to come Scott, Robin, and Nell will be among those who will deserve to be credited with putting math instruction in our nation back on track.

Thank you for taking an interest in our work. Please join us at www.commoncore.org.

Lynne Munson
President and Executive Director
Common Core
Washington, DC
June 20, 2013

Common Core's K-5 Math Staff

Scott Baldridge, Lead Mathematician and Writer
Robin Ramos, Lead Writer, PreKindergarten-5
Jill Diniz, Lead Writer, 6-12
Ben McCarty, Mathematician

Nell McAnelly, Project Director
Tiah Alphonso, Associate Director
Jennifer Loftin, Associate Director
Catriona Anderson, Curriculum Manager,
    PreKindergarten-5

Sherri Adler, PreKindergarten
Debbie Andorka-Aceves, PreKindergarten

Kate McGill Austin, Kindergarten
Nancy Diorio, Kindergarten
Lacy Endo-Peery, Kindergarten
Melanie Gutierrez, Kindergarten
Nuhad Jamal, Kindergarten
Cecilia Rudzitis, Kindergarten
Shelly Snow, Kindergarten

Beth Barnes, First Grade
Lily Cavanaugh, First Grade
Ana Estela, First Grade
Kelley Isinger, First Grade
Kelly Spinks, First Grade
Marianne Strayton, First Grade
Hae Jung Yang, First Grade

Wendy Keehfus-Jones, Second Grade
Susan Midlarsky, Second Grade
Jenny Petrosino, Second Grade
Colleen Sheeron, Second Grade
Nancy Sommer, Second Grade
Lisa Watts-Lawton, Second Grade
MaryJo Wieland, Second Grade
Jessa Woods, Second Grade

Eric Angel, Third Grade
Greg Gorman, Third Grade
Susan Lee, Third Grade
Cristina Metcalf, Third Grade
Ann Rose Santoro, Third Grade
Kevin Tougher, Third Grade
Victoria Peacock, Third Grade
Saffron VanGalder, Third Grade

Katrina Abdussalaam, Fourth Grade
Kelly Alsup, Fourth Grade
Patti Dieck, Fourth Grade
Mary Jones, Fourth Grade
Soojin Lu, Fourth Grade
Tricia Salerno, Fourth Grade
Gail Smith, Fourth Grade
Eric Welch, Fourth Grade
Sam Wertheim, Fourth Grade
Erin Wheeler, Fourth Grade

Leslie Arceneaux, Fifth Grade
Adam Baker, Fifth Grade
Janice Fan, Fifth Grade
Peggy Golden, Fifth Grade
Halle Kananak, Fifth Grade
Shauntina Kerrison, Fifth Grade
Pat Mohr, Fifth Grade
Chris Sarlo, Fifth Grade

Additional Writers

Bill Davidson, Fluency Specialist
Robin Hecht, UDL Specialist
Simon Pfeil, Mathematician

Document Management Team

Tam Le, Document Manager
Jennifer Merchan, Copy Editor

New York State Common Core

Mathematics Curriculum

Table of Contents

GRADE 3 • MODULE 3

Multiplication and Division with Units of 0, 1, 6–9, and Multiples of 10

Grade 3 • Module 3

Multiplication and Division with Units of 0, 1, 6–9, and Multiples of 10

OVERVIEW

This 25-day module builds directly on students' work with multiplication and division in Module 1. By this point, Module 1 instruction coupled with fluency practice in Module 2 has students well on their way to meeting the Grade 3 fluency expectation for multiplying and dividing within 100 (**3.OA.7**). Module 3 extends the study of factors from 2, 3, 4, 5, and 10 to include all units from 0 to 10, as well as multiples of 10 within 100. Similar to the organization of Module 1, the introduction of new factors in Module 3 spreads across topics. This allows students to build fluency with facts involving a particular unit before moving on. The factors are sequenced to facilitate systematic instruction with increasingly sophisticated strategies and patterns.

Topic A begins by revisiting the commutative property. Students study familiar facts from Module 1 to identify known facts using units of 6, 7, 8, and 9 (**3.OA.5, 3.OA.7**). They realize that they already know more than half of their facts by recognizing, for example, that if they know 2 × 8, they also know 8 × 2 through commutativity. This begins a study of arithmetic patterns that becomes an increasingly prominent theme in the module (**3.OA.9**). The subsequent lesson carries this study a step further; students apply the commutative property to relate 5 × 8 and 8 × 5, and then add one more group of 8 to solve 6 × 8 and, by extension, 8 × 6. The final lesson in this topic builds fluency with familiar multiplication and division facts, preparing students for the work ahead by introducing the use of a letter to represent the unknown in various positions (**3.OA.3, 3.OA.4**).

Topic B introduces units of 6 and 7, factors that are well suited to Level 2 skip-counting strategies and to the Level 3 distributive property strategy, already familiar from Module 1. Students learn to compose up to, then over the next decade. For example, to solve a fact using units of 7 they might count 7, 14, and then mentally add 14 + 6 + 1 to make 21. This strategy previews the associative property using addition and illuminates arithmetic patterns as students apply count-bys to solve problems (**3.OA.9**). In the next lesson, students apply the distributive property (familiar from Module 1) as a strategy to multiply and divide. They decompose larger unknown facts into smaller known facts to solve. For example, 48 ÷ 6 becomes (30 ÷ 6) + (18 ÷ 6), or 5 + 3 (**3.OA.5, 3.OA.7**). Topic B's final lesson emphasizes word problems, providing opportunities to analyze and model. Students apply the skill of using a letter to represent the unknown in various positions within multiplication and division problems (**3.OA.3, 3.OA.4, 3.OA.7**).

Topic C anticipates the formal introduction of the associative property with a lesson on making use of structure to problem solve. Students learn the conventional order for performing operations when parentheses are and are not present in an equation (**3.OA.8**). With this knowledge in place, the associative property emerges in the next lessons as a strategy to multiply using units up to 8 (**3.OA.5**). Units of 6 and 8 are particularly useful for presenting this Level 3 strategy. Rewriting 6 as 2 × 3 or 8 as 2 × 4 makes shifts in grouping readily apparent (see example below), and also utilizes familiar factors 2, 3, and 4 as students learn the new material. The following strategy may be used to solve a problem like 8 × 5:

	Module 3:	Multiplication and Division with Units of 0, 1, 6–9, and Multiples of 10	
	Date:	7/31/13	ii

© 2013 Common Core, Inc. All rights reserved. commoncore.org

$$8 \times 5 = (4 \times 2) \times 5$$
$$8 \times 5 = 4 \times (2 \times 5)$$
$$8 \times 5 = 4 \times 10$$

In the final lesson of Topic C, students relate division using units up to 8 with multiplication. They understand division as both a quantity divided into equal groups and an unknown factor problem for which—given the large size of units—skip-counting to solve can be more efficient than dividing (**3.OA.3, 3.OA.4, 3.OA.7**).

Topic D introduces units of 9 over three days, exploring a variety of arithmetic patterns that become engaging strategies for quickly learning facts with automaticity (**3.OA.3, 3.OA.7, 3.OA.9**). Nines are placed late in the module so that students have enough experience with multiplication and division to recognize, analyze, and apply the rich patterns found in the manipulation of these facts. As with other topics, the sequence ends with interpreting the unknown factor to solve multiplication and division problems (**3.OA.3, 3.OA.4, 3.OA.5, 3.OA.7**).

In Topic E, students begin by working with facts using units of 0 and 1. From a procedural standpoint, these are simple facts that require little time for students to master; however, understanding the concept of nothing (zero) is among the more complex, particularly as it relates to division. This unique combination of simple and complex explains the late introduction of 0 and 1 in the sequence of factors. Students study the results of multiplying and dividing with those units to identify relationships and patterns (**3.OA.7, 3.OA.9**). The topic closes with a lesson devoted to two-step problems involving all four operations (**3.OA.8**). In this lesson, students work with equations involving unknown quantities and apply the rounding skills learned in Module 2 to make estimations that help them assess the reasonableness of their solutions (**3.OA.8**).

In Topic F, students multiply by multiples of 10 (**3.NBT.3**). To solve a fact like 2 × 30, they first model the basic fact 2 × 3 on the place value chart. Place value understanding helps them to notice that the product shifts one place value to the left when multiplied by 10: 2 × 3 tens can be found by simply locating the same basic fact in the tens column.

In the subsequent lesson, place value understanding becomes more abstract as students model place value strategies using the associative property (**3.NBT.3, 3.OA.5**). 2 × 30 = 2 × (3 × 10) = (2 × 3) × 10. The final lesson focuses on solving two-step word problems involving multiples of 10 and equations with unknown quantities (**3.OA.8**). As in Lesson 18, students estimate to assess the reasonableness of their solutions (**3.OA.8**).

Distribution of Instructional Minutes

This diagram represents a suggested distribution of instructional minutes based on the emphasis of particular lesson components in different lessons throughout the module.

■ **Fluency Practice**
□ **Concept Development**
▨ **Application Problems**
■ **Student Debrief**

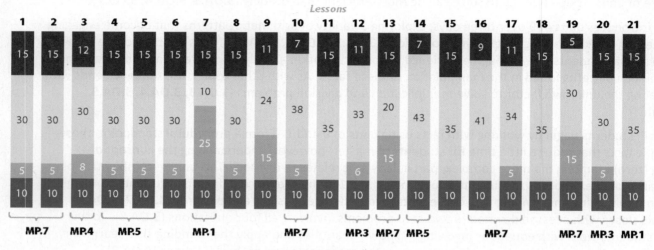

Lessons

MP = Mathematical Practice

Focus Grade Level Standards

Represent and solve problems involving multiplication and division.[1]

3.OA.3   Use multiplication and division within 100 to solve word problems in situations involving equal groups, arrays, and measurement quantities, e.g., by using drawings and equations with a symbol for the unknown number to represent the problem. (See Glossary, Table 2.)

3.OA.4   Determine the unknown whole number in a multiplication or division equation relating three whole numbers. *For example, determine the unknown number that makes the equation true in each of the equations $8 \times ? = 48$, $5 = \_ \div 3$, $6 \times 6 = ?$.*

Understand properties of multiplication and the relationship between multiplication and division.[2]

3.OA.5   Apply properties of operations as strategies to multiply and divide. (Students need not use formal terms for these properties.) *Examples: If $6 \times 4 = 24$ is known, then $4 \times 6 = 24$ is also*

---

[1] The balance of this cluster is addressed in Module 1.
[2] The balance of this cluster is addressed in Module 1.

Module 3:	Multiplication and Division with Units of 0, 1, 6–9, and Multiples of 10
Date:	7/31/13

iv

known. (Commutative property of multiplication.) 3 × 5 × 2 can be found by 3 × 5 = 15, then 15 × 2 = 30, or by 5 × 2 = 10, then 3 × 10 = 30. (Associative property of multiplication.) Knowing that 8 × 5 = 40 and 8 × 2 = 16, one can find 8 × 7 as 8 × (5 + 2) = (8 × 5) + (8 × 2) = 40 + 16 = 56. (Distributive property.)

Multiply and divide within 100.[3]

3.OA.7   Fluently multiply and divide within 100, using strategies such as the relationship between multiplication and division (e.g., knowing that 8 × 5 = 40, one knows 40 ÷ 5 = 8) or properties of operations. By the end of Grade 3, know from memory all products of two one-digit numbers.

Solve problems involving the four operations, and identify and explain patterns in arithmetic.[4]

3.OA.8   Solve two-step word problems using the four operations. Represent these problems using equations with a letter standing for the unknown quantity. Assess the reasonableness of answers using mental computation and estimation strategies including rounding. (This standard is limited to problems posed with whole numbers and having whole-number answers; students should know how to perform operations in the conventional order when there are no parentheses to specify a particular order, i.e., Order of Operations.)

3.OA.9   Identify arithmetic patterns (including patterns in the addition table or multiplication table), and explain them using properties of operations. *For example, observe that 4 times a number is always even, and explain why 4 times a number can be decomposed into two equal addends.*

Use place value understanding and properties of operations to perform multi-digit arithmetic. (A range of algorithms may be used.)[5]

3.NBT.3   Multiply one-digit whole numbers by mutliples of 10 in the range 10–90 (e.g., 9 × 80, 5 × 60) using strategies based on place value and properties of operations.

Foundational Standards

2.OA.3   Determine whether a group of objects (up to 20) has an odd or even number of members, e.g., by pairing objects or counting them by 2s; write an equation to express an even number as a sum of two equal addends.

2.OA.4   Use addition to find the total number of objects arranged in rectangular arrays with up to 5 rows and up to 5 columns; write an equation to express the total as a sum of equal addends.

2.NBT.2   Count within 1000; skip-count by 5s, 10s, and 100s.

---

[3] From this point forward, fluency practice with multiplication and division facts is part of the students' on-going experience.
[4] After being fully taught in Module 3, this standard (as well as 3.OA.3) continues being practiced throughout the remainder of the school year.
[5] The balance of this cluster is addressed in Module 2.

3.OA.1 Interpret products of whole numbers, e.g., interpret 5 × 7 as the total number of objects in 5 groups of 7 objects each. *For example, describe a context in which a total number of objects can be expressed as 5 × 7.*

3.OA.2 Interpret whole-number quotients of whole numbers, e.g., interpret 56 ÷ 8 as the number of objects in each share when 56 objects are partitioned equally into 8 shares, or as a number of shares when 56 objects are partitioned into equal shares of 8 objects each. *For example, describe a context in which a number of shares or a number of groups can be expressed as 56 ÷ 8.*

3.OA.6 Understand division as an unknown-factor problem. *For example, find 32 ÷ 8 by finding the number that makes 32 when multiplied by 8.*

Focus Standards for Mathematical Practice

MP.1 **Make sense of problems and persevere in solving them.** Students engage in exploratory lessons to discover and interpret patterns, and apply their observations to solving multi-step word problems involving all four operations.

MP.3 **Construct viable arguments and critique the reasoning of others.** As students compare solution strategies, they construct arguments and critique the reasoning of their peers. This practice is particularly exemplified in daily Application Problems and problem-solving specific lessons in which students share and explain their work with one another.

MP.4 **Model with mathematics.** Students use arrays, tape diagrams, and equations to represent word problem situations.

MP.5 **Use appropriate tools strategically.** Students analyze problems and select the appropriate tools and pathways to solutions. This is particularly evident as students select problem-solving strategies, and use arithmetic properties as simplifying strategies when appropriate.

MP.7 **Look for and make use of structure.** In this module, patterns emerge as tools for problem solving. Students make use of structure as they utilize the distributive property to establish the 9 = 10 − 1 pattern, for example, or when they check the solution to a fact using units of 9 by making sure the sum of the digits in the product adds up to 9. They make use of the relationship between multiplication and division as they determine unknown factors and interpret the meanings thereof.

Overview of Module Topics and Lesson Objectives

Standards		Topics and Objectives	Days
3.OA.4 **3.OA.5** **3.OA.7** **3.OA.9** 3.OA.1 3.OA.2 3.OA.3 3.OA.6	A	**The Properties of Multiplication and Division** Lesson 1: Study commutativity to find known facts of 6, 7, 8, and 9. Lesson 2: Apply the distributive and commutative properties to relate multiplication facts $5 \times n + n$ to $6 \times n$ and $n \times 6$ where n is the size of the unit. Lesson 3: Multiply and divide with familiar facts using a letter to represent the unknown.	3
3.OA.3 **3.OA.4** **3.OA.5** **3.OA.7** **3.OA.9** 3.OA.1 3.OA.2 3.OA.6	B	**Multiplication and Division Using Units of 6 and 7** Lesson 4: Count by units of 6 to multiply and divide using number bonds to decompose. Lesson 5: Count by units of 7 to multiply and divide using number bonds to decompose. Lesson 6: Use the distributive property as a strategy to multiply and divide using units of 6 and 7. Lesson 7: Interpret the unknown in multiplication and division to model and solve problems using units of 6 and 7.	4
3.OA.3 **3.OA.4** **3.OA.5** **3.OA.7** 3.OA.1 3.OA.2 3.OA.6 3.OA.8	C	**Multiplication and Division Using Units up to 8** Lesson 8: Understand the function of parentheses and apply to solving problems. Lesson 9: Model the associative property as a strategy to multiply. Lesson 10: Use the distributive property as a strategy to multiply and divide. Lesson 11: Interpret the unknown in multiplication and division to model and solve problems.	4
		Mid-Module Assessment: Topics A–C (assessment ½ day, return ½ day, remediation or further applications 1 day)	2

Standards		Topics and Objectives	Days
3.OA.3 **3.OA.4** **3.OA.5** **3.OA.7** **3.OA.9** 3.OA.1 3.OA.2 3.OA.6	D	**Multiplication and Division Using Units of 9** Lesson 12: Apply the distributive property and the fact 9 = 10 − 1 as a strategy to multiply. Lessons 13– 14: Identify and use arithmetic patterns to multiply. Lesson 15: Interpret the unknown in multiplication and division to model and solve problems.	4
3.OA.3 **3.OA.7** **3.OA.8** **3.OA.9** 3.OA.1 3.OA.2 3.OA.4 3.OA.6	E	**Analysis of Patterns and Problem Solving Including Units of 0 and 1** Lesson 16: Reason about and explain arithmetic patterns using units of 0 and 1 as they relate to multiplication and division. Lesson 17: Identify patterns in multiplication and division facts using the multiplication table. Lesson 18: Solve two-step word problems involving all four operations and assess the reasonableness of solutions.	3
3.OA.5 **3.OA.8** **3.OA.9** **3.NBT.3** 3.OA.1	F	**Multiplication of Single-Digit Factors and Multiples of 10** Lesson 19: Multiply by multiples of 10 using the place value chart. Lesson 20: Use place value strategies and the associative property $n \times (m \times 10) = (n \times m) \times 10$ (where n and m are less than 10) to multiply by multiples of 10. Lesson 21: Solve two-step word problems involving multiplying single-digit factors and multiples of 10.	3
		End-of-Module Assessment: Topics A–F (assessment ½ day, return ½ day, remediation or further application 1 day)	2
Total Number of Instructional Days			**25**

Terminology

New or Recently Introduced Terms

- Even, odd (number)
- Multiple (specifically with reference to naming multiples of 9 and 10, e.g., 20, 30, 40, etc.)
- Multiplier (the factor representing the number of units)
- Product (the quantity resulting from multiplying two or more numbers together)

Familiar Terms and Symbols[6]

- Array (a set of numbers or objects that follow a specific pattern)
- Commutative Property (e.g., 2 × 3 = 3 × 2)
- Distribute (with reference to the distributive property; e.g., in 12 × 3 = (10 × 3) + (2 × 3), the 3 is multiplier for each part of the decomposition)
- Divide, division (partitioning a total into equal groups to show how many equal groups add up to a specific number, e.g., 15 ÷ 5 = 3)
- Equal groups (with reference to multiplication and division; one factor is the number of objects in a group and the other is a multiplier that indicates the number of groups)
- Equation (a statement that two expressions are equal, e.g., 3 × 4 = 12)
- Factors (numbers that are multiplied to obtain a product)
- Multiply, multiplication (an operation showing how many times a number is added to itself, e.g., 5 × 3 = 15)
- Number bond (model used to show part–part–whole relationships)
- Ones, twos, threes, etc. (units of one, two, or three)
- Parentheses (the symbols ( ) used around a fact or numbers within an equation)
- Quotient (the answer when one number is divided by another)
- Row, column (in reference to rectangular arrays)
- Tape diagram (a method for modeling problems)
- Unit (one segment of a partitioned tape diagram)
- Unknown (the "missing" factor or quantity in multiplication or division)
- Value (how much)

---

[6] These are terms and symbols students have used or seen previously.

	Module 3:	Multiplication and Division with Units of 0, 1, 6–9, and	ix
		Multiples of 10	
	Date:	7/31/13	

Suggested Tools and Representations

- Array
- Tape Diagram (a method for modeling problems)

Scaffolds[7]

The scaffolds integrated into *A Story of Units* give alternatives for how students access information as well as express and demonstrate their learning. Strategically placed margin notes are provided within each lesson elaborating on the use of specific scaffolds at applicable times. They address many needs presented by English language learners, students with disabilities, students performing above grade level, and students performing below grade level. Many of the suggestions are applicable to more than one population. The charts included in Module 1 provide a general overview of the lesson-aligned scaffolds, organized by Universal Design for Learning (UDL) principles. To read more about the approach to differentiated instruction in *A Story of Units*, please refer to "How to Implement *A Story of Units*."

Assessment Summary

Type	Administered	Format	Standards Addressed
Mid-Module Assessment Task	After Topic C	Constructed response with rubric	3.OA.3 3.OA.4 3.OA.5 3.OA.7 3.OA.9
End-of-Module Assessment Task	After Topic F	Constructed response and timed fluency with rubric	3.OA.3 3.OA.4 3.OA.5 3.OA.7 3.OA.8 3.OA.9 3.NBT.3

---

[7] Students with disabilities may require Braille, large print, audio, or special digital files. Please visit the website, www.p12.nysed.gov/specialed/aim, for specific information on how to obtain student materials that satisfy the National Instructional Materials Accessibility Standard (NIMAS) format.

Topic A
The Properties of Multiplication and Division

3.OA.4, 3.OA.5, 3.OA.7, 3.OA.9, 3.OA.1, 3.OA.2, 3.OA.3, 3.OA.6

Focus Standard:	3.OA.4	Determine the unknown whole number in a multiplication or division equation relating three whole numbers. *For example, determine the unknown number that makes the equation true in each of the equations 8 × ? = 48, 5 = _ ÷ 3, 6 × 6 = ?*
	3.OA.5	Apply properties of operations as strategies to multiply and divide. (Students need not use formal terms for these properties.) *Examples: If 6 × 4 = 24 is known, then 4 × 6 = 24 is also known. (Commutative property of multiplication.) 3 × 5 × 2 can be found by 3 × 5 = 15, then 15 × 2 = 30, or by 5 × 2 = 10, then 3 × 10 = 30. (Associative property of multiplication.) Knowing that 8 × 5 = 40 and 8 × 2 = 16, one can find 8 × 7 as 8 × (5 + 2) = (8 × 5) + (8 × 2) = 40 + 16 = 56. (Distributive property.)*
	3.OA.7	Fluently multiply and divide within 100, using strategies such as the relationship between multiplication and division (e.g., knowing that 8 × 5 = 40, one knows 40 ÷ 5 = 8) or properties of operations. By the end of Grade 3, know from memory all products of two one-digit numbers.
	3.OA.9	Identify arithmetic patterns (including patterns in the addition table or multiplication table), and explain them using properties of operations. *For example, observe that 4 times a number is always even, and explain why 4 times a number can be decomposed into two equal addends.*
Instructional Days:	3	
Coherence -Links from:	G2–M6	Foundations of Multiplication and Division
	G3–M1	Properties of Multiplication and Division and Solving Problems with Units of 2–5 and 10
	G3–M4	Multiplication and Area
-Links to:	G4–M3	Multi-Digit Multiplication and Division

In Lesson 1, students study the commutativity of familiar Module 1 facts that use units of 2, 3, 4, 5, and 10. Through study they "discover" facts that they already know using units of 6, 7, 8, and 9. For example, students recognize that if they know 3 × 6 = 18, then they also know 6 × 3 = 18. They write out familiar facts and those known through commutativity, organizing them in rows and columns to form the beginning of a table through which arithmetic patterns become visible. Students finish this lesson encouraged about the work to come after seeing that they already know more than half of their facts.

Topic A:	The Properties of Multiplication and Division
Date:	7/31/13

3.A.1

In Lesson 2, students apply commutativity in conjunction with the $n + 1$ strategy to solve unknown facts. For example, students relate 5×8 and 8×5, and then add one more group of 8 (n) to solve 6×8 and, by extension, 8×6. Adding one more group to a known fact in order to find an unknown fact continues to bridge Module 1 and Module 3 learning as students are reminded of their prior work with the distributive property.

Lesson 3 introduces using a letter to represent the unknown in various positions within multiplication and division problems. In Module 1 students represented the unknown on tape diagrams, and occasionally in equations, using a question mark. This lesson uses familiar facts to introduce the new abstraction of letter as placeholder.

A Teaching Sequence Towards Mastery of The Properties of Multiplication and Division
Objective 1: Study commutativity to find known facts of 6, 7, 8, and 9. (Lesson 1)
Objective 2: Apply the distributive and commutative properties to relate multiplication facts $5 \times n + n$ to $6 \times n$ and $n \times 6$ where n is the size of the unit. (Lesson 2)
Objective 3: Multiply and divide with familiar facts using a letter to represent the unknown. (Lesson 3)

Lesson 1

Objective: Study commutativity to find known facts of 6, 7, 8, and 9.

Suggested Lesson Structure

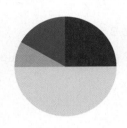

- ■ Fluency Practice   (15 minutes)
- ■ Application Problem   (5 minutes)
- ■ Concept Development   (30 minutes)
- ■ Student Debrief   (10 minutes)

  Total Time   **(60 minutes)**

Fluency Practice (15 minutes)

- Sprint: Mixed Multiplication **3.OA.7**   (9 minutes)
- Group Counting **3.OA.1**   (3 minutes)
- Commutative Property of Multiplication **3.OA.5**   (3 minutes)

Sprint: Mixed Multiplication (9 minutes)

Materials: (S) Mixed Multiplication Sprint

Note: This Sprint reviews familiar multiplication facts from Module 1 while preparing students for today's lesson on using commutativity with known facts to find unknown facts.

Group Counting (3 minutes)

Note: Group counting reviews interpreting multiplication as repeated addition. Counting by sixes, sevens, eights, and nines in this activity anticipates multiplication using those units later in the module.

Direct students to count forward and backward, occasionally changing the direction of the count:

- ▪ Sixes to 60
- ▪ Sevens to 70
- ▪ Eights to 80
- ▪ Nines to 90

NOTES ON
MULTIPLE MEANS OF
ENGAGEMENT:

Group Counting in Module 3 no longer explicitly includes twos, threes, fours, and fives. However, you may want to include those units if your class has not yet mastered those facts.

Whisper/talking, hum/talking, or think/talking threes and fours can also work as a scaffold to build fluency with sixes and eights.

Lesson 1:   Study commutativity to find known facts of 6, 7, 8, and 9.   3.A.3
Date: 7/31/13

Commutative Property of Multiplication (3 minutes)

Materials: (S) Personal white boards

Note: This activity reviews the commutative property from Module 1 and anticipates its use in today's lesson.

- T: (Project array with 3 groups of 2 circles.) Write two multiplication sentences and two division sentences for this array.
- S: (Write 3 × 2 = 6, 2 × 3 = 6, 6 ÷ 2 = 3, and 6 ÷ 3 = 2.)

Continue with the following suggested sequence: 2 groups of 9, 3 groups of 7, and 5 groups of 8.

Application Problem (5 minutes)

Geri brings 3 water jugs to her soccer game to share with teammates. Each jug contains 6 liters of water. How many liters of water does Geri bring?

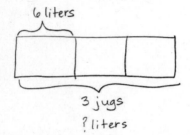

NOTES ON
MULTIPLE MEANS OF
ENGAGEMENT:

Extend for students working above grade level with a related word problem with larger factors.

For example, "A runner drinks 3 liters of water during a race. The track team has 8 runners. How many liters of water will they need for the race?"

Note: This problem reviews multiplication with 3 units of 6 to solve word problems while also reinforcing measurement concepts. It leads into the discussion of commutativity in the Concept Development.

Concept Development (30 minutes)

Materials: (S) Personal white boards, Problem Set

Part 1: Explore commutativity as it relates to multiplication.

Draw or project the tape diagrams shown at right.

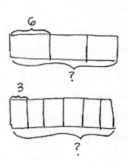

- T: Talk to your partner. Which tape diagram represents the Application Problem? How do you know? (Allow time for discussion.)
- T: Draw both tape diagrams on your board. Write a multiplication sentence for each. (Allow time for students to work and finish.)
- T: How are the multiplication sentences related?

S: They use the same numbers. → Both have a product of 18. → They use the same factors, but in a different order. The product is the same.

MP.7

T: This is an example of the commutative property that we studied in Module 1. What does this property tell us about the product and its factors?

S: Even if the order of the factors changes, the product stays the same!

T: Earlier in the year we learned our threes, including 3×6. If we know 3×6, what other fact do we know?

S: 6×3!

T: What is the product of both 3×6 and 6×3?

S: 18!

T: To show that 3×6 and 6×3 equal the same amount, we can write $3 \times 6 = 6 \times 3$. (Model.)

T: Using commutativity as a strategy, we know many more facts than just the ones we've practiced!

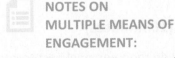

**NOTES ON
MULTIPLE MEANS OF
ENGAGEMENT:**

Review the commutative property by exploring arrays—concrete or pictorial. Review 3 twos is 2 threes, for example, by 6 students standing in 2 rows of 3, and then 3 rows of 2.

When drawing the array, use color to differentiate 6 threes from 3 sixes.

Continue with the following suggested sequence:

- $2 \times 7 = 7 \times 2$
- 5 eights = 8 fives

Part 2: Use the multiplication chart to find known facts through commutativity.

T: Problem 1(a) on your Problem Set shows a multiplication chart. The shaded numbers along the left column and the top are factors. The numbers inside the chart are products. Each un-shaded box represents the product of 1 multiplication fact. Find the total number of facts on your multiplication chart. (Allow time for students to count.) How many facts are on the chart?

S: 100 facts.

T: Let's use the chart to locate the product of 3 and 6. Put your finger on Row 3 and slide it to the right until it's also in the 6 column. The number in the square where the row and column meet is the product, which has been done for you. What do you see in the chart is the product of 3 and 6?

S: 18.

T: Let's now locate the product of 6 and 3. Find the square where the row for 6 and the column for 3 meet. Use commutativity to write the product of 6 and 3 in that square on your chart.

S: (Write 18.)

T: We can use commutativity to solve many new facts and fill in the products on the chart. Write the products for all the facts that we've already studied on the chart, then fill in those you can solve using commutativity. (Allow time for students to work.)

T: Shade in the facts you completed. (Allow time for students to work.) How many are left to learn?

S: 16!

T: Look carefully at those 16 facts. Are there any that you will be able to solve using the commutative property once you know one?

S: Yes! There are 12 facts that we can use the
      commutative property to solve. That means we
      only need to know 6 of them.

T: Really there are only 10 new facts to learn before
      you know all the facts up to 10 × 10!

Problem Set (10 minutes)

Students should do their personal best to complete the
Problem Set within the allotted 10 minutes. Some
problems do not specify a method for solving. This is an
intentional reduction of scaffolding that invokes MP.5, Use
Appropriate Tools Strategically. Students should solve
these problems using the RDW approach used for
Application Problems.

For some classes, it may be appropriate to modify the
assignment by specifying which problems students should
work on first. With this option, let the careful sequencing
of the Problem Set guide your selections so that problems
continue to be scaffolded. Balance word problems with
other problem types to ensure a range of practice. Assign
incomplete problems for homework or at another time
during the day.

Student Debrief (10 minutes)

Lesson Objective: Study commutativity to find known
facts of 6, 7, 8, and 9.

The Student Debrief is intended to invite reflection and
active processing of the total lesson experience.

Invite students to review their solutions for the Problem
Set. They should check work by comparing answers with a
partner before going over answers as a class. Look for
misconceptions or misunderstandings that can be
addressed in the Debrief. Guide students in a conversation
to debrief the Problem Set and process the lesson.

You may choose to use any combination of the questions
below to lead the discussion.

- How did commutativity help you solve more facts
  than you thought you knew in Problem 1(a)?

- Invite students to share their processes for
  finding the multiplication facts for the array in

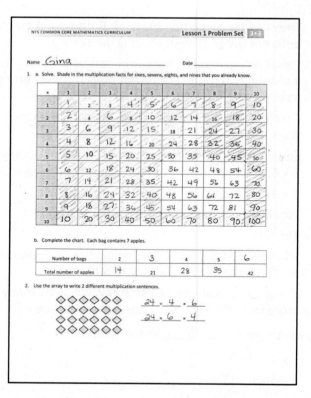

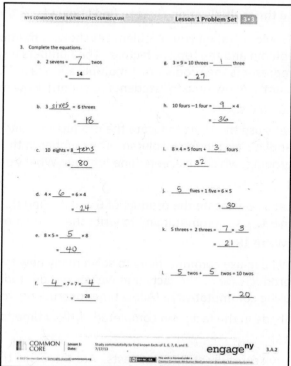

Problem 2.

- In Problems 3(a), 3(b), and 3(c), what do you notice about the words and numbers on each side of the equal sign? How are they related?

- How did you know to subtract 1 three in Problem 3(g)? What would that problem look like rewritten as an equation?

Exit Ticket (3 minutes)

After the Student Debrief, instruct students to complete the Exit Ticket. A review of their work will help you assess the students' understanding of the concepts that were presented in the lesson today and plan more effectively for future lessons. You may read the questions aloud to the students.

NOTES ON MULTIPLE MEANS FOR ACTION AND EXPRESSION:

English language learners and others will benefit from reviewing *commutative property* and *commutativity* during the Debrief. Allow students to explain the property to a partner in their first language, and/or record the term, with an example, in a personal math dictionary.

A
                                                        # Correct _____

Multiply.

1	2 x 1 =		23	2 x 7 =	
2	2 x 2 =		24	5 x 5 =	
3	2 x 3 =		25	5 x 6 =	
4	4 x 1 =		26	5 x 7 =	
5	4 x 2 =		27	4 x 5 =	
6	4 x 3 =		28	4 x 6 =	
7	1 x 6 =		29	4 x 7 =	
8	2 x 6 =		30	3 x 5 =	
9	1 x 8 =		31	3 x 6 =	
10	2 x 8 =		32	3 x 7 =	
11	3 x 1 =		33	2 x 7 =	
12	3 x 2 =		34	2 x 8 =	
13	3 x 3 =		35	2 x 9 =	
14	5 x 1 =		36	5 x 7 =	
15	5 x 2 =		37	5 x 8 =	
16	5 x 3 =		38	5 x 9 =	
17	1 x 7 =		39	4 x 7 =	
18	2 x 7 =		40	4 x 8 =	
19	1 x 9 =		41	4 x 9 =	
20	2 x 9 =		42	3 x 7 =	
21	2 x 5 =		43	3 x 8 =	
22	2 x 6 =		44	3 x 9 =	

© Bill Davidson

COMMON CORE	Lesson 1:	Study commutativity to find known facts of 6, 7, 8, and 9.	
	Date:	7/31/13	3.A.8

B   Improvement _____   # Correct _____

Multiply.

#			#		
1	5 x 1 =		23	5 x 7 =	
2	5 x 2 =		24	2 x 5 =	
3	5 x 3 =		25	2 x 6 =	
4	3 x 1 =		26	2 x 7 =	
5	3 x 2 =		27	3 x 5 =	
6	3 x 3 =		28	3 x 6 =	
7	1 x 7 =		29	3 x 7 =	
8	2 x 7 =		30	4 x 5 =	
9	1 x 9 =		31	4 x 6 =	
10	2 x 9 =		32	4 x 7 =	
11	2 x 1 =		33	5 x 7 =	
12	2 x 2 =		34	5 x 8 =	
13	2 x 3 =		35	5 x 9 =	
14	4 x 1 =		36	2 x 7 =	
15	4 x 2 =		37	2 x 8 =	
16	4 x 3 =		38	2 x 9 =	
17	1 x 6 =		39	3 x 7 =	
18	2 x 6 =		40	3 x 8 =	
19	1 x 8 =		41	3 x 9 =	
20	2 x 8 =		42	4 x 7 =	
21	5 x 5 =		43	4 x 8 =	
22	5 x 6 =		44	4 x 9 =	

© Bill Davidson

Lesson 1:   Study commutativity to find known facts of 6, 7, 8, and 9.
Date: 7/31/13

3.A.9

Name _____ Date _____

1. a. Solve. Shade in the multiplication facts for sixes, sevens, eights, and nines that you already know.

×	1	2	3	4	5	6	7	8	9	10
1		2	3							
2		4		8				16		
3						18				
4					20					
5										50
6		12								
7										
8										
9										
10										

b. Complete the chart. Each bag contains 7 apples.

Number of bags	2		4	5	
Total number of apples		21			42

2. Use the array to write two different multiplication sentences.

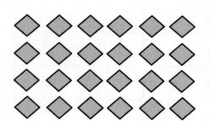

_____ = _____ × _____

_____ = _____ × _____

3.   Complete the equations.

a.   2 sevens = _____ twos

$$= \underline{\textbf{14}}$$

b.   3 _____ = 6 threes

$$= \underline{\qquad}$$

c.   10 eights = 8_____

$$= \underline{\qquad}$$

d.   4 × _____ = 6 × 4

$$= \underline{\qquad}$$

e.   8 × 5 = _____ × 8

$$= \underline{\qquad}$$

f.   _____ × 7 = 7 × _____

$$= \underline{\ 28 \ }$$

g.   3 × 9 = 10 threes − _____ three

$$= \underline{\qquad}$$

h.   10 fours − 1 four = _____ × 4

$$= \underline{\qquad}$$

i.   8 × 4 = 5 fours + _____ fours

$$= \underline{\qquad}$$

j.   _____ fives + 1 five = 6 × 5

$$= \underline{\qquad}$$

k.   5 threes + 2 threes = _____ × _____

$$= \underline{\qquad}$$

l.   _____ twos + _____ twos = 10 twos

$$= \underline{\qquad}$$

Name _____   Date _____

1. Use the array to write two different multiplication facts.

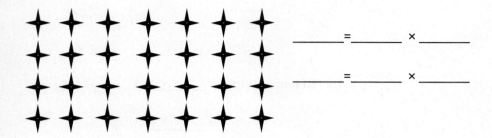

_____ = _____ × _____

_____ = _____ × _____

2. Karen says, "If I know 3 × 8 = 24, then I know the answer to 8 × 3!" Explain how this is true.

Name _____　Date _____

1. Complete the charts below.

   a. A tricycle has 3 wheels.

Number of tricycles	3		5		7
Total number of wheels		12		18	

   b. A tiger has 4 legs.

Number of tigers			7	8	9
Total number of legs	20	24			

   c. A pack has 5 erasers.

Number of packs	6				10
Total number of erasers		35	40	45	

2. Write two multiplication facts for each array.

   _____ = _____ × _____

   _____ = _____ × _____

   _____ = _____ × _____

   _____ = _____ × _____

3.   Match the expressions.

3×6 7 threes

3 sevens 2×10

2 eights 9×5

5×9 8×2

10 twos 6×3

---

4.   Complete the equations.

a.   2 sixes = _____ twos

      = __12__

b.   _____ × 6 = 6 threes

          = _____

c. 4×8 = _____ × 4

          = _____

d. $4 \times$ _____ = _____ × 4

                      = __28__

e.   5 twos + 2 twos = _____ × _____

                      = _____

f.   _____ fives + 1 five = 6×5

                      = _____

Lesson 2

Objective: Apply the distributive and commutative properties to relate multiplication facts 5 × *n* + *n* to 6 × *n* and *n* × 6 where *n* is the size of the unit.

Suggested Lesson Structure

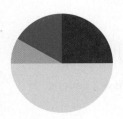

- ■ Fluency Practice   (15 minutes)
- ■ Application Problem   (5 minutes)
- ■ Concept Development   (30 minutes)
- ■ Student Debrief   (10 minutes)
  - **Total Time**   **(60 minutes)**

Fluency Practice (15 minutes)

- Sprint: Commutative Property of Multiplication **3.OA.5**   (9 minutes)
- Group Counting **3.OA.1**   (4 minutes)
- Make Tens **3.OA.5**   (2 minutes)

Sprint: Commutative Property of Multiplication (9 minutes)

Materials: (S) Commutative Property of Multiplication Sprint

Note: This activity reviews Lesson 1.

Group Counting (4 minutes)

Note: Group counting reviews interpreting multiplication as repeated addition. Counting by sixes, sevens, eights, and nines in this activity anticipates multiplication using those units later in the module. Focusing on the mentioned transitions bolsters student understanding of the distributive property of multiplication.

Direct students to count forward and backward, occasionally changing the direction of the count:

- ▪ Sixes to 60, emphasizing the 30 to 36 transition
- ▪ Sevens to 70, emphasizing the 35 to 42 transition
- ▪ Eights to 80, emphasizing the 40 to 48 transition
- ▪ Nines to 90, emphasizing the 45 to 54 transition

Lesson 2:	Apply the distributive and commutative properties to relate multiplication facts 5 x *n* + *n* to 6 x *n* and *n* x 6 where *n* is the size of the unit.	
Date:	7/31/13	

Make Tens (2 minutes)

Note: This fluency prepares students for the skip-counting strategies used to multiply units of 6 and 7 in Lessons 4 and 5.

    T: (Write 9 + __ = 10.) Say the missing addend.
    S: 1.

Continue with the following suggested sequence: 1 + __ = 10, 5 + __ = 10, 8 + __ = 10, 2 + __ = 10, 6 + __ = 10, 7 + __ = 10, 4 + __ = 10, and 3 + __ = 10.

Application Problem (5 minutes)

Jocelyn says 7 fives has the same answer as 3 sevens + 2 sevens. Is she correct? Explain why or why not.

Note: This problem reviews the commutative property from Lesson 1, and also previews the first fact used in the Concept Development to ensure all students' automaticity with the answer.

Jocelyn is correct.
3 sevens + 2 sevens is 5 sevens.
Using the commutative property,
we know that 5 sevens is equal
to 7 fives. If we write it as
equations, it would look like
this : 5 × 7 = 7 × 5 and the
answer to both facts is 35.

Concept Development (30 minutes)

Materials: (S) Personal white boards

    T: (Draw 1 circle with a 7 inside.) This circle represents 1
         unit of 7. As I draw circles, count the sevens with me.
         (Draw circles one on top of the other until you make
         one column of 5 circles.)

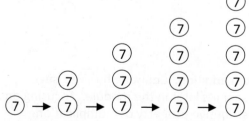

MP.7

    S: 1 seven, 2 sevens, 3 sevens, 4 sevens, 5 sevens.
    T: Whisper the multiplication fact for 5 sevens.
    S: 5 × 7.
    T: Use commutativity to name a related fact.
    S: 7 × 5.
    T: What are 5 sevens, 5 × 7, and 7 × 5 all equal to?
    S: 35.
    T: Let's use our familiar fives facts to find facts we haven't learned yet. (Draw a dot above the first 5

NOTES ON MULTIPLE MEANS OF ACTION AND EXPRESSION:

This lesson moves from pictorial representations in the vignette to abstract in the examples suggested for continued guided practice. Depending on the needs of your class, start out concretely. Have students manipulate cubes rather than draw or look at dots. As they become comfortable with the material, transition to pictorial circles, and, if appropriate, eventually to an abstract example.

COMMON CORE

Lesson 2:

Date:

Apply the distributive and commutative properties to relate multiplication facts 5 x *n* + *n* to 6 x *n* and *n* x 6 where *n* is the size of the unit.

7/31/13

3.A.16

dots in another color, shown right.) What is 5 sevens + 1 seven?

S: 6 sevens.

T: (Write 35 + 7.) Tell your partner how this expression shows the total of 6 sevens.

S: 35 is the total of 5 sevens, and 7 is the total of 1 seven. → 35 + 7 shows 5 sevens + 1 seven in number form. → It's the break apart and distribute strategy we learned before! The dots show 6 sevens broken into 5 sevens and 1 seven, because we know those facts and they're easy!

MP.7

T: What is the total of 6 sevens?

S: 42!

T: Using commutativity, which 2 multiplication facts did we just solve?

S: 6 × 7 and 7 × 6.

T: Compare 5 × 7 and 6 × 7. What is the difference between them?

S: 6 × 7 has one more group of 7 than 5 × 7. → That's what the teacher showed with the dots, 5 sevens and 6 sevens.

T: By noticing that 6 × 7 is only 1 more group of 7 than 5 × 7, we used the total of 5 × 7 to help us make an easy addition problem to find 6 × 7.

NOTES ON
MULTIPLE MEANS OF
REPRESENTATION:

Problem 1 of the Problem Set reviews 6 × 7 used in the vignette using blocks. Although the blocks were not used in the lesson, it is familiar enough to feel friendly for students and provides an opportunity to discuss the difference in models during the Debrief.

Continue with the following suggested sequence. Use the model of the dots as necessary, changing the value of 1 dot to match the problem.

-   5 × 9 to find 6 × 9 and 9 × 6
-   5 × 6 to find 6 × 6

Problem Set (10 minutes)

Students should do their personal best to complete the Problem Set within the allotted 10 minutes. For some classes, it may be appropriate to modify the assignment by specifying which problems they work on first. Some problems do not specify a method for solving. Students solve these problems using the RDW approach used for Application Problems.

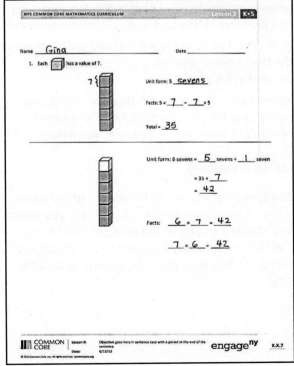

Lesson 2:

Date:

Apply the distributive and commutative properties to relate multiplication facts 5 x *n* + *n* to 6 x *n* and *n* x 6 where *n* is the size of the unit.

7/31/13

3.A.17

Student Debrief (10 minutes)

Lesson Objective: Apply the distributive and commutative properties to relate multiplication facts 5 x n + n to 6 x n and n x 6 where n is the size of the unit.

The Student Debrief is intended to invite reflection and active processing of the total lesson experience.

Invite students to review their solutions for the Problem Set. They should check work by comparing answers with a partner before going over answers as a class. Look for misconceptions or misunderstandings that can be addressed in the Debrief. Guide students in a conversation to debrief the Problem Set and process the lesson.

You may choose to use any combination of the questions below to lead the discussion.

- What pattern did you notice between Problems 1 and 2?

- Explain to your partner how 1 fact can help you solve 2 new facts.

- Explain why you used multiplication or division to solve Problem 4. How does a division sentence in this problem relate to a multiplication sentence?

- How does the strategy we learned today relate to the break apart and distribute strategy we studied in Module 1?

- How might you use the strategy we practiced today to solve other problems? For example, how might you use 5 × 7 to help you solve 7 × 7?

Exit Ticket (3 minutes)

After the Student Debrief, instruct students to complete the Exit Ticket. A review of their work will help you assess the students' understanding of the concepts that were presented in the lesson today and plan more effectively for future lessons. You may read the questions aloud to the students.

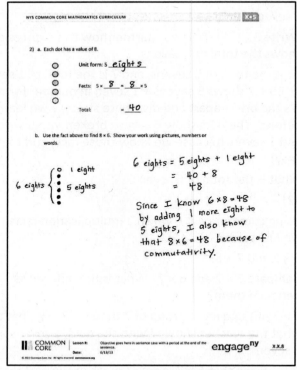

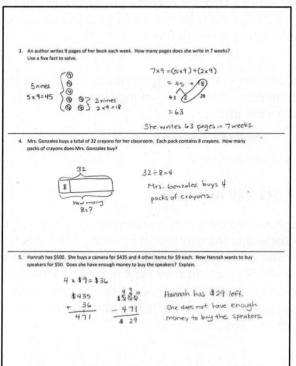

Lesson 2:

Date:

Apply the distributive and commutative properties to relate multiplication facts 5 x n + n to 6 x n and n x 6 where n is the size of the unit.

7/31/13

3.A.18

A

Multiply.

Correct _____

1	2 x 2 =		23	5 x 6 =	
2	2 x 3 =		24	6 x 5 =	
3	3 x 2 =		25	5 x 7 =	
4	2 x 4 =		26	7 x 5 =	
5	4 x 2 =		27	5 x 8 =	
6	2 x 5 =		28	8 x 5 =	
7	5 x 2 =		29	5 x 9 =	
8	2 x 6 =		30	9 x 5 =	
9	6 x 2 =		31	5 x 10 =	
10	2 x 7 =		32	10 x 5 =	
11	7 x 2 =		33	3 x 3 =	
12	2 x 8 =		34	3 x 4 =	
13	8 x 2 =		35	4 x 3 =	
14	2 x 9 =		36	3 x 6 =	
15	9 x 2 =		37	6 x 3 =	
16	2 x 10 =		38	3 x 7 =	
17	10 x 2 =		39	7 x 3 =	
18	5 x 3 =		40	3 x 8 =	
19	3 x 5 =		41	8 x 3 =	
20	5 x 4 =		42	3 x 9 =	
21	4 x 5 =		43	9 x 3 =	
22	5 x 5 =		44	4 x 4 =	

© Bill Davidson

Lesson 2:

Date:

Apply the distributive and commutative properties to relate multiplication facts 5 x n + n to 6 x n and n x 6 where n is the size of the unit.

7/31/13

3.A.19

B   Improvement _____   # Correct _____

Multiply.

1	5 x 2 =			23	2 x 6 =	
2	2 x 5 =			24	6 x 2 =	
3	5 x 3 =			25	2 x 7 =	
4	3 x 5 =			26	7 x 2 =	
5	5 x 4 =			27	2 x 8 =	
6	4 x 5 =			28	8 x 2 =	
7	5 x 5 =			29	2 x 9 =	
8	5 x 6 =			30	9 x 2 =	
9	6 x 5 =			31	2 x 10 =	
10	5 x 7 =			32	10 x 2 =	
11	7 x 5 =			33	3 x 3 =	
12	5 x 8 =			34	3 x 4 =	
13	8 x 5 =			35	4 x 3 =	
14	5 x 9 =			36	3 x 6 =	
15	9 x 5 =			37	6 x 3 =	
16	5 x 10 =			38	3 x 7 =	
17	10 x 5 =			39	7 x 3 =	
18	2 x 2 =			40	3 x 8 =	
19	2 x 3 =			41	8 x 3 =	
20	3 x 2 =			42	3 x 9 =	
21	2 x 4 =			43	9 x 3 =	
22	4 x 2 =			44	3 x 3 =	

© Bill Davidson

Lesson 2:   Apply the distributive and commutative properties to relate
multiplication facts 5 x *n* + *n* to 6 x *n* and *n* x 6 where *n* is the
size of the unit.

Date: 7/31/13

3.A.20

Name _____   Date _____

1. Each 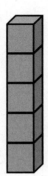 has a value of 7.

Unit form: 5 _____

Facts: 5 × _____ = _____ × 5

Total = _____

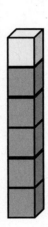

Unit form: 6 sevens = _____ sevens + _____ seven

= 35 + _____

= _____

Facts: _____ × _____ = _____

_____ × _____ = _____

COMMON CORE | Lesson 2:   Apply the distributive and commutative properties to relate
multiplication facts 5 x *n* + *n* to 6 x *n* and *n* x 6 where *n* is the
size of the unit.   **3.A.21**
Date: 7/31/13

2. a. Each dot has a value of 8.

Unit form: 5 _____

Facts: 5 × _____ = _____× 5

Total: = _____

b. Use the fact above to find 8 × 6. Show your work using pictures, numbers, or words.

COMMON CORE

Lesson 2:   Apply the distributive and commutative properties to relate
multiplication facts 5 x *n* + *n* to 6 x *n* and *n* x 6 where *n* is the
size of the unit.
Date: 7/31/13

3.A.22

3. An author writes 9 pages of her book each week. How many pages does she write in 7 weeks?
    Use a fives fact to solve.

4. Mrs. Gonzalez buys a total of 32 crayons for her classroom. Each pack contains 8 crayons. How many
    packs of crayons does Mrs. Gonzalez buy?

5. Hannah has $500. She buys a camera for $435 and 4 other items for $9 each. Now Hannah wants to buy
    speakers for $50. Does she have enough money to buy the speakers? Explain.

Lesson 2:

Date: 7/31/13

Apply the distributive and commutative properties to relate
multiplication facts 5 x n + n to 6 x n and n x 6 where n is the
size of the unit.

3.A.23

Name _____   Date _____

Use a fives fact to help you solve 7 × 6. Show your work using pictures, numbers, or words.

Lesson 2:   Apply the distributive and commutative properties to relate
           multiplication facts 5 x *n* + *n* to 6 x *n* and *n* x 6 where *n* is the
           size of the unit.
Date: 7/31/13

3.A.24

Name _____   Date _____

1. Each has a value of 9.

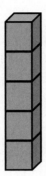

Unit form: _____

Facts: 5 × _____ = _____ × 5

Total = _____

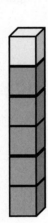

Unit form: 6 nines = _____ nines + _____ nine

= 45 + _____

= _____

Facts: _____ × _____ = _____

_____ × _____ = _____

COMMON CORE | **Lesson 2:** | Apply the distributive and commutative properties to relate multiplication facts 5 x *n* + *n* to 6 x *n* and *n* x 6 where *n* is the size of the unit. | 3.A.25

Date: 7/31/13

2. There are 6 blades on each windmill. How many total blades are on 7 windmills? Use a fives fact to solve.

3. Juanita organizes her magazines into 3 equal piles. She has a total of 18 magazines. How many magazines are in each pile?

4. Markuo spends $27 on some plants. Each plant costs $9. How many plants does he buy?

Lesson 2:

Date: 7/31/13

Apply the distributive and commutative properties to relate multiplication facts 5 x *n* + *n* to 6 x *n* and *n* x 6 where *n* is the size of the unit.

3.A.26

Lesson 3

Objective: Multiply and divide with familiar facts using a letter to represent the unknown.

Suggested Lesson Structure

- ■ Fluency Practice   (12 minutes)
- ■ Application Problem   (8 minutes)
- □ Concept Development   (30 minutes)
- ■ Student Debrief   (10 minutes)
- **Total Time**   **(60 minutes)**

Fluency Practice (12 minutes)

- Familiar Facts **3.OA.4**   (5 minutes)
- Multiply Using the Distributive Property **3.OA.5**   (5 minutes)
- Make Tens **3.OA.5**   (2 minutes)

Familiar Facts (5 minutes)

Materials: (S) Personal white boards

Note: This fluency reviews the relationship between multiplication and division from Module 1 in anticipation of their use in today's lesson.

    T: (Write 5 × 3 = ____.) Say the multiplication sentence.

    S: 5 × 3 = 15.

    T: (Write 5 × 3 = 15. To the right, write 15 ÷ 3 = ____.) On your boards, write the division sentence.

    S: (Write 15 ÷ 3 = 5.)

Repeat process for 4 × 3 and 7 × 2.

    T: (Write ____ × 2 = 10.) Say the missing factor.

    S: 5.

    T: (Write 10 ÷ 2 = ____.) On your boards, write the division sentence.

    S: (Write 10 ÷ 2 = 5.)

Repeat process for ____ × 3 = 6 and ____ × 2 = 16.

    T: (Write 20 = ____ × 10.) Say the missing factor.

    S: 2.

T: (Write 20 ÷ 10 = ____.) On your boards, write the division sentence.

S: (Write 20 ÷ 10 = 2.)

Repeat process for 18 = ____ × 3 and 45 = ____ × 5.

Multiply Using the Distributive Property (5 minutes)

Materials: (S) Personal white boards

Note: This fluency reviews the n + 1 strategy from Lesson 2.

NOTES ON
MULTIPLE MEANS OF
REPRESENTATION:

Use color to customize the presentation of the Multiply Using the Distributive Property fluency. Using a different color for each row of 9 may help students count groups of 9. The various colors can additionally help student interpret each column of the array as fives.

T: (Project a 5 × 9 array, covering a sixth row of 9.) How many groups of 9 are there?

S: 5.

T: Let's find how many are in the array counting by fives. (Point as students count.)

S: 5, 10, 15, 20, 25, 30, 35, 40, 45.

T: Let's find how many are in the array counting by nines. (Point as students count.)

S: 9, 18, 27, 36, 45.

T: Write two multiplication sentences for this array.

S: (Write 9 × 5 = 45 and 5 × 9 = 45.)

T: (Reveal the sixth row of 9.) How many groups of 9 are there now?

S: 6.

T: Add 1 more group of 9 to 45. (Write 45 + 9 = ____.) On your boards, write the addition sentence.

S: (Write 45 + 9 = 54.)

T: On your boards, write two multiplication sentences for this array.

S: (Write 9 × 6 = 54 and 6 × 9 = 54.)

Continue with the following suggested sequence: 5 × 8 → 6 × 8, 5 × 7 → 6 × 7, and 5 × 6 → 6 × 6.

Make Tens (2 minutes)

Note: This fluency prepares students for the skip-counting strategies used to multiply units of 6 and 7 in Lessons 4 and 5.

T: I'll say a number between 0 and 10. You say the number that you add to it to make a ten. 9.

S: 1.

Continue with the following suggested sequence: 8, 7, 6, 5, 9, 1, 8, 2, 7, 3, 6, 4, 8, 4, 7, 3, 6, 1, 2, 5, 9.

	Lesson 3:	Multiply and divide with familiar facts using a letter to represent the unknown.	3.A.28
	Date:	7/31/13	

Application Problem (8 minutes)

Twenty-four people line up to use the canoes at the park. Three people are assigned to each canoe. How many canoes are used?

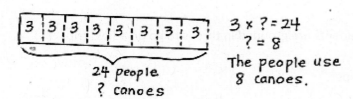

Note: Students may choose to model either as division or as multiplication. In the Concept Development this problem provides a context for using a letter to represent the unknown.

NOTES ON MULTIPLE MEANS OF REPRESENTATION:

Challenge above grade level learners by adding complexity to the Application Problem.

For example: Twenty-eight people lined up for canoes. Three people are assigned to each canoe. What are at least two possible solutions to make it possible for those people who don't make a threesome to go canoeing?

Concept Development (30 minutes)

Materials: (S) Personal white boards

Problem 1: Use a letter to represent the unknown in multiplication.

T: (Show a student's tape diagram and equation for the Application Problem, or example work above.) This is Student A's work on the Application Problem. What do the question marks in her work represent?

S: The unknown. → The number of canoes that are used.

T: We can use a letter to represent the unknown value instead of a question mark. For this problem, we might choose letter *c* to help us express that the unknown stands for how many *canoes* are used in the problem. How will using a letter to express the unknown value change the way we model and solve?

S: There will be *c*'s where the question marks were on the tape diagram and in the equation. I don't think it changes the way you solve though.

T: Let's confirm your thinking. On your board, solve the Application Problem, this time using letter *c* to express the unknown on your model and in your equation. Solve, and then compare with your work on the Application Problem.

S: (Solve and compare, possible work below.)

`MP.4`

NOTES ON MULTIPLE MEANS OF REPRESENTATION:

Clarify unknowns for English language learners and others by pre-teaching using a few simple equations with letters, such as $2 + 2 = h$; $h = 4$, or the Familiar Facts fluency in Lesson 4.

MP.4

T: In a complete sentence, what is the value of *c*?

S: The value of *c* is 8 canoes.

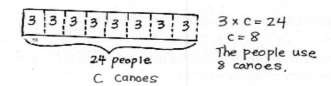

Problem 2: Use a letter to represent the unknown in division.

(Project or show the following problem: Twenty-one students are grouped in threes to go on a field trip. How many groups of students are there?)

T: Read the problem with your partner, then whisper what the unknown represents.

S: (Read problem.) The unknown represents the number of groups.

T: Before we solve, talk with your partner about which letter you might choose to express the unknown on your model and in your equation.

S: We could use *s* for students. → I think *n* will remind me we are looking for the number of groups. → *g* is best because it stands for *groups*.

T: Model the problem and write an equation to solve. Let's use the letter *g* to express the unknown.

S: (Students model and write $21 \div 3 = g$.)

T: In a complete sentence, tell the value of *g*.

S: The value of *g* is 7 groups.

Continue with the following suggested sequence to show unknowns in various positions:

- $24 = 4 \times r$
- $5 = 50 \div m$
- $27 \div b = 3$
- $d \div 6 = 3$

Call attention to the way that you write the value of the unknown (e.g., *n* = 14 after finding it). Students should emulate this in their work.

Depending on time, extend the lesson by assigning each student (or pair of students) a letter of the alphabet. Task them with writing a simple word problem in which their assigned letter represents the unknown. They first solve their own problem, and then exchange with another student to solve a new one.

NOTES ON CHOOSING VARIABLES:

Point out that some letters may potentially be confused with other symbols. Letters *s*, *o*, *l*, *x*, and *t* respectively resemble 5, 0, 1, the multiplication symbol (×), and the addition symbol (+). Encourage students to use other letters if possible.

NOTES ON NUMBER CHOICES:

This lesson intentionally uses known facts from Module 1. Ideally students are fairly automatic with these facts so that focus stays on naming the unknown represented by the letter rather than the calculation.

COMMON CORE

Lesson 3:   Multiply and divide with familiar facts using a letter to represent the unknown.
Date: 7/31/13

3.A.30

Problem Set (15 minutes)

Students should do their personal best to complete the Problem Set within the allotted 10 minutes.
For some classes, it may be appropriate to modify the assignment by specifying which problems they work on first. Some problems do not specify a method for solving. Students solve these problems using the RDW approach used for Application Problems.

Student Debrief (10 minutes)

Lesson Objective: Multiply and divide with familiar facts using a letter to represent the unknown.

The Student Debrief is intended to invite reflection and active processing of the total lesson experience.

Invite students to review their solutions for the Problem Set. They should check work by comparing answers with a partner before going over answers as a class. Look for misconceptions or misunderstandings that can be addressed in the Debrief. Guide students in a conversation to debrief the Problem Set and process the lesson.

You may choose to use any combination of the questions below to lead the discussion.

- Invite students to share the steps they took to model and solve Problem 4, the problem that likely posed the greatest challenge.

- Share student work for Problem 3 that shows different approaches (e.g., $4 \times p = 28$ and $28 \div 4 = p$). Discuss the thinking behind each approach to review division as both an *unknown factor* and *equal groups* problem.

- Why is using a letter to represent the unknown more helpful than using a question mark?

Exit Ticket (3 minutes)

After the Student Debrief, instruct students to complete the Exit Ticket. A review of their work will help you assess the students' understanding of the concepts that were presented in the lesson today and plan more effectively for future lessons. You may read the questions aloud to the students.

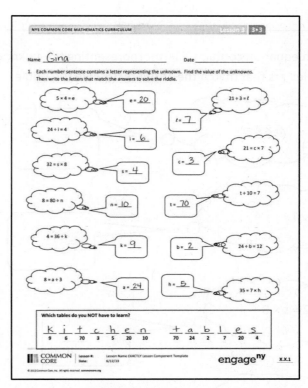

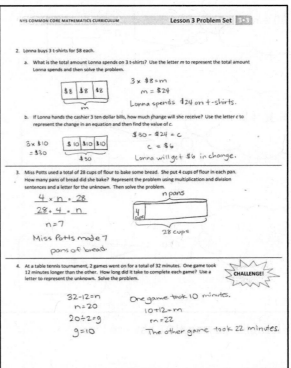

Lesson 3:   Multiply and divide with familiar facts using a letter to represent
              the unknown.
Date: 7/31/13

3.A.31

© 2013 Common Core, Inc. All rights reserved. commoncore.org

Name _____   Date _____

1. Each equation contains a letter representing the unknown. Find the value of the unknowns, then write the letters that match the answers to solve the riddle.

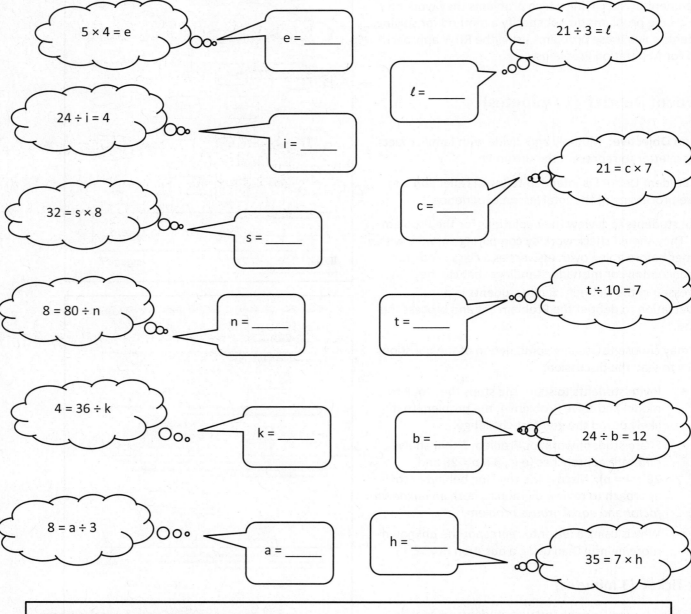

$5 \times 4 = e$ e = _____

$21 \div 3 = l$ l = _____

$24 \div i = 4$ i = _____

$21 = c \times 7$ c = _____

$32 = s \times 8$ s = _____

$t \div 10 = 7$ t = _____

$8 = 80 \div n$ n = _____

$4 = 36 \div k$ k = _____

$24 \div b = 12$ b = _____

$8 = a \div 3$ a = _____

$35 = 7 \times h$ h = _____

Which tables do you NOT have to learn?

___ ___ ___ ___ ___ ___ ___   ___ ___ ___ ___ ___ ___
 9   6   70   3   5   20   10   70   24   2   7   20   4

2. Lonna buys 3 t-shirts for $8 each.

    a. What is the total amount Lonna spends on 3 t-shirts? Use the letter *m* to represent the total amount Lonna spends, and then solve the problem.

    b. If Lonna hands the cashier 3 ten dollar bills, how much change will she receive? Use the letter *c* to represent the change in an equation, and then find the value of *c*.

3. Miss Potts used a total of 28 cups of flour to bake some bread. She put 4 cups of flour in each pan. How many pans of bread did she bake? Represent the problem using multiplication and division sentences and a letter for the unknown. Then, solve the problem.

    _____ × _____ = _____

    _____ ÷ _____ = _____

4. At a table tennis tournament, two games went on for a total of 32 minutes. One game took 12 minutes longer than the other. How long did it take to complete each game? Use letters to represent the unknowns. Solve the problem.

Name _____ Date _____

Find the value of the unknown in Problems 1–4.

1. $z = 5 \times 9$

   z = _____

2. $30 \div 6 = v$

   v = _____

3. $8 \times w = 24$

   w = _____

4. $y \div 4 = 7$

   y = _____

5. Mr. Strand waters his rose bushes for a total of 15 minutes. He waters each rose bush for 3 minutes. How many rose bushes does Mr. Strand water? Represent the problem using multiplication and division sentences and a letter for the unknown. Then, solve the problem.

   _____ × _____ = _____

   _____ ÷ _____ = _____

COMMON CORE

Lesson 3:   Multiply and divide with familiar facts using a letter to represent the unknown.

Date: 7/31/13

3.A.34

Name _____   Date _____

1. a.   Complete the pattern.

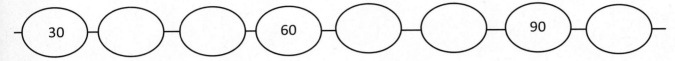

30   60   90

   b.   Find the value of the unknown.

   $10 \times 2 = d$ d = __20__ $10 \times 6 = w$ w = _____

   $3 \times 10 = e$ e = _____ $10 \times 7 = n$ n = _____

   $f = 4 \times 10$ f = _____ $g = 8 \times 10$ g = _____

   $p = 5 \times 10$ p = _____

2.   Each equation contains a letter representing the unknown. Find the value of the unknown.

$8 \div 2 = n$	n = _____
$3 \times a = 12$	a = _____
$p \times 8 = 40$	p = _____
$18 \div 6 = c$	c = _____
$d \times 4 = 24$	d = _____
$h \div 7 = 5$	h = _____
$6 \times 3 = f$	f = _____
$32 \div y = 4$	y = _____

3. Pedro buys 4 books at the fair for $7 each.
   a. What is the total amount Pedro spends on 4 books? Use the letter *b* to represent the total amount Pedro spends, and then solve the problem.

   b. Pedro hands the cashier 3 ten dollar bills. How much change will he receive? Write an equation to solve. Use the letter *c* to represent the unknown.

4. On field day, the first grade dash is 25 meters long. The third grade dash is twice the distance of the first grade dash. How long is the third grade dash? Use a letter to represent the unknown and solve.

COMMON CORE | Lesson 3: | Multiply and divide with familiar facts using a letter to represent the unknown.
Date: | 7/31/13

3.A.36

Mathematics Curriculum

Topic B

Multiplication and Division Using Units of 6 and 7

3.OA.3, 3.OA.4, 3.OA.5, 3.OA.7, 3.OA.9, 3.OA.1, 3.OA.2, 3.OA.6

Focus Standard:	3.OA.3	Use multiplication and division within 100 to solve word problems in situations involving equal groups, arrays, and measurement quantities, e.g., by using drawings and equations with a symbol for the unknown number to represent the problem. (See Glossary, Table 2.)
	3.OA.4	Determine the unknown whole number in a multiplication or division equation relating three whole numbers. *For example, determine the unknown number that makes the equation true in each of the equations 8 × ? = 48, 5 = _ ÷ 3, 6 × 6 = ?*
	3.OA.5	Apply properties of operations as strategies to multiply and divide. (Students need not use formal terms for these properties.) *Examples: If 6 × 4 = 24 is known, then 4 × 6 = 24 is also known. (Commutative property of multiplication.) 3 × 5 × 2 can be found by 3 × 5 = 15, then 15 × 2 = 30, or by 5 × 2 = 10, then 3 × 10 = 30. (Associative property of multiplication.) Knowing that 8 × 5 = 40 and 8 × 2 = 16, one can find 8 × 7 as 8 × (5 + 2) = (8 × 5) + (8 × 2) = 40 + 16 = 56. (Distributive property.)*
	3.OA.7	Fluently multiply and divide within 100, using strategies such as the relationship between multiplication and division (e.g., knowing that 8 × 5 = 40, one knows 40 ÷ 5 = 8) or properties of operations. By the end of Grade 3, know from memory all products of two one-digit numbers.
	3.OA.9	Identify arithmetic patterns (including patterns in the addition table or multiplication table), and explain them using properties of operations. *For example, observe that 4 times a number is always even, and explain why 4 times a number can be decomposed into two equal addends.*
Instructional Days:	4	
Coherence -Links from:	G2–M3	Place Value, Counting, and Comparison of Numbers to 1000
	G2–M6	Foundations of Multiplication and Division
	G3–M1	Properties of Multiplication and Division and Solving Problems with Units of 2–5 and 10
** -Links to:**	G3–M4	Multiplication and Area
	G4–M3	Multi-Digit Multiplication and Division
	G4–M5	Fraction Equivalence, Ordering, and Operations
	G4–M7	Exploring Multiplication

In Lessons 4 and 5, students count by sixes and sevens, composing up to and then over the next decade. Students might count, 6, 12, 18, and then mentally add 18 + 2 + 4 to make 24. This skip-counting method utilizes make ten strategies from Grades 1 and 2. Initially, students use number bonds to decompose and identify appropriate number pairs. In the example above, 18 needs 2 more to make 20. The next six can be decomposed as 2 and 4. Eventually students are able to use mental math as they manipulate numbers and skip-count to multiply. Although a formal introduction to the associative property comes in Topic C, these lessons preview the concept using addition:

- 6 + 6 = 6 + 4 + 2
- 18 + 6 = 18 + 2 + 4
- 36 + 6 = 36 + 4 + 2
- 48 + 6 = 48 + 2 + 4

Lesson 6 builds on Lesson 2 with a formal re-introduction of the distributive property using the 5 + n pattern to multiply and divide. Students understand that multiples of 6 can be thought of as (5 + 1) × n to make 5 and 1 more groups, or 6 groups of n. Similarly, multiples of 7 can be thought of as (5 + 2) × n to make 5 and 2 more groups, or 7 groups of n. In division students decompose the dividend using a multiple of 5, and then add the quotients of the smaller division facts to find the quotient of the larger unknown division fact. For example:

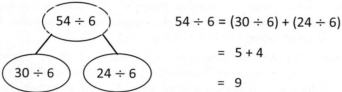

$$54 \div 6 = (30 \div 6) + (24 \div 6)$$
$$= 5 + 4$$
$$= 9$$

Use of the 5 + n pattern as a strategy builds on concepts in Lessons 2, 4, and 5, and facilitates mental math, particularly using units of 6.

In Lesson 7, students use tape diagrams to analyze multiplication and division word problems and determine the unknown. This is the first time they use a letter to represent the unknown in word problem contexts, and also using new units.

A Teaching Sequence Towards Mastery of Multiplication and Division Using Units of 6 and 7

Objective 1: Count by units of 6 to multiply and divide using number bonds to decompose.
           (Lesson 4)

Objective 2: Count by units of 7 to multiply and divide using number bonds to decompose.
           (Lesson 5)

Objective 3: Use the distributive property as a strategy to multiply and divide using units of 6 and 7.
           (Lesson 6)

Objective 4: Interpret the unknown in multiplication and division to model and solve problems using
           units of 6 and 7.
           (Lesson 7)

Topic B:	Multiplication and Division Using Units of 6 and 7
Date:	7/31/13

3.B.2

Lesson 4

Objective: Count by units of 6 to multiply and divide using number bonds to decompose.

Suggested Lesson Structure

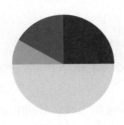

■ Fluency Practice   (15 minutes)
■ Application Problem   (5 minutes)
■ Concept Development   (30 minutes)
■ Student Debrief   (10 minutes)

Total Time   **(60 minutes)**

Fluency Practice (15 minutes)

- Group Counting **3.OA.1**   (4 minutes)
- Familiar Facts **3.OA.4**   (4 minutes)
- Multiply Using the Distributive Property **3.OA.5**   (4 minutes)
- Make Ten Game **3.OA.5**   (3 minutes)

Group Counting (4 minutes)

Note: Group counting reviews interpreting multiplication as repeated addition. Counting by sixes and sevens prepares students for multiplication using those units in this topic. Group counting eights and nines anticipates multiplication using those units later in the module. Direct students to count forward and backward, occasionally changing the direction of the count:

- Sixes to 60
- Sevens to 70
- Eights to 80
- Nines to 90

Familiar Facts (4 minutes)

Materials: (S) Personal white boards

Note: This fluency reviews the relationship between multiplication and division from Module 1, as well as using a letter to represent the unknown from Lesson 3.

T: (Write $6 \times 2 = a$.) On your boards, write the value of a.

S: (Write $a = 12$.)

Lesson 4:   Count by units of 6 to multiply and divide using number bonds to
Date: decompose.
             7/31/13

3.B.3

T: (Write $6 \times 2 = 12$. To the right, write $12 \div 6 = b$.) On your white boards, write the division sentence.

S: (Write $12 \div 6 = 2$.)

Repeat the process for: $7 \times 3 = c$, $21 \div 7 = d$, $e \times 4 = 24$, $24 \div 4 = f$, $g \times 2 = 18$, $18 \div 2 = h$, $16 = i \times 2$, $16 \div 8 = j$, $45 = 5 \times k$, and $45 \div 9 = m$.

Multiply Using the Distributive Property (4 minutes)

Materials: (S) Personal white boards

Note: This fluency reviews the $n + 1$ strategy from Lesson 2.

T: (Project a 5×6 array, covering a sixth row of 6.) How many groups of 6 are there?

S: 5.

T: Let's find how many are in the array counting by fives. (Point as students count.)

S: 5, 10, 15, 20, 25, 30.

T: Let's find how many are in the array counting by sixes. (Point as students count.)

S: 6, 12, 18, 24, 30.

T: Write two multiplication sentences for this array.

S: (Write $6 \times 5 = 30$ and $5 \times 6 = 30$.)

T: (Reveal the sixth row of 6.) How many groups of 6 are there now?

S: 6.

T: Add 1 more group of 6 to 30. (Write $30 + 6 = $ ____.) On your white boards, write the addition sentence.

S: (Write $30 + 6 = 36$.)

T: On your white boards, write a multiplication sentence for this array.

S: (Write $6 \times 6 = 36$.)

Continue with the following suggested sequence: $5 \times 8 \rightarrow 6 \times 8$, $5 \times 7 \rightarrow 6 \times 7$, and $5 \times 9 \rightarrow 6 \times 9$.

Make Ten Game (3 minutes)

Materials: (S) Number cards (1–9)

Note: This fluency prepares students for today's Concept Development.

(Students play in pairs. Each pair has a set of 9 cards, each with a number 1–9.)

T: (Write ____ + ____ = 10.) Spread the cards out in front of you.

T: Put your hands behind your back. I'll write a number in the first blank. When you know the number that belongs in the second blank, touch the card that shows the number. The first person to touch the card keeps it. Whoever has the most cards at the end wins. (Write $8 + $ ____ = 10.)

S: (Touch the 2 card. The first to touch it keeps the card.)

Continue with the following suggested sequence: 5, 2, 7, 1, 4, 3, 6, students replace cards, 1, 5, 3, 2, 4, 7, 6, students replace cards, 4, 7, 3, 9, 6.

	Lesson 4:	Count by units of 6 to multiply and divide using number bonds to decompose.	
	Date:	7/31/13	3.B.4

Application Problem (5 minutes)

Marshall puts 6 pictures on each of the 6 pages in his photo album. How many pictures does he put in the photo album in all?

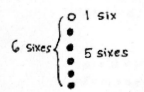

6 sixes = 5 sixes + 1 six
       = 30 + 6
       = 36
Marshall puts 36 pictures in his photo album.

Note: This problem is designed to review the Lesson 2 concept of applying the distributive property to relate multiplication by $n + 1$ to multiplication by n.

NOTES ON MULTIPLE MEANS OF ENGAGEMENT:

In order to encourage students to apply the distributive property, you may adjust the numbers in the Application Problem. For example, a student above grade level may mentally solve 6 times 6, yet choose to use the distributive property to multiply 6 times 13.

Concept Development (30 minutes)

Materials: (S) Personal white boards

Part 1: Use number bonds to decompose and skip-count using units of 6.

T: Some of you may have skip-counted by six to get the answer to Marshall's problem. When we're skip-counting by six, how do we get the next number in our sequence?

S: Add 6!

T: Like this? (Write equation, as shown.)

T: Think back to our fluency practice today. What number should I add to 6 to make ten?

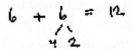

S: 4!

T: Write my equation on your board. Then, draw a number bond to break apart the second six, showing how to solve using a make ten strategy. (Draw number bond as shown.)

T: 6 plus 4 equals?

S: 10!

T: Write it next to 6 + 6. (Write equation as shown.)

T: 10 plus 2 equals?

S: 12!

T: Write that under 6 + 4 = 10. (Write equation as shown.)

T: So, what is 6 plus 6?

NOTES ON MULTIPLE MEANS OF REPRESENTATION:

Learners differ in their ability to process information. Help students organize board notes to support their understanding. For example, you may choose to label, write out, illustrate, and/or put to music the steps of the make ten strategy.

Lesson 4:   Count by units of 6 to multiply and divide using number bonds to decompose.
Date: 7/31/13

3.B.5

S: 12!

Have students repeat the process for the next two minutes to see how high they can count by six: 12 + 6 = 18, 18 + 6 = 24, 24 + 6 = 30, 30 + 6 = 36, 36 +6 = 42, 42 + 6 = 48, 48 +6 = 54, 54 + 6 = 60

T: What patterns did you notice counting by six?

S: Sometimes we broke apart the six to complete the ten like in 18 + 6. Other times we broke apart the two-digit number to complete the ten like in 12 + 6.

T: How did adding 6 and 6 help you add 36 and 6?

S: You add it the same way by breaking the six into 4 and 2 to complete the ten. → You can also think of 36 + 6 as 3 tens more than 6 + 6.

T: How did adding 18 and 6 help you add 48 and 6?

MP.5

S: We broke apart the six into 2 and 4 to complete the ten. → 48 + 6 is also just 3 tens more than 18 + 6.

T: Why is a make ten strategy with number bonds helpful for counting by sixes?

S: Adding sixes is harder than adding with tens.

T: What other count-bys is it helpful for? Is it helpful for the fives?

S: No, because adding by fives is easy to do mentally.

T: Is it helpful for sevens?

S: I think so. Sevens are hard to skip-count by too.

T: Yes, we'll find out tomorrow.

T: Now that we discussed how the make ten strategy makes our skip-counting sixes more efficient, let's try it out to solve multiplication and division problems.

Part 2: Use skip-counting sixes to solve multiplication and division problems.

T: Skip-count by six 10 times. Write the count-by sequence on your board. You can also record your addition on your white board.

T: What is the last number in your sequence?

S: 60!

T: 60 is the same as how many sixes?

S: 10 sixes.

Sample Student Board of Count-by

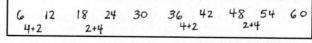

T: Tell a partner what multiplication problem we just solved, then write it on your white board.

S: 6 times 10 equals 60. (Write 6 × 10 = 60.)

T: We just used our count by six sequence to help us find that 6 times 10 equals 60.

T: We can also use skip-counting to solve division problems. Write the last number in your sequence

COMMON CORE | Lesson 4:   Count by units of 6 to multiply and divide using number bonds to decompose.
Date: 7/31/13   3.B.6

© 2013 Common Core, Inc. All rights reserved. commoncore.org

on your white board, followed by a division symbol.

T: What did we count by to get to 60?

S: Sixes!

T: Write 6 after the division symbol, followed by an equals sign.

T: How many times did we count by six to get to 60?

S: 10 times!

T: Write 10 as the answer to this division problem. Read your equation to a partner.

T: Turn and talk to a partner, what do you notice about the multiplication and division problems we solved?

S: They use the same numbers. → The division fact uses the same numbers as the multiplication fact, just in a different order. → 60 divided by 6 equals 10 is the related division fact for 6 times 10 equals 60.

T: That's right, they are related facts. Now you have learned another strategy to solve multiplication and division facts with sixes!

Continue with the following suggested sequence to help develop strategies for and learn the following facts. You may want to refer students back to the times table chart in Lesson 1 to focus their attention on the 16 new facts:

- 6 × 6
- 6 × 7
- 6 × 8
- 6 × 9

Problem Set (10 minutes)

Students should do their personal best to complete the Problem Set within the allotted 10 minutes. For some classes, it may be appropriate to modify the assignment by specifying which problems they work on first. Some problems do not specify a method for solving. Students solve these problems using the RDW approach used for Application Problems.

Student Debrief (10 minutes)

Lesson Objective: Count by units of 6 to multiply and divide using number bonds to decompose.

The Student Debrief is intended to invite reflection and active processing of the total lesson experience.

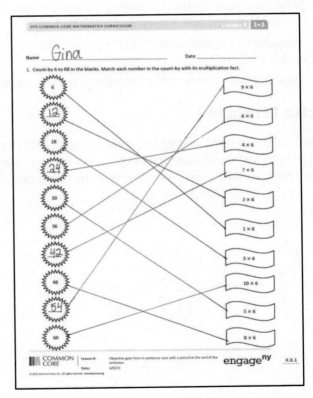

COMMON CORE

Lesson 4:   Count by units of 6 to multiply and divide using number bonds to decompose.

Date: 7/31/13

3.B.7

Invite students to review their solutions for the Problem Set. They should check work by comparing answers with a partner before going over answers as a class. Look for misconceptions or misunderstandings that can be addressed in the Debrief. Guide students in a conversation to debrief the Problem Set and process the lesson.

You may choose to use any combination of the questions below to lead the discussion.

- With a partner, list the related division facts for each number in the skip-counting sequence in Problem 1.
- What other multiplication and division problems can you solve with the sequence you already have in Problem 2?
- How was using the skip-counting strategy different in Problem 4 than in the other problems?
- How does your method of adding 18 and 6 help you add 18 tens and 6 tens, and $480 and $60?
- How did the Application Problem connect to today's lesson?
- How did the fluency help prepare you for the lesson?

Exit Ticket (3 minutes)

After the Student Debrief, instruct students to complete the Exit Ticket. A review of their work will help you assess the students' understanding of the concepts that were presented in the lesson today and plan more effectively for future lessons. You may read the questions aloud to the students.

COMMON CORE

Lesson 4:   Count by units of 6 to multiply and divide using number bonds to decompose.

Date: 7/31/13

3.B.8

© 2013 Common Core, Inc. All rights reserved. commoncore.org

Name _____   Date _____

1. Skip-count by six to fill in the blanks. Match each number in the count-by with its multiplication fact.

6	9×6
___	6×6
18	4×6
___	7×6
30	2×6
36	1×6
___	3×6
48	10×6
___	5×6
60	8×6

2. Count by six to fill in the blanks below.

6, _____, _____, _____

Complete the multiplication equation that represents the final number in your count-by.

6 × _____ = _____

Complete the division equation that represents your count-by.

_____ ÷ 6 = _____

3. Count by six to fill in the blanks below.

6, _____, _____, _____, _____, _____, _____

Complete the multiplication equation that represents the final number in your count-by.

6 × _____ = _____

Complete the division equation that represents your count-by.

_____ ÷ 6 = _____

4. Mrs. Byrne's class skip-counts by six for a group counting activity. When she points up, they count up by six and when she points down, they count down by six. The arrows show when she changes direction.

   a. Fill in the blanks below to show the group counting answers.

   ↑ 0, 6, _____, 18, _____ ↓ _____, 12 ↑ _____, 24, 30, _____ ↓ 30, 24, _____ ↑ 24, _____, 36, _____, 48

   b. Mrs. Byrne says the last number that the class counts is the product of 6 and another number. Write a multiplication sentence and a division sentence to show she's right.

        6 × _____ = 48   48 ÷ 6 = _____

5. Julie counts by six to solve 6 × 7. She says the answer is 36. Is she right? Explain your answer.

Lesson 4: Count by units of 6 to multiply and divide using number bonds to decompose.
Date: 7/31/13

3.B.10

Name _____   Date _____

1. Sylvia solves 6 × 9 by adding 48 + 6. Show how Sylvia breaks apart and bonds her numbers to complete the ten. Then solve.

2. Skip-count by six to solve the following:

   a.   8 × 6 = _____   b.   54 ÷ 6 = _____

COMMON CORE | **Lesson 4:**   Count by units of 6 to multiply and divide using number bonds to decompose.

Date: 7/31/13   3.B.11

Name _____   Date _____

1. Use number bonds to help you skip-count by six by either making a ten or adding to the ones.

a. 6 + 6 = __**10**__ + __**2**__ = _____
         4   2

b. 12 + 6 = __**10**__ + __**8**__ = _____
      10 2

c. 18 + 6 = _____ + _____ = _____
        2   4

d. 24 + 6 = _____ + _____ = _____
      20 4

e. 30 + 6 = _____

f. 36 + 6 = _____ + _____ = _____
        4   2

g. 42 + 6 = _____ + _____ = _____

h. 48 + 6 = _____ + _____ = _____

i. 54 + 6 = _____ + _____ = _____

COMMON CORE   Lesson 4:   Count by units of 6 to multiply and divide using number bonds to
                             decompose.
               Date: 7/31/13   3.B.12

© 2013 Common Core, Inc. All rights reserved. commoncore.org

2. Count by six to fill in the blanks below.

6, _____, _____, _____, _____

Complete the multiplication equation that represents the final number in your count-by.

6 × _____ = _____

Complete the division equation that represents your count-by.

_____ ÷ 6 = _____

3. Count by six to fill in the blanks below.

6, _____, _____, _____, _____, _____

Complete the multiplication equation that represents the final number in your count-by.

6 × _____ = _____

Complete the division equation that represents your count-by.

_____ ÷ 6 = _____

4. Count by 6 to solve 48 ÷ 6. Show your work below.

COMMON CORE

Lesson 4:   Count by units of 6 to multiply and divide using number bonds to decompose.

Date: 7/31/13

3.B.13

Lesson 5

Objective: Count by units of 7 to multiply and divide using number bonds to decompose.

Suggested Lesson Structure

■ Fluency Practice   (15 minutes)
■ Application Problem   (5 minutes)
■ Concept Development   (30 minutes)
■ Student Debrief   (10 minutes)
  Total Time   **(60 minutes)**

Fluency Practice (15 minutes)

- Multiply by 6 **3.OA.7**   (7 minutes)
- Group Counting **3.OA.1**   (4 minutes)
- Make Seven Game **3.OA.5**   (4 minutes)

Multiply by 6 (7 minutes)

Materials: (S) Multiply by 6 Pattern Sheet (1–5)

Note: This activity builds fluency with multiplication facts using units of 6. It works toward students knowing from memory all products of two one-digit numbers.

    T: (Write 6 × 5 = _____.) Let's skip-count by sixes to find the answer. I'll raise a finger for each six. (Count with fingers to 5 as students count.)

    S: 6, 12, 18, 24, 30.

    T: (Circle 30 and write 6 × 5 = 30 above it. Write 6 × 3 = _____.) Let's skip-count up by sixes again. (Count with fingers to 3 as students count.)

    S: 6, 12, 18.

    T: Let's see how we can skip-count down to find the answer, too. Start at 30 with 5 fingers, 1 for each six. (Count down with your fingers as students say numbers.)

    S: 30 (5 fingers), 24 (4 fingers), 18 (3 fingers).

Repeat the process for 6 × 4.

    T: (Distribute the Multiply by 6 Pattern Sheet.) Let's practice multiplying by 6. Be sure to work left to right across the page.

Lesson 5:   Count by units of 7 to multiply and divide using number bonds to decompose.
Date: 7/31/13

3.B.14

Directions for administration of Multiply By Pattern Sheets:

- Distribute Multiply By Pattern Sheet.
- Allow a maximum of two minutes for students to complete as many problems as possible.
- Direct students to work left to right across the page.
- Encourage skip-counting strategies to solve unknown facts.

Group Counting (4 minutes)

Note: Group counting reviews interpreting multiplication as repeated addition. Counting by sevens prepares students for multiplication using those units in this lesson. Group counting eights and nines anticipates multiplication using those units later in the module. Direct students to count forward and backward, occasionally changing the direction of the count.

- Sevens to 70
- Eights to 80
- Nines to 90

Make Seven Game (4 minutes)

Note: This activity prepares students for the skip-counting strategy used to multiply using units of 7 in today's lesson.

Students play in pairs. Each pair has a set of 6 cards, each with a number (1–6).

- T: (Write ___ + ___ = 7.) Spread the cards out in front of you.
- T: Put your hands behind your back. I'll write a number in the first blank. When you know the number that belongs in the second blank, touch the card that shows the number. The first person to touch the card keeps it. Whoever has the most cards at the end wins. (Write 5 + __ = 7.)
- S: (Touch the 2 card. The first to touch it keeps the card.)

Continue with the following suggested sequence: 1, 4, 2, 3, and 5.

Application Problem (5 minutes)

Gracie draws 7 rows of stars. In each row, she draws 4 stars. How many stars does Gracie draw in all? Use a letter to represent the unknown and solve.

Note: This problem reviews the G3–M1 concept of multiplying using units of 4. It will be used in the Concept Development to lead into skip-counting by sevens. Be sure to circulate and find a student's work to be used as an example in the Concept Development (find a student who counted by four 7 times to solve the problem).

$7 \times 4 = g$

$g = 28$

Gracie draws 28 stars.

Concept Development (30 minutes)

Materials: (S) Personal white boards

Part 1: Use number bonds to decompose and make ten as a strategy for skip-counting units of 7.

T: I noticed that Student A solved the Application Problem by skip-counting by four 7 times. Is there another count-by strategy that could be used to solve this problem?

S: Skip-count by seven 4 times.

T: Let's show that work on our boards. Write 7 on your board.

T: How do we get the next number in our count?

S: Add 7!

T: Can we use a number bond to add 7 by making ten like we did yesterday with sixes?

S: Yes, we can break apart 7 into 3 and 4, and then use the 3 to make ten with the first 7.

T: Work with a partner to use number bonds to show how you make ten to count by seven 4 times.

T: Check your work with mine. (Project work as shown.)

T: What is the last number in the sequence when you count by seven 4 times?

S: 28!

T: Is the answer the same even though Student A counted by four 7 times?

S: Yes, it's the same because we just switched the order of the factors. → The product is the same, but the order of the factors is different. It's the commutative property.

T: Work with a partner to complete your sequence by counting by seven 10 times. Use number bonds to make ten. (Circulate and check student work.)

T: Everyone, at my signal, read your count by seven sequence.

NOTES ON
MULTIPLE MEANS OF
REPRESENTATION:

For English language learners you may pre-teach and/or clarify unfamiliar math terms, such as *sequence, row, factors, product, number bond, count by,* and *skip-count.*

Depending on your learners' needs, give explicit prompts for every step of using the make ten strategy to count by seven 4 times. Alternatively, you may scaffold with a checklist or template.

Count by seven 4 times:

$0 + 7 = 7$

$7 + 7 = 14$
    /\
    3 4

$14 + 7 = 21$
     /\
     6 1

$21 + 7 = 28$
 /\
 20 1

Remaining count by seven:

$28 + 7 = 35$
    /\
    2 5

$35 + 7 = 42$
    /\
    5 2

$42 + 7 = 49$
   /\
   40 2

$49 + 7 = 56$
    /\
    1 6

$56 + 7 = 63$
    /\
    4 3

$63 + 7 = 70$
   /\
   60 3

Lesson 5:   Count by units of 7 to multiply and divide using number bonds to decompose.

Date: 7/31/13

3.B.16

Part 2: Skip-count by seven to solve multiplication and division problems.

T: Let's use our sequence to solve multiplication and division problems with seven. I am going to say a multiplication or division problem. Write the problem on your board and use your sequence to find the answer. At my signal, show your board.

T: Let's do a practice one together. Turn and talk to a partner, how can you use your skip-counting sequence to solve 42 divided by 7?

S: I can count 6 sevens in the sequence, which takes me to 42. So, 42 divided by 7 equals 6.

T: Write the equation on your board.

T: At my signal, show me your board.

T: Ok, here we go, next problem! 49 divided by 7 equals? (After students work, signal.)

Continue with the following suggested sequence:

- 7 × 6
- 7 × e = 56
- f ÷ 7 equals 9

Problem Set (10 minutes)

Students should do their personal best to complete the Problem Set within the allotted 10 minutes. For some classes, it may be appropriate to modify the assignment by specifying which problems they work on first. Some problems do not specify a method for solving. Students solve these problems using the RDW approach used for Application Problems.

NOTES ON MULTIPLE MEANS OF ENGAGEMENT:

Some learners may prefer to use the distributive or commutative property to solve 7 times 6. Encourage their personal choices of efficient strategies. Challenge learners to present a multiplication fact they would solve using skip-counting. Ask, "How do you choose your strategy to solve?"

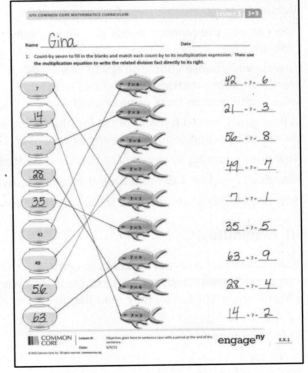

COMMON CORE   Lesson 5:   Count by units of 7 to multiply and divide using number bonds to decompose.
                Date: 7/31/13

© 2013 Common Core, Inc. All rights reserved. commoncore.org

3.B.17

Student Debrief (10 minutes)

Lesson Objective: Count by units of 7 to multiply and divide using number bonds to decompose.

The Student Debrief is intended to invite reflection and active processing of the total lesson experience.

Invite students to review their solutions for the Problem Set. They should check work by comparing answers with a partner before going over answers as a class. Look for misconceptions or misunderstandings that can be addressed in the Debrief. Guide students in a conversation to debrief the Problem Set and process the lesson. You may choose to use any combination of the questions below to lead the discussion.

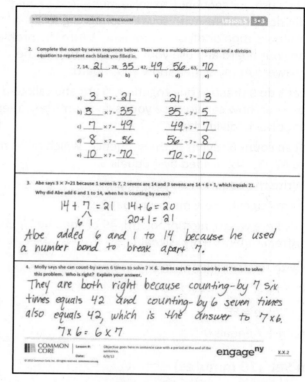

- Take turns with a partner reading the multiplication facts in Problem 1 and the related division facts.
- How can you use number bonds to help you solve Problem 2?
- How do you choose your strategy to solve? What are some different strategies that can help you solve multiplication facts using units of 7?

MP.5

- In Problem 3, would it make sense for Abe to use number bonds to find the next number after 21 in the count by seven sequence? Why or why not?
- How does counting by seven help you solve multiplication and division problems with seven?
- How does Problem 4 demonstrate the commutative property?
- How does today's lesson relate to our previous work of adding 1 unit to 5 units?

Exit Ticket (3 minutes)

After the Student Debrief, instruct students to complete the Exit Ticket. A review of their work will help you assess the students' understanding of the concepts that were presented in the lesson today and plan more effectively for future lessons. You may read the questions aloud to the students.

Multiply.

6 x 1 = _____   6 x 2 = _____   6 x 3 = _____   6 x 4 = _____

6 x 5 = _____   6 x 1 = _____   6 x 2 = _____   6 x 1 = _____

6 x 3 = _____   6 x 1 = _____   6 x 4 = _____   6 x 1 = _____

6 x 5 = _____   6 x 1 = _____   6 x 2 = _____   6 x 3 = _____

6 x 2 = _____   6 x 4 = _____   6 x 2 = _____   6 x 5 = _____

6 x 2 = _____   6 x 1 = _____   6 x 2 = _____   6 x 3 = _____

6 x 1 = _____   6 x 3 = _____   6 x 2 = _____   6 x 3 = _____

6 x 4 = _____   6 x 3 = _____   6 x 5 = _____   6 x 3 = _____

6 x 4 = _____   6 x 1 = _____   6 x 4 = _____   6 x 2 = _____

6 x 4 = _____   6 x 3 = _____   6 x 4 = _____   6 x 5 = _____

6 x 4 = _____   6 x 5 = _____   6 x 1 = _____   6 x 5 = _____

6 x 2 = _____   6 x 5 = _____   6 x 3 = _____   6 x 5 = _____

6 x 4 = _____   6 x 2 = _____   6 x 4 = _____   6 x 3 = _____

6 x 5 = _____   6 x 3 = _____   6 x 2 = _____   6 x 4 = _____

6 x 3 = _____   6 x 5 = _____   6 x 2 = _____   6 x 4 = _____

© Bill Davidson

 | **Lesson 5:** Count by units of 7 to multiply and divide using number bonds to decompose.
Date: 7/31/13

3.B.19

Name _____   Date _____

1. Skip-count by seven to fill in the blanks and match each count-by to its multiplication expression. Then use the multiplication equation to write the related division fact directly to the right.

7

7 × 6

_____ ÷ 7 = _____

_____

7 × 3

_____ ÷ 7 = _____

21

7 × 8

_____ ÷ 7 = _____

_____

7 × 7

_____ ÷ 7 = _____

_____

7 × 1

_____ ÷ 7 = _____

42

7 × 5

_____ ÷ 7 = _____

49

7 × 9

_____ ÷ 7 = _____

_____
7 × 4

_____ ÷ 7 = _____

_____

7 × 2

_____ ÷ 7 = _____

COMMON CORE

Lesson 5: Count by units of 7 to multiply and divide using number bonds to decompose.

Date: 7/31/13

3.B.20

2. Complete the count by seven sequence below. Then write a multiplication equation and a division equation to represent each blank you filled in.

7, 14, _____, 28, _____, 42, _____, _____, 63, _____
a)   b)   c)   d)   e)

a) _____ × 7 = _____   _____ ÷ 7 = _____

b) _____ × 7 = _____   _____ ÷ 7 = _____

c) _____ × 7 = _____   _____ ÷ 7 = _____

d) _____ × 7 = _____   _____ ÷ 7 = _____

e) _____ × 7 = _____   _____ ÷ 7 = _____

3. Abe says 3 × 7 = 21 because 1 seven is 7, 2 sevens are 14 and 3 sevens are 14 + 6 + 1, which equals 21. Why did Abe add 6 and 1 to 14, when he is counting by seven?

4. Molly says she can count by seven 6 times to solve 7 × 6. James says he can count by six 7 times to solve this problem. Who is right? Explain your answer.

COMMON CORE

Lesson 5: Count by units of 7 to multiply and divide using number bonds to decompose.

Date: 7/31/13

3.B.21

Name _____ Date _____

Complete the **count by seven** sequence below. Then write a multiplication equation and a division equation to represent each number in the sequence.

7, 14, _____, 28, _____, 42, _____, _____, 63, _____

a. _____ × 7 = _____   _____ ÷ 7 = _____

b. _____ × 7 = _____   _____ ÷ 7 = _____

c. _____ × 7 = _____   _____ ÷ 7 = _____

d. _____ × 7 = _____   _____ ÷ 7 = _____

e. _____ × 7 = _____   _____ ÷ 7 = _____

f. _____ × 7 = _____   _____ ÷ 7 = _____

g. _____ × 7 = _____   _____ ÷ 7 = _____

h. _____ × 7 = _____   _____ ÷ 7 = _____

i. _____ × 7 = _____   _____ ÷ 7 = _____

j. _____ × 7 = _____   _____ ÷ 7 = _____

COMMON CORE

Lesson 5: Count by units of 7 to multiply and divide using number bonds to decompose.

Date: 7/31/13

3.B.22

Name _____   Date _____

1. Use number bonds to help you skip-count by seven by making ten or adding to the ones.

(a) 7 + 7 = __10__ + __4__ = _____
    /\
   3 4

(b) 14 + 7 = _____ + _____ = _____
     /\
    6 1

(c) 21 + 7 = _____ + _____ = _____
    /\
  20 1

(d) 28 + 7 = _____ + _____ = _____
     /\
    2 5

(e) 35 + 7 = _____
     /\
    5 2

(f) 42 + 7 = _____ + _____ = _____

(g) 49 + 7 = _____ + _____ = _____

(h) 56 + 7 = _____ + _____ = _____

2. Skip-count by seven to fill in the blanks. Then use the multiplication equation to write the related division fact directly to the right.

_____	$7 \times 10 = $ _____	_____ $\div 7 = $ _____
_____	$7 \times 9 = $ _____	_____ $\div 7 = $ _____
_____	$7 \times 8 = $ _____	_____ $\div 7 = $ _____
49	$7 \times 7 = $ _____	_____ $\div 7 = $ _____
_____	$7 \times 6 = $ _____	_____ $\div 7 = $ _____
_____	$7 \times 5 = $ _____	_____ $\div 7 = $ _____
28	$7 \times 4 = $ _____	_____ $\div 7 = $ _____
_____	$7 \times 3 = $ _____	_____ $\div 7 = $ _____
_____	$7 \times 2 = $ _____	_____ $\div 7 = $ _____
7	$7 \times 1 = $ _____	_____ $\div 7 = $ _____

COMMON CORE

Lesson 5:

Date:

Count by units of 7 to multiply and divide using number bonds to decompose.

7/31/13

3.B.24

Lesson 6

Objective: Use the distributive property as a strategy to multiply and divide using units of 6 and 7.

Suggested Lesson Structure

■ Fluency Practice   (15 minutes)
■ Application Problem   (5 minutes)
■ Concept Development   (30 minutes)
■ Student Debrief   (10 minutes)
   Total Time   **(60 minutes)**

Fluency Practice (15 minutes)

- Multiply by 6 **3.OA.7**   (8 minutes)
- Group Counting **3.OA.1**   (4 minutes)
- Decompose Multiples of 6 and 7 **3.OA.5**   (3 minutes)

Multiply by 6 (8 minutes)

Materials: (S) Multiply by 6 Pattern Sheet (6–10)

Note: This activity builds fluency with multiplication facts using units of 6. It works toward students knowing from memory all products of two one-digit numbers. See G3–M3–Lesson 5 for directions for administration of Multiply By Pattern Sheet.

T: (Write $6 \times 7 =$ ____.) Let's skip-count up by sixes. I'll raise a finger for each six. (Count with fingers to 7 as students count.)

S: 6, 12, 18, 24, 30, 36, 42.

T: Let's skip-count by sixes starting at 30. Why is 30 a good place to start?

S: It's a fact we already know, so we can use it to figure out a fact we don't know.

T: Let's see how we can skip-count down to find the answer, too. Start at 60 with 10 fingers, 1 for each six. (Count down with your fingers as students say numbers.)

S: 60 (10 fingers), 54 (9 fingers), 48 (8 fingers), 42 (7 fingers).

Continue with the following suggested sequence: 6×9, 6×6, and 6×8.

> **NOTES ON**
> **MULTIPLE MEANS OF**
> **ENGAGEMENT:**
>
> Multiply by 6 is carefully scaffolded to support student success. However, you may adjust the activity to suit your students' diverse needs. For example, focus on one skill, such as skip-counting down to solve. Or, have students choose and solve the three hardest facts using three different strategies.

Lesson 6:	Use the distributive property as a strategy to multiply and divide using units of 6 and 7.	3.B.25
Date:	7/31/13	

T: (Distribute Multiply by 6 Pattern Sheet.) Let's practice multiplying by 6. Be sure to work left to right across the page.

Group Counting (4 minutes)

Note: Group counting reviews interpreting multiplication as repeated addition. Counting by sevens prepares students for multiplication using those units in this lesson. Group counting eights and nines anticipates multiplication using those units later in the module.

Direct students to count forward and backward, occasionally changing the direction of the count.

- Sevens to 70
- Eights to 80
- Nines to 90

Decompose Multiples of 6 and 7 (3 minutes)

Materials: (S) Personal white boards

Note: This activity prepares students to use the distributive property with number bonds in today's lesson.

T: (Project a number bond with a whole of 48 and a part of 12.) On your boards, fill in the missing part in the addition number bond.

Continue with the following suggested sequence: a whole of 54 and 24 as a part, a whole of 49 and 14 as a part, and a whole of 63 and 21 as a part.

Application Problem (5 minutes)

Mabel cuts 9 pieces of ribbon for an art project. Each piece of ribbon is 7 centimeters long. What is the total length of the pieces of ribbon that Mabel cuts?

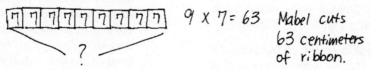

$9 \times 7 = 63$ Mabel cuts 63 centimeters of ribbon.

Note: This problem reviews multiplication using units of seven. It is the same problem that is used in the first example in the concept development. Here it is given a context, while in the Concept Development it is not because the focus shifts to using the distributive property.

COMMON CORE

Lesson 6:   Use the distributive property as a strategy to multiply and divide
             using units of 6 and 7.
Date: 7/31/13

3.B.26

Concept Development (30 minutes)

Materials: (S) Personal white boards

Part 1: Apply the distributive property to multiply using units of 6 and 7.

T: We used 9 × 7 to solve the Application Problem. Say 9 × 7 in unit form.

S: 9 sevens.

T: Model 9 × 7 using a tape diagram. Then, write the fact under the diagram. (Allow students time to work.)

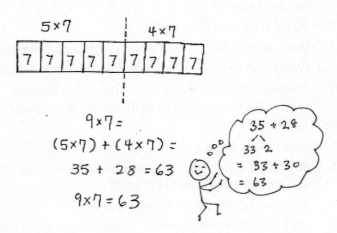

T: Recently, we used the break apart and distribute strategy to help solve larger multiplication facts. Talk with your partner. How did we do that?

S: We broke apart a bigger fact into 2 easy facts. → That made it easier to solve because we just added the products of the 2 easy facts.

T: Breaking the bigger fact into 5 plus something helped us make those 2 smaller facts. 9 sevens can be broken into 5 sevens plus how many sevens?

S: 5 sevens plus 4 sevens.

T: Draw a dotted line separating the 5 sevens from 4 sevens on your tape diagram. Label the sides of your tape diagram with multiplication facts.

S: (Draw line, label 5 × 7 and 4 × 7.)

T: Let's use those facts to rewrite 5 sevens plus 4 sevens like this. (Write: (5 × 7) + (4 × 7).) Remind your partner why this expression is the same as 9 × 7.

S: It's the same because the 5 and the 4 together make 9. → And the 7 just got distributed to the 2 parts.

T: Now solve. Check your work with your partner's. (Allow students time to work.)

T: What is 9 × 7?

S: 63.

Continue with the following suggested sequence:

- 8 × 6
- 8 × 7

A NOTE ON
MULTIPLE MEANS OF
ENGAGEMENT:

Alternatively, challenge students working above grade level to use, compare, and present three different multiplication strategies to solve 8 × 6, including the 5 plus something strategy.

Lesson 6: Use the distributive property as a strategy to multiply and divide using units of 6 and 7.

Date: 7/31/13

3.B.27

Part 2: Use addition number bonds to apply the distributive property to divide using units of 6 and 7.

T: We also used the break apart and distribute strategy earlier
    this year with arrays and division. Instead of using arrays
    today, let's use number bonds.

T: Write 48 ÷ 6 on your board and circle it.

T: We need to break apart 48 ÷ 6 into two smaller division expressions. Why would 30 make a good
    breaking point?

S: 30 ÷ 6 is an easy fives fact.

T: Write and circle 30 ÷ 6 as a part on your number bond.

S: (Write and circle 30 ÷ 6 as a part on the number bond.)

T: We have 30 ÷ 6 as one of our parts. What division
    expression do we need to write for the other part?

S: 18 ÷ 6.

T: How do you know?

S: 30 plus 18 equals 48. → I know because we used 30
    and we need 18 more to get to 48.

T: Write and circle 18 ÷ 6 as the other part.

T: Let's show that work with an equation. Write 48 ÷ 6 =
    (30 ÷ 6) + (18 ÷ 6). Put parentheses around the two
    expressions to show that we do these 2 division facts
    first.

T: How can we use the quotients of these two division
    expressions to find the quotient of 48 ÷ 6?

S: Add the quotient of 30 ÷ 6 and the quotient of 18 ÷ 6.

T: (Write addition sign as shown.) Add the two quotients
    to solve for 48 ÷ 6.

S: (Write 5 + 3 = 8.)

T: 48 ÷ 6 is…

S: 8!

T: Write the answer below your equation. This is a great
    problem to solve this way since adding to 30 is so easy.
    What is another 5 fact that results in an easy number?

S: 5 times 8 is 40. 5 times 4 is 20. → The even numbers!

T: What fact would you like to try next?

S: Let's do a big number divided by 8. → 56 divided by 8!

Repeat the process with 56 ÷ 8.

NOTES ON
MULTIPLE MEANS OF
ENGAGEMENT:

You may want to clarify that the two
smaller division expressions must be
divided by 6 expressions. Emphasize
the value of this strategy as a way to
solve sixes facts by using familiar fives,
fours, threes, or twos facts.
Alternatively, challenge students to
present, compare, and justify the use
of a different number bond for 48 ÷ 6.

Sample Teacher Board:

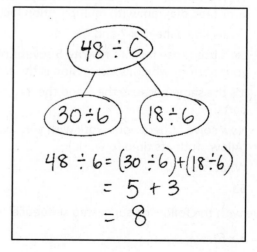

COMMON CORE

Lesson 6:   Use the distributive property as a strategy to multiply and divide
              using units of 6 and 7.
Date: 7/31/13

3.B.28

© 2013 Common Core, Inc. All rights reserved. commoncore.org

Problem Set (10 minutes)

Students should do their personal best to complete the Problem Set within the allotted 10 minutes. For some classes, it may be appropriate to modify the assignment by specifying which problems they work on first. Some problems do not specify a method for solving. Students solve these problems using the RDW approach used for Application Problems.

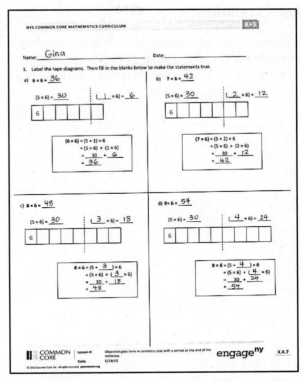

Student Debrief (10 minutes)

Lesson Objective: Use the distributive property as a strategy to multiply and divide using units of 6 and 7.

The Student Debrief is intended to invite reflection and active processing of the total lesson experience.

Invite students to review their solutions for the Problem Set. They should check work by comparing answers with a partner before going over answers as a class. Look for misconceptions or misunderstandings that can be addressed in the Debrief. Guide students in a conversation to debrief the Problem Set and process the lesson. You may choose to use any combination of the questions below to lead the discussion.

- What pattern did you notice in Problems 1(a) through 1(d)? What multiplication fact is used in all of these problems? How does this fact help you solve these problems?

- What division fact did you use to complete the number bond in Problem 3? Why?

- Explain to a partner what your picture looks like for Problem 4. How does your picture show the break apart and distribute strategy?

- What number bond did you use to solve Problem 5? Explain your choice. Explain why Kelly couldn't break apart 42 ÷ 7 into 30 ÷ 7 and 12 ÷ 7.

- How does using the break apart and distribute strategy help you multiply and divide using known facts to find larger, unknown facts?

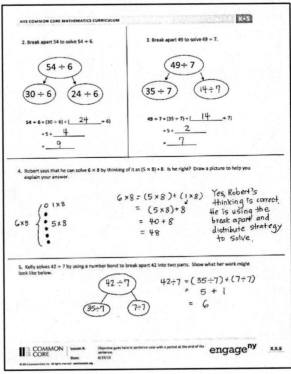

COMMON CORE   Lesson 6:   Use the distributive property as a strategy to multiply and divide using units of 6 and 7.
Date: 7/31/13

3.B.29

Exit Ticket (3 minutes)

After the Student Debrief, instruct students to complete the Exit Ticket. A review of their work will help you assess the students' understanding of the concepts that were presented in the lesson today and plan more effectively for future lessons. You may read the questions aloud to the students.

Lesson 6:   Use the distributive property as a strategy to multiply and divide
                using units of 6 and 7.

Date: 7/31/13

3.B.30

Multiply.

6 x 1 = _____	6 x 2 = _____	6 x 3 = _____	6 x 4 = _____
6 x 5 = _____	6 x 6 = _____	6 x 7 = _____	6 x 8 = _____
6 x 9 = _____	6 x 10 = _____	6 x 5 = _____	6 x 6 = _____
6 x 5 = _____	6 x 7 = _____	6 x 5 = _____	6 x 8 = _____
6 x 5 = _____	6 x 9 = _____	6 x 5 = _____	6 x 10 = _____
6 x 6 = _____	6 x 5 = _____	6 x 6 = _____	6 x 7 = _____
6 x 6 = _____	6 x 8 = _____	6 x 6 = _____	6 x 9 = _____
6 x 6 = _____	6 x 7 = _____	6 x 6 = _____	6 x 7 = _____
6 x 8 = _____	6 x 7 = _____	6 x 9 = _____	6 x 7 = _____
6 x 8 = _____	6 x 6 = _____	6 x 8 = _____	6 x 7 = _____
6 x 8 = _____	6 x 9 = _____	6 x 9 = _____	6 x 6 = _____
6 x 9 = _____	6 x 7 = _____	6 x 9 = _____	6 x 8 = _____
6 x 9 = _____	6 x 8 = _____	6 x 6 = _____	6 x 9 = _____
6 x 7 = _____	6 x 9 = _____	6 x 6 = _____	6 x 8 = _____
6 x 9 = _____	6 x 7 = _____	6 x 6 = _____	6 x 8 = _____

© Bill Davidson

Lesson 6:   Use the distributive property as a strategy to multiply and divide using units of 6 and 7.

Date: 7/31/13

3.B.31

Name:_____   Date:_____

1. Label the tape diagrams. Then fill in the blanks below to make the statements true.

a. **6 × 6 =** _____

(5 × 6) = _____   (_____ × 6) = _____

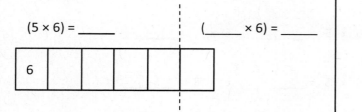

$$(6 × 6) = (5 + 1) × 6$$
$$= (5 × 6) + (1 × 6)$$
$$= \underline{\ 30\ } + \underline{\ \ \ \ \ \ }$$
$$= \underline{\ \ \ \ \ \ }$$

b. **7 × 6 =** _____

(5 × 6) = _____   (_____ × 6) = _____

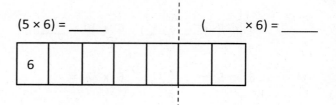

$$(7 × 6) = (5 + 2) × 6$$
$$= (5 × 6) + (2 × 6)$$
$$= \underline{\ 30\ } + \underline{\ \ \ \ \ \ }$$
$$= \underline{\ \ \ \ \ \ }$$

c. **8 × 6 =** _____

(5 × 6) = _____   (_____ × 6) = _____

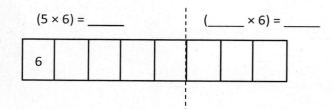

$$8 × 6 = (5 + \underline{\ \ \ \ \ }) × 6$$
$$= (5 × 6) + (\underline{\ \ \ \ } × 6)$$
$$= \underline{\ 30\ } + \underline{\ \ \ \ \ \ }$$
$$= \underline{\ \ \ \ \ \ }$$

d. **9 × 6 =** _____

(5 × 6) = _____   (_____ × 6) = _____

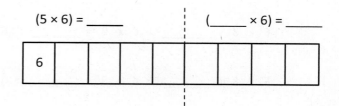

$$9 × 6 = (5 + \underline{\ \ \ \ \ }) × 6$$
$$= (5 × 6) + (\underline{\ \ \ \ } × 6)$$
$$= \underline{\ 30\ } + \underline{\ \ \ \ \ \ }$$
$$= \underline{\ \ \ \ \ \ }$$

COMMON CORE | **Lesson 6:** Use the distributive property as a strategy to multiply and divide using units of 6 and 7.
Date: 7/31/13

3.B.32

2. Break apart 54 to solve 54 ÷ 6.

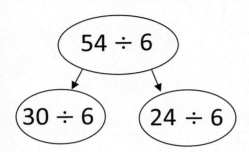

$$54 ÷ 6 = (30 ÷ 6) + (\underline{\hspace{2cm}} ÷ 6)$$

$$= 5 + \underline{\hspace{2cm}}$$

$$= \underline{\hspace{2cm}}$$

3. Break apart 49 to solve 49 ÷ 7.

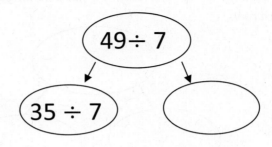

$$49 ÷ 7 = (35 ÷ 7) + (\underline{\hspace{2cm}} ÷ 7)$$

$$= 5 + \underline{\hspace{2cm}}$$

$$= \underline{\hspace{2cm}}$$

4. Robert says that he can solve 6 × 8 by thinking of it as (5 × 8) + 8. Is he right? Draw a picture to help you explain your answer.

5. Kelly solves 42 ÷ 7 by using a number bond to break apart 42 into two parts. Show what her work might look like below.

COMMON CORE

Lesson 6:   Use the distributive property as a strategy to multiply and divide using units of 6 and 7.

Date: 7/31/13

3.B.33

Name:_____   Date:_____

1. A parking lot has space for 48 cars. Each row has 6 parking spaces. Break apart 48 to find how many cars can park in each row.

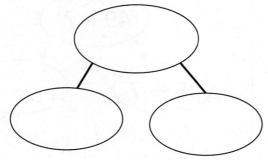

2. Malia solves 6 × 7 using (5 × 7) + 7. Leonidas solves 6 × 7 using (6 × 5) + (6 × 2). Who is correct? Draw a picture to help you explain your answer.

COMMON CORE | **Lesson 6:** Use the distributive property as a strategy to multiply and divide using units of 6 and 7.
Date: 7/31/13

3.B.34

Name:_____   Date:_____

1.   Label the tape diagrams. Then fill in the blanks below to make the statements true.

a. **6 × 7 =** _____

(5 × 7) = _____   (_____ × 7) = _____

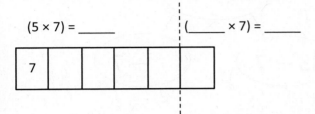

$$(6 \times 7) = (5 + 1) \times 7$$
$$= (5 \times 7) + (1 \times 7)$$
$$= \underline{\ 35\ } + \underline{\quad}$$
$$= \underline{\quad}$$

b. **7 × 7 =** _____

(5 × 7) = _____   (_____ × 7) = _____

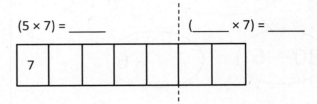

$$(7 \times 7) = (5 + 2) \times 7$$
$$= (5 \times 7) + (2 \times 7)$$
$$= \underline{\ 35\ } + \underline{\quad}$$
$$= \underline{\quad}$$

c. **8 × 7 =** _____

(5 × 7) = _____   (_____ × 7) = _____

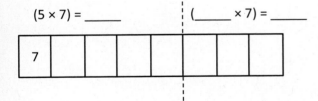

$$8 \times 7 = (5 + \underline{\quad}) \times 7$$
$$= (5 \times 7) + (\underline{\quad} \times 7)$$
$$= \underline{\ 35\ } + \underline{\quad}$$
$$= \underline{\quad}$$

d. **9 × 7 =** _____

(5 × 7) = _____   (_____ × 7) = _____

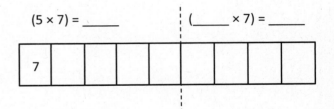

$$9 \times 7 = (5 + \underline{\quad}) \times 7$$
$$= (5 \times 7) + (\underline{\quad} \times 7)$$
$$= \underline{\ 35\ } + \underline{\quad}$$
$$= \underline{\quad}$$

COMMON CORE | **Lesson 6:**   Use the distributive property as a strategy to multiply and divide   **3.B.35**
                   | using units of 6 and 7.
                   | **Date:**   7/31/13

2. Break apart 54 to solve $54 \div 6$.

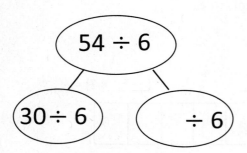

$54 \div 6 = (30 \div 6) + (\underline{\hspace{2cm}} \div 6)$

$= 5 + \underline{\hspace{2cm}}$

$= \underline{\hspace{2cm}}$

3. Break apart 56 to solve $56 \div 7$.

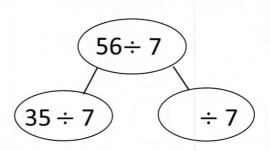

$56 \div 7 = (\underline{\hspace{1cm}} \div \underline{\hspace{1cm}}) + (\underline{\hspace{1cm}} \div \underline{\hspace{1cm}})$

$= 5 + \underline{\hspace{1.5cm}}$

$= \underline{\hspace{1.5cm}}$

4. Forty-two third grade students sit in 6 equal rows in the auditorium. How many students sit in each row? Show your thinking.

5. Ronaldo solves 7×6 by thinking of it as $(5 \times 7) + 7$. Is he correct? Explain Ronaldo's strategy.

COMMON CORE | Lesson 6: | Use the distributive property as a strategy to multiply and divide using units of 6 and 7.
| | Date: | 7/31/13

3.B.36

© 2013 Common Core, Inc. All rights reserved. commoncore.org

Lesson 7

Objective: Interpret the unknown in multiplication and division to model and solve problems using units of 6 and 7.

Suggested Lesson Structure

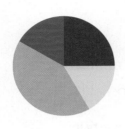

- ■ Fluency Practice   (15 minutes)
- ■ Concept Development   (10 minutes)
- ■ Application Problems   (25 minutes)
- ■ Student Debrief   (10 minutes)

Total Time   **(60 minutes)**

Fluency Practice (15 minutes)

- Multiply by 7 **3.OA.7**   (7 minutes)
- Group Counting **3.OA.1**   (4 minutes)
- Decompose the Multiplication Sentence **3.OA.5**   (4 minutes)

Multiply by 7 (7 minutes)

Materials: (S) Multiply by 7 Pattern Sheet (1–5)

Note: This activity builds fluency with multiplication facts using units of 7. It works toward students knowing from memory all products of two one-digit numbers. See G3–M3–Lesson 5 for the directions for administration of Multiply By Pattern Sheets.

T: (Write 7 × 5 = _____.) Let's skip-count by sevens to find the answer. I'll raise a finger for each seven. (Count with fingers to 5 as students count.)

S: 7, 14, 21, 28, 35.

T: (Circle 35 and write 7 × 5 = 35 above it. Write 7 × 3 = _____.) Let's skip-count up by sevens again. (Count with fingers to 3 as students count.)

S: 7, 14, 21.

T: Let's see how we can skip-count down to find the answer, too. Start at 35 with 5 fingers, 1 for each seven. (Count down with your fingers as students say numbers.)

S: 35 (5 fingers), 28 (4 fingers), 21 (3 fingers).

Repeat the process for 7 × 4.

T: (Distribute the Multiply by 7 Pattern Sheet.) Let's practice multiplying by 7. Be sure to work left to right across the page.

Lesson 7:   Interpret the unknown in multiplication and division to model and
solve problems using units of 6 and 7.
Date: 7/31/13

3.B.37

Group Counting (4 minutes)

Note: Group counting reviews interpreting multiplication as repeated addition. Counting by sixes reviews multiplication using those units in this topic and prepares students for today's lesson. Group counting eights and nines anticipates multiplication using those units later in the module. Direct students to count forward and backward, occasionally changing the direction of the count.

- Sixes to 60
- Eights to 80
- Nines to 90

Decompose the Multiplication Sentence (4 minutes)

Materials: (S) Personal white boards

Note: This activity reviews using the distributive property in Lesson 6.

- T: (Write $6 \times 6 = (5 + \underline{\ \ }) \times 6$.) On your boards, write out and complete the equation.
- S: (Write $(6 \times 6) = (5 + 1) \times 6$.)
- T: (Write $= (\underline{\ \ } \times 6) + (\underline{\ \ } \times 6)$.) Write out and complete the equation.
- S: (Write $(5 \times 6) + (1 \times 6)$.)
- T: Write an addition equation. Below it, write your answer.
- S: (Write $30 + 6$ and 36 below it.)

Continue with the following suggested sequence: 8×6, 7×6, and 9×6.

NOTES ON MULTIPLE MEANS FOR ACTION AND EXPRESSION:

Scaffold Decompose the multiplication sentence with pre-made sentence frames where students can simply fill in the blank, or solicit oral student responses only. Alternatively, have students draw number bonds or arrays while you model the equation.

$$
\begin{aligned}
\mathbf{(6 \times 6)} &= (5 + 1) \times 6 \\
&= (5 \times 6) + (1 \times 6) \\
&= 30 + 6 \\
&= 36
\end{aligned}
$$

Concept Development (10 minutes)

Materials: (S) Personal white boards

Thad sees 7 beetles when he weeds his garden. Each beetle has 6 legs. How many legs are there on all 7 beetles?

- T: Talk to a partner, what kind of picture can we draw to model this problem?
- S: We can draw 7 beetles, each with 6 legs. → We can draw an array with 7 rows and 6 dots in each row. → We can draw a tape diagram with 7 parts and 6 in each part.
- T: Draw and label a tape diagram to model this problem. Use the letter *b*, for the beetles' legs, to represent the unknown. (Draw and label tape diagram as shown.)
- T: What does the letter on your tape diagram represent?

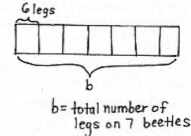

b = total number of legs on 7 beetles

Lesson 7:	Interpret the unknown in multiplication and division to model and solve problems using units of 6 and 7.
Date:	7/31/13

3.B.38

© 2013 Common Core, Inc. All rights reserved. commoncore.org

S: The unknown. → The total number of legs on 7 beetles.

T: Next to your tape diagram, write an equation for the problem and solve it. At the signal, show your board. (Signal after students write equation.)

S: (Show $7 \times 6 = b$, $b = 42$.)

T: Talk to a partner, what strategy did you use to find b?

T: Write a sentence to answer the problem, and then read your sentence to a partner.

If time allows, repeat the process with $48 \div 6$, providing a context for the problem.

Application Problems (25 minutes)

NOTES ON
MULTIPLE MEANS OF
REPRESENTATION:

Materials: (S) Problem Set (page 2)

During this time, students work together in groups to complete the second page of the Problem Set. When the group work is done, they meet with members of other groups to discuss answers and problem solving strategies.

Divide students into groups of four. Each group will be assigned a word problem to model and solve from page 2 of the Problem Set. Depending on your class size, there will be multiple groups solving the same problem. Circulate and clear up any misconceptions as students work.

Depending on the level of English proficiency of your English language learners, you may make the problems and discussion available in their first language, if possible. Alternatively, provide extra time, reduce the amount of work, and/or provide sentence frames for discussion. You may even want to read out the words in Problem 1 as students match it to the correct equation.

After students have solved, bring the class back together and redistribute the students into new groups. New groups should be comprised of at least four students who each solved a different word problem. They will then take turns discussing how their group solved their designated problem, paying special attention to the various strategies that were used. Allow 10 minutes for discussion.

Problem Set (10 minutes)

The second page of the Problem Set is designed to be completed in the group work activity, as described above. The first page of the Problem Set can be completed during this time.

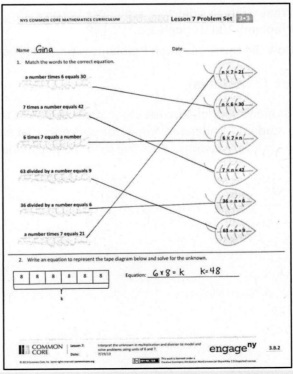

COMMON
CORE

Lesson 7:

Date:

Interpret the unknown in multiplication and division to model and solve problems using units of 6 and 7.

7/31/13

3.B.39

Student Debrief (10 minutes)

Lesson Objective: Interpret the unknown in multiplication and division to model and solve problems using units of 6 and 7.

The Student Debrief is intended to invite reflection and active processing of the total lesson experience.

Invite students to review their solutions for the Problem Set. They should check work by comparing answers with a partner before going over answers as a class. Look for misconceptions or misunderstandings that can be addressed in the Debrief. Guide students in a conversation to debrief the Problem Set and process the lesson.

You may choose to use any combination of the questions below to lead the discussion.

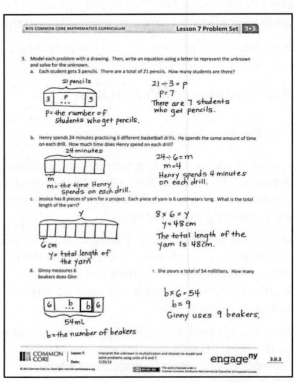

- What is the value of *n* in each equation in Problem 1?

- What equation did you use to solve Problem 2?

- Explain to a partner what your drawing looks like for Problem 3(a).

- In each problem, what was unknown? Was it the group size or number of groups?

- What strategies did your group use to solve Problems 3(a) through 3(d)? Why?

- How did the Application Problems connect to today's lesson?

Exit Ticket (3 minutes)

After the Student Debrief, instruct students to complete the Exit Ticket. A review of their work will help you assess the students' understanding of the concepts that were presented in the lesson today and plan more effectively for future lessons. You may read the questions aloud to the students.

COMMON CORE

Lesson 7:   Interpret the unknown in multiplication and division to model and solve problems using units of 6 and 7.
Date: 7/31/13

3.B.40

© 2013 Common Core, Inc. All rights reserved. commoncore.org

Multiply.

7 x 1 = _____   7 x 2 = _____   7 x 3 = _____   7 x 4 = _____

7 x 5 = _____   7 x 1 = _____   7 x 2 = _____   7 x 1 = _____

7 x 3 = _____   7 x 1 = _____   7 x 4 = _____   7 x 1 = _____

7 x 5 = _____   7 x 1 = _____   7 x 2 = _____   7 x 3 = _____

7 x 2 = _____   7 x 4 = _____   7 x 2 = _____   7 x 5 = _____

7 x 2 = _____   7 x 1 = _____   7 x 2 = _____   7 x 3 = _____

7 x 1 = _____   7 x 3 = _____   7 x 2 = _____   7 x 3 = _____

7 x 4 = _____   7 x 3 = _____   7 x 5 = _____   7 x 3 = _____

7 x 4 = _____   7 x 1 = _____   7 x 4 = _____   7 x 2 = _____

7 x 4 = _____   7 x 3 = _____   7 x 4 = _____   7 x 5 = _____

7 x 4 = _____   7 x 5 = _____   7 x 1 = _____   7 x 5 = _____

7 x 2 = _____   7 x 5 = _____   7 x 3 = _____   7 x 5 = _____

7 x 4 = _____   7 x 2 = _____   7 x 4 = _____   7 x 3 = _____

7 x 5 = _____   7 x 3 = _____   7 x 2 = _____   7 x 4 = _____

7 x 3 = _____   7 x 5 = _____   7 x 2 = _____   7 x 4 = _____

© Bill Davidson

COMMON CORE | **Lesson 7:**   Interpret the unknown in multiplication and division to model and
                      | solve problems using units of 6 and 7.
                      | **Date:**   7/31/13

3.B.41

Name _____ Date _____

1. Match the words to the correct equation.

a number times 6 equals 30

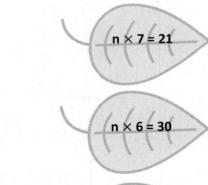

n × 7 = 21

7 times a number equals 42

n × 6 = 30

6 times 7 equals a number

6 × 7 = n

63 divided by a number equals 9

7 × n = 42

36 divided by a number equals 6

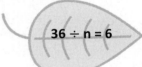

36 ÷ n = 6

a number times 7 equals 21

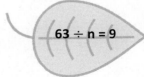

63 ÷ n = 9

2. Write an equation to represent the tape diagram below and solve for the unknown.

8	8	8	8	8	8

k

Equation: _____

3. Model each problem with a drawing. Then, write an equation using a letter to represent the unknown and solve for the unknown.

a. Each student gets 3 pencils. There are a total of 21 pencils. How many students are there?

b. Henry spends 24 minutes practicing 6 different basketball drills. He spends the same amount of time on each drill. How much time does Henry spend on each drill?

c. Jessica has 8 pieces of yarn for a project. Each piece of yarn is 6 centimeters long. What is the total length of the yarn?

d. Ginny measures 6 milliliters of water into each beaker. She pours a total of 54 milliliters. How many beakers does Ginny use?

Lesson 7:	Interpret the unknown in multiplication and division to model and solve problems using units of 6 and 7.	3.B.43
Date:	7/31/13	

Name _____ Date _____

1. Three boys and three girls each buy 7 bookmarks. How many bookmarks do they buy altogether? Write an equation using a letter to represent the unknown. Then solve for the unknown.

2. Seven friends equally share the cost of a $56 meal. How much does each person pay? Write an equation using a letter to represent the unknown. Then solve for the unknown.

COMMON CORE

Lesson 7: Interpret the unknown in multiplication and division to model and solve problems using units of 6 and 7.

Date: 7/31/13

3.B.44

Name _____ Date _____

1. Match the words on the arrow to the correct equation on the target.

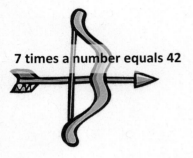

7 times a number equals 42

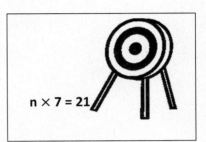

$n \times 7 = 21$

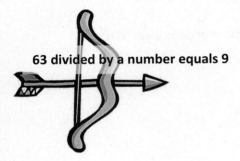

63 divided by a number equals 9

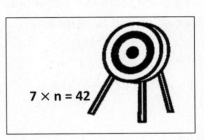

$7 \times n = 42$

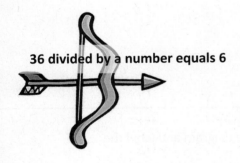

36 divided by a number equals 6

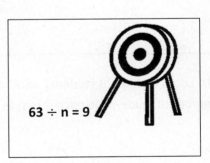

$63 \div n = 9$

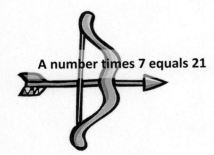

A number times 7 equals 21

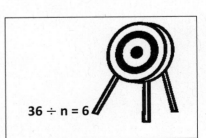

$36 \div n = 6$

COMMON CORE | Lesson 7: | Interpret the unknown in multiplication and division to model and solve problems using units of 6 and 7.
Date: | 7/31/13

3.B.45

© 2013 Common Core, Inc. All rights reserved. commoncore.org

2. Ari sells 6 boxes of pens at the school store.

   a. Each box of pens sells for $7. Draw a tape diagram and label the total amount of money he makes as *m*. Write an equation and solve for *m*.

   b. Each box contains 6 pens. Draw a tape diagram and label the total number of pens as *p*. Write an equation and solve for *p*.

3. Mr. Lucas divides 28 students into 7 equal groups for a project. Draw a tape diagram and label the number of students in each group as *n*. Write an equation and solve for *n*.

Lesson 7:

Date:

Interpret the unknown in multiplication and division to model and solve problems using units of 6 and 7.

7/31/13

3.B.46

Topic C

Multiplication and Division Using Units up to 8

3.OA.3, 3.OA.4, 3.OA.5, 3.OA.7, 3.OA.1, 3.OA.2, 3.OA.6, 3.OA.8

Focus Standard:	3.OA.3	Use multiplication and division within 100 to solve word problems in situations involving equal groups, arrays, and measurement quantities, e.g., by using drawings and equations with a symbol for the unknown number to represent the problem. (See Glossary, Table 2.)
	3.OA.4	Determine the unknown whole number in a multiplication or division equation relating three whole numbers. *For example, determine the unknown number that makes the equation true in each of the equations $8 \times ? = 48$, $5 = \_ \div 3$, $6 \times 6 = ?$*
	3.OA.5	Apply properties of operations as strategies to multiply and divide. (Students need not use formal terms for these properties.) *Examples: If $6 \times 4 = 24$ is known, then $4 \times 6 = 24$ is also known. (Commutative property of multiplication.) $3 \times 5 \times 2$ can be found by $3 \times 5 = 15$, then $15 \times 2 = 30$, or by $5 \times 2 = 10$, then $3 \times 10 = 30$. (Associative property of multiplication.) Knowing that $8 \times 5 = 40$ and $8 \times 2 = 16$, one can find 8×7 as $8 \times (5 + 2) = (8 \times 5) + (8 \times 2) = 40 + 16 = 56$. (Distributive property.)*
	3.OA.7	Fluently multiply and divide within 100, using strategies such as the relationship between multiplication and division (e.g., knowing that $8 \times 5 = 40$, one knows $40 \div 5 = 8$) or properties of operations. By the end of Grade 3, know from memory all products of two one-digit numbers.
Instructional Days:	4	
Coherence -Links from:	G2–M3	Place Value, Counting, and Comparison of Numbers to 1000
	G2–M6	Foundations of Multiplication and Division
	G3–M1	Properties of Multiplication and Division and Solving Problems with Units of 2–5 and 10
-Links to:	G3–M4	Multiplication and Area
	G4–M3	Multi-Digit Multiplication and Division
	G4–M5	Fraction Equivalence, Ordering, and Operations
	G4–M7	Exploring Multiplication

Students are informally familiar with parentheses from having seen them in distributive property lessons in Module 1. In Lesson 8 they understand parentheses as tools for grouping, and learn the conventional order for performing Grade 3 operations. This practice anticipates the application of parentheses that students will make in Lesson 9 as they formally study the associative property.

In Lesson 9, students model and demonstrate how to multiplicatively compose or decompose to make problems using units up to 8 easier to solve. For example, 8×5 may be thought of as

$8 \times 5 = (4 \times 2) \times 5$

$= 4 \times (2 \times 5)$

$= 4 \times 10$

Lessons 10 and 11 in this topic parallel Lessons 6 and 7 in Topic B. In Lesson 10, students use the $5 + n$ pattern as a strategy for solving multiplication and division problems using units of 8 with the distributive property. They learn that multiples of 8 can be thought of as $(5 + 3) \times n$. In division problems they practice decomposing the dividend using multiples of 5. They recognize the efficacy of using this strategy when the quotient of a division equation is greater than 5, and also realize that the dividend must be decomposed into numbers that are divisible by the divisor. For example, to solve $64 \div 8$, 64 can be decomposed as 40 and 24 because both are divisible by 8.

In Lesson 11, students analyze, model, and solve multiplication and division word problems using units of 8. They understand division as both a quantity divided into equal groups, as well as an unknown factor problem. They draw models and write equations to interpret and solve problems, using a letter to represent the unknown in various positions.

A Teaching Sequence Towards Mastery of Multiplication and Division Using Units up to 8
Objective 1: **Understand the function of parentheses and apply to solving problems.**   **(Lesson 8)**
Objective 2: **Model the associative property as a strategy to multiply.**   **(Lesson 9)**
Objective 3: **Use the distributive property as a strategy to multiply and divide.**   **(Lesson 10)**
Objective 4: **Interpret the unknown in multiplication and division to model and solve problems.**   **(Lesson 11)**

Lesson 8

Objective: Understand the function of parentheses and apply to solving problems.

Suggested Lesson Structure

■ Fluency Practice	(15 minutes)
■ Application Problem	(5 minutes)
■ Concept Development	(30 minutes)
■ Student Debrief	(10 minutes)
Total Time	**(60 minutes)**

Fluency Practice (15 minutes)

- Multiply by 7 **3.OA.7**   (6 minutes)
- Group Counting **3.OA.1**   (4 minutes)
- Add 6 and 7 Mentally **2.NBT.5**   (5 minutes)

Multiply by 7 (6 minutes)

Materials: (S) Multiply by 7 Pattern Sheet (6–10)

Note: This activity builds fluency with multiplication facts using units of 7. It works toward students knowing from memory all products of two one-digit numbers. See G3–M3–Lesson 5 for the directions for administration of Multiply By Pattern Sheet.

> T: (Write 7 × 6 = _____.) Let's skip-count up by sevens to solve. I'll raise a finger for each seven. (Count with fingers to 6 as students count.)
>
> S: 7, 14, 21, 28, 35, 42.
>
> T: Let's skip-count down to find the answer, too. Start at 70. (Count down with fingers as students count.)
>
> S: 70, 63, 56, 49, 42.

Continue with the following suggested sequence: 7 × 8 and 7 × 7, and 7 × 9.

> T: (Distribute the Multiply by 7 Pattern Sheet.) Let's practice multiplying by 7. Be sure to work left to right across the page.

**NOTES ON
MULTIPLE MEANS OF
ENGAGEMENT:**

Multiply by 7 is carefully scaffolded to support student success. However, you may adjust the activity to suit your students' diverse needs. For example, focus on one skill, such as skip-counting down to solve. Or, have students review and solidify their memorization of skip-counting up by seven by group counting first.

Group Counting (4 minutes)

Note: Group counting reviews interpreting multiplication as repeated addition. Counting by sixes reviews multiplication using those units in Topic B. Group counting eights prepares students for multiplication in this topic, and nines anticipates multiplication using those units later in the module. Direct students to count forward and backward, occasionally changing the direction of the count.

- Sixes to 60
- Eights to 80
- Nines to 90

Add 6 and 7 Mentally (5 minutes)

Materials: (S) Personal white boards

Note: This activity reviews the make ten strategy used for skip-counting by sixes and sevens in Lessons 4 and 5.

T: (Project 6 + 6 = ___.) Say the equation.

S: 6 + 6.

T: 6 and what make ten?

S: 4.

T: (Draw a number bond beneath the second 6.) On your boards, break apart the second 6, taking out the 4.

$$6 + 6 = 12$$
$$\underset{4 \quad 2}{\diagdown}$$

S: (Write the number bond.)

T: Say the addition sentence.

S: 6 + 6 = 12.

Continue with the following possible sequence: 12 + 6, 18 + 6, 24 + 6, 30 + 6, 36 + 6, 42 + 6, 48 + 6, 54 + 6, 7 + 7, 14 + 7, 21 + 7, 28 + 7, 35 + 7, 42 + 7, 49 + 7, 56 + 7, and 63 + 7.

Application Problem (5 minutes)

Richard has 2 cartons with 6 eggs in each. As he opens the cartons, he drops 2 eggs. How many unbroken eggs does Richard have left?

6 eggs	6 eggs

?

2 × 6 eggs = 12 eggs

12 eggs − 2 eggs = 10 eggs

Richard has 10 eggs left.

Note: This problem provides context for solving equations involving multiple operations, which is central to the Concept Development.

Concept Development (30 minutes)

Materials: (S) Personal white boards

Part 1: Solve equations containing parentheses.

T: The two equations used to solve the Application Problem are $2 \times 6 = 12$ and $12 - 2 = 10$. (Show picture to the right.) This picture shows both. Talk to your partner: How could we include all of this information in one equation?

S: We can rewrite them as one equation. Maybe $2 \times 6 - 2 = 10$?

T: Let's check to make sure the new equation equals 10. Should we multiply first or subtract first? Does it matter?

S: I don't think it matters. → Before we multiplied first, so let's do that again.

T: Let's find out. Solve the equation twice. The first time you solve it, multiply first. The second time you solve, subtract first. (Allow time for students to calculate.)

S: When I multiplied first I still got 10, but when I subtracted first I got 8!

T: For this problem the order *does* matter. We can use parentheses in our equation to show what to do first. Remind me, which part of the equation do we need to do first and why?

S: 2×6, because we have to find the total number of eggs Richard has in 2 cartons first.

T: Watch how I use parentheses to show that. (Write: $(2 \times 6) - 2 = 10$.)

T: What is the product of 2×6?

S: 12!

T: Rewrite 2×6 as 12. What equation is left?

S: $12 - 2$!

T: What does $12 - 2$ equal?

S: 10!

T: In a complete sentence, how many eggs does Richard have left?

S: Richard has 10 eggs left.

> **NOTES ON MULTIPLE MEANS OF ENGAGEMENT:**
>
> Alternatively, challenge students working above grade level to write equations in which multiple operations are used on both sides of the equation. For example, a student might extend $(2 \times 6) - 2 = 10$, as $(2 \times 6) - 2 = (7 - 2) \times 2$.

Continue with the following suggested sequence:

- $4 + 2 = 6$ and $6 \times 6 = 36$ → $(4 + 2) \times 6 = 36$
- $12 \div 3 = 4$ and $15 - 4 = 11$ → $15 - (12 \div 3) = 11$

Note: Have students refer back to the original problem, as the situation dictates the placement of the parentheses.

	Lesson 8:	Understand the function of parenthesis and apply to solving problems.
	Date:	7/31/13

3.C.5

Part 2: Explore how moving the parentheses can change the answer in an equation.

Write or project the following equation and the picture to the right: $(25 - 10) \div 5 = 3$.

T: Check my work. Is it correct?

S: Yes, because $25 - 10$ equals 15, and $15 \div 5$ equals 3.

T: Let's divide 10 by 5 first. What should we do with the parentheses to show that?

S: Move them over! → Make them go around $10 \div 5$.

T: Now the equation looks like this. (Write $25 - (10 \div 5) = n$.) Write the equation on your board. Why is there a letter where the 3 was before?

S: We should write 3 because the numbers didn't change. → We don't know if it equals 3 anymore.

T: Really? Why not? The numbers are the same as before.

S: The parentheses moved.

T: Do the problem with your partner. Does this equation still have an answer of 3?

S: (Work and discuss.) No, the answer is 23!

T: Why is the answer different?

S: We divided first. → One way we divided 15 by 5. → The other way we subtracted 2 from 25. → We divided and then subtracted. Before, we subtracted and then divided.

T: What does this tell you about the way we use parentheses to group the math in equations? Is it important? Why or why not?

S: The parentheses tell us what math gets done first. → Yes it's important, because moving the parentheses can change the answer.

Continue with the following possible suggestions:

- $(2 + 3) \times 7$ and $2 + (3 \times 7)$
- $(3 \times 4) \div 2$ and $3 \times (4 \div 2)$

Problem Set (10 minutes)

Students should do their personal best to complete the Problem Set within the allotted 10 minutes. For some classes, it may be appropriate to modify the assignment by specifying which problems they work on first. Some problems do not specify a method for solving. Students solve these problems using the RDW approach used for Application Problems.

COMMON CORE   Lesson 8: Understand the function of parenthesis and apply to solving problems.

Date: 7/31/13   3.C.6

© 2013 Common Core, Inc. All rights reserved. commoncore.org

Student Debrief (10 minutes)

Lesson Objective: Understand the function of parentheses and apply to solving problems.

The Student Debrief is intended to invite reflection and active processing of the total lesson experience.

Invite students to review their solutions for the Problem Set. They should check work by comparing answers with a partner before going over answers as a class. Look for misconceptions or misunderstandings that can be addressed in the Debrief. Guide students in a conversation to debrief the Problem Set and process the lesson.

You may choose to use any combination of the questions below to lead the discussion.

- Look at Problem 1(j). Would the answer be the same if I solved $(12 ÷ 2) + (12 ÷ 4)$? Why not? (Lead students to understand that they cannot distribute in this problem.)
- Look at Problem 1(l). Would the answer be the same if I solved $(9 ÷ 3) + (15 ÷ 3)$? Why?
- Invite students to share how they discovered where the parentheses belonged in Problem 2.
- Why does moving the parentheses in an equation only change the answer sometimes?

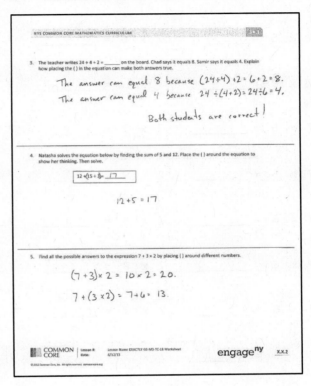

Exit Ticket (3 minutes)

After the Student Debrief, instruct students to complete the Exit Ticket. A review of their work will help you assess the students' understanding of the concepts that were presented in the lesson today and plan more effectively for future lessons. You may read the questions aloud to the students.

Multiply.

7 x 1 = _____   7 x 2 = _____   7 x 3 = _____   7 x 4 = _____

7 x 5 = _____   7 x 6 = _____   7 x 7 = _____   7 x 8 = _____

7 x 9 = _____   7 x 10 = _____   7 x 5 = _____   7 x 6 = _____

7 x 5 = _____   7 x 7 = _____   7 x 5 = _____   7 x 8 = _____

7 x 5 = _____   7 x 9 = _____   7 x 5 = _____   7 x 10 = _____

7 x 6 = _____   7 x 5 = _____   7 x 6 = _____   7 x 7 = _____

7 x 6 = _____   7 x 8 = _____   7 x 6 = _____   7 x 9 = _____

7 x 6 = _____   7 x 7 = _____   7 x 6 = _____   7 x 7 = _____

7 x 8 = _____   7 x 7 = _____   7 x 9 = _____   7 x 7 = _____

7 x 8 = _____   7 x 6 = _____   7 x 8 = _____   7 x 7 = _____

7 x 8 = _____   7 x 9 = _____   7 x 9 = _____   7 x 6 = _____

7 x 9 = _____   7 x 7 = _____   7 x 9 = _____   7 x 8 = _____

7 x 9 = _____   7 x 8 = _____   7 x 6 = _____   7 x 9 = _____

7 x 7 = _____   7 x 9 = _____   7 x 6 = _____   7 x 8 = _____

7 x 9 = _____   7 x 7 = _____   7 x 6 = _____   7 x 8 = _____

© **Bill Davidson**

COMMON CORE | Lesson 8: | Understand the function of parenthesis and apply to solving problems.
Date: | 7/31/13

3.C.8

Name _____   Date _____

1. Solve.

   a. $(12 - 4) + 6 =$ _____

   b. $12 - (4 + 6) =$ _____

   c. _____ $= 15 - (7 + 3)$

   d. _____ $= (15 - 7) + 3$

   e. _____ $= (3 + 2) \times 6$

   f. _____ $= 3 + (2 \times 6)$

   g. $4 \times (7 - 2) =$ _____

   h. $(4 \times 7) - 2 =$ _____

   i. _____ $= (12 \div 2) + 4$

   j. _____ $= 12 \div (2 + 4)$

   k. $9 + (15 \div 3) =$ _____

   l. $(9 + 15) \div 3 =$ _____

   m. $60 \div (10 - 4) =$ _____

   n. $(60 \div 10) - 4 =$ _____

   o. _____ $= 35 + (10 \div 5)$

   p. _____ $= (35 + 10) \div 5$

2. Use parentheses to show the order you would need to do the operations to make the equation true.

a. $16 - 4 + 7 = 19$	b. $16 - 4 + 7 = 5$
c. $2 = 22 - 15 + 5$	d. $12 = 22 - 15 + 5$
e. $3 + 7 \times 6 = 60$	f. $3 + 7 \times 6 = 45$
g. $5 = 10 \div 10 \times 5$	h. $50 = 100 \div 10 \times 5$
i. $26 - 5 \div 7 = 3$	j. $36 = 4 \times 25 - 16$

3. The teacher writes 24 ÷ 4 + 2 = _____ on the board. Chad says it equals 8. Samir says it equals 4. Explain how placing the ( ) in the equation can make both answers true.

4. Natasha solves the equation below by finding the sum of 5 and 12. Place the ( ) around the equation to show her thinking. Then solve.

> 12 + 15 ÷ 3 = _____

5. Find two possible answers to the expression 7 + 3 × 2 by placing ( ) around different numbers.

COMMON CORE | **Lesson 8:**   Understand the function of parenthesis and apply to solving problems.

Date: 7/31/13

© 2013 Common Core, Inc. All rights reserved. commoncore.org

3.C.10

Name _____   Date _____

1. Use parentheses to make the equations true.

    a. $24 = 32 - 14 + 6$

    b. $12 = 32 - 14 + 6$

    c. $2 + 8 \times 7 = 70$

    d. $2 + 8 \times 7 = 58$

2. Marcos solves $24 \div 6 + 2 = $ _____. He says it equals 6. Iris says it equals 3. Show and explain how the position of parentheses in the equation can make both answers true.

Name _____   Date _____

1. Solve.

   a. $9 - (6 + 3) =$ _____

   b. $(9 - 6) + 3 =$ _____

   c. _____ $= 14 - (4 + 2)$

   d. _____ $= (14 - 4) + 2$

   e. _____ $= (4 + 3) \times 6$

   f. _____ $= 4 + (3 \times 6)$

   g. $(18 \div 3) + 6 =$ _____

   h. $18 \div (3 + 6) =$ _____

2. Use parentheses to make the equations true.

   a. $14 - 8 + 2 = 4$

   b. $14 - 8 + 2 = 8$

   c. $2 + 4 \times 7 = 30$

   d. $2 + 4 \times 7 = 42$

   g. $12 = 18 \div 3 \times 2$

   h. $3 = 18 \div 3 \times 2$

   e. $5 = 50 \div 5 \times 2$

   f. $20 = 50 \div 5 \times 2$

COMMON CORE | Lesson 8: | Understand the function of parenthesis and apply to solving problems.

Date: | 7/31/13

© 2013 Common Core, Inc. All rights reserved.commoncore.org

3.C.12

3. Determine if the equation is true or false.

a. $(15 - 3) \div 2 = 6$	Example: True
b. $(10 - 7) \times 6 = 18$	
c. $(35 - 7) \div 4 = 8$	
d. $28 = 4 \times (20 - 13)$	
e. $35 = (22 - 8) \div 5$	

4. Jerome finds that $(3 \times 6) \div 2$ and $18 \div 2$ are equal. Explain why this is true.

5. Place parentheses in the equation below so that you solve by finding the difference between 28 and 3.
    Find the answer.

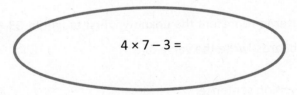

$4 \times 7 - 3 =$

6. Johnny says that the answer to $2 \times 6 \div 3$ is 4 no matter where the parentheses are. Do you agree?
    Place parentheses around different numbers to show his thinking.

COMMON CORE

Lesson 8:

Date:

Understand the function of parenthesis and apply to solving problems.
7/31/13

3.C.13

Lesson 9

Objective: Model the associative property as a strategy to multiply.

Suggested Lesson Structure

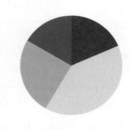

- ■ Fluency Practice   (11 minutes)
- ■ Application Problems   (15 minutes)
- ■ Concept Development   (24 minutes)
- ■ Student Debrief   (10 minutes)
- **Total Time**   **(60 minutes)**

Fluency Practice (11 minutes)

- Divide by 6 and 7 **3.OA.7**   (3 minutes)
- Group Counting **3.OA.1**   (4 minutes)
- Write In the Parentheses **3.OA.7**   (4 minutes)

Divide by 6 and 7 (3 minutes)

Materials: (S) Personal white boards

Note: This fluency reviews using a letter to represent the unknown, first taught in G3–M3–Lesson 3.

- T: (Write $a \times 6 = 12$.) On your boards, write the value of a.
- S: (Write $a = 2$.)
- T: (Write $12 \div 6 = a$.) Say the division sentence.
- S: $12 \div 6 = 2$.

Continue with the following suggested sequence: $a \times 6 = 30$, $b \times 6 = 24$, $c \times 6 = 36$, $d \times 6 = 60$, $e \times 6 = 54$, $f \times 7 = 35$, $g \times 7 = 28$, $h \times 7 = 42$, $j \times 7 = 70$, and $k \times 7 = 56$.

Group Counting (4 minutes)

Note: Group counting reviews interpreting multiplication as repeated addition. Group counting eights prepares students for multiplication in this topic, and nines anticipates multiplication using those units later in the module.

Direct students to count forward and backward, occasionally changing the direction of the count:

- Eights to 80
- Nines to 90

Lesson 9:   Model the associative property as a strategy to multiply.
Date: 7/31/13

3.C.14

Write In the Parentheses (4 minutes)

Materials: (S) Personal white boards

Note: This fluency reviews the use of parentheses, taught in G3–M3–Lesson 8.

- T: (Write 10 − 5 + 3 = 8.) On your boards, copy the equation. Then insert parentheses to make the statement true.
- S: (Write (10 − 5) + 3 = 8.)

Continue with the following suggested sequence: 10 − 5 + 3 = 2, 10 = 20 − 7 + 3, 16 = 20 − 7 + 3, 8 + 2 × 4 = 48, 8 + 2 × 4 = 40, 12 = 12 ÷ 2 × 2, 3 = 12 ÷ 2 × 2, 10 = 35 − 5 × 5, and 20 − 10 ÷ 5 = 2.

Application Problems (15 minutes)

Materials: (S) Application Problems Sheet

Note: These problems give students practice solving equations with parentheses. This sequence of problems is specifically designed so that students recognize that the position of the parentheses does not change the answer in multiplication problems with more than two factors. (The same is true for addition. Problem 1 hints at this.) Debrief the Application Problems so that this is clear to students with respect to multiplication; this understanding will be critical for the Concept Development. You may choose to begin the discussion by having them analyze the difference between the problems they circled and those they did not.

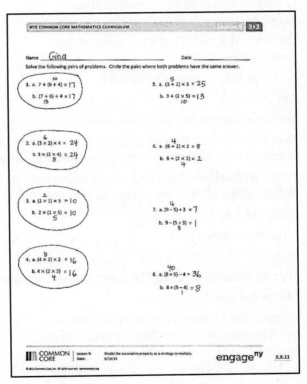

Concept Development (24 minutes)

Materials: (S) Personal white boards

- T: (Write 16 × 3.) This is a difficult problem for a third grader to solve. Let's simplify it. Work with your partner to list factors that have a product of 16. Write them on your personal board.
- S: 4 times 4 makes 16! → 8 and 2 also works.
- T: 4, 8, and 2 are much friendlier factors than 16. Let's rewrite 16 as 8 × 2. (Write (8 ×2) × 3.) Why do you think I put 8 × 2 in parentheses?
- S: The parentheses show that when you group those numbers together and multiply, you get 16.

A NOTE ON
MULTIPLE MEANS FOR
ACTION AND
EXPRESSION:

One way to scaffold listing factors of 16 is to give students 16 beans they can put into equal groups.

T: Even with the 16 rewritten, this problem isn't too friendly because I still have to multiply 16 × 3 in the last step. Suppose I move the parentheses to change the way the numbers are grouped. Will it completely change my answer?

S: No, we saw it's okay to move the parentheses when it's all multiplication in our Application Problems.

T: Write the equation on your board. Use the parentheses to group the numbers differently. Check your work with your partner's.

S: (Write 8 × (2 × 3) and check work with a partner.)

T: (Draw array.) My array shows how I regrouped the numbers to show 8 groups of (2 × 3). Is this problem friendlier than 16 × 3?

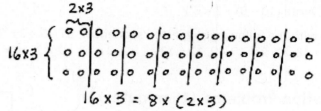

S: Oh, it's just 8 × 6! That's the same as 48! That was easy!

T: So, what is the answer to 16 × 3?

S: 48!

T: Tell your partner the steps we took to simplify the problem and solve.

S: First we rewrote 16 as a multiplication problem with two easier factors. Then we grouped the numbers with parentheses to make a multiplication problem that was easy to solve.

T: When we brainstormed factors with a product of 16, some of you thought of 4 × 4. Let's see if rewriting the 16 that way helps us simplify. Rewrite 16 × 3 using 4 × 4.

S: (Write (4 × 4) × 3.)

T: Is it easy to solve yet?

S: No!

T: Try and simplify by using the parentheses to group the numbers differently.

S: (Write 4 × (4 × 3).)

T: (Draw array.) Here is the array that shows our 4 groups of (4 × 3). Did the problem get easier?

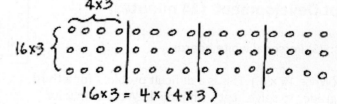

S: Not really. It's still 4 × 12, and that's hard.

T: Let's compare the two arrays. What do you notice?

S: They show 16 × 3 in different ways. → The first array shows 8 groups of 6 and the second array show 4 groups of 12. → The second array has fewer groups but multiplies a larger number. → So, both arrays still show a total of 48, but the first array breaks it up into easier numbers.

T: True. If we use repeated addition to find the answer to 4 × 12 we'll find the answer is still 48. We didn't do anything wrong, but rewriting the 16 as 4 × 4 and moving the parentheses didn't do what

Lesson 9: Model the associative property as a strategy to multiply.
Date: 7/31/13

3.C.16

we wanted it to. It didn't help us simplify. With your partner, compare the two arrays. What happened when we rewrote 16 as 4 × 4 and 8 × 2? What does the comparison tell you about this strategy?

S: It doesn't always work. → It means you have to be careful about which numbers you choose. → Yeah, some are helpful and some aren't. → Sometimes you might have to try more than one pair of numbers before you find the pair that helps you simplify.

Continue with 15 × 3. You may want to point out that the order in which 15 is rewritten can make a difference. For example, ask students to notice which is easier:

a. (3 × 5) ×3   b. (5 × 3) ×3
   3 × (5 × 3)   5 × (3 × 3)
   3 × 15   5 × 9

Problem Set (10 minutes)

Students should do their personal best to complete the Problem Set within the allotted 10 minutes. For some classes, it may be appropriate to modify the assignment by specifying which problems they work on first. Some problems do not specify a method for solving. Students solve these problems using the RDW approach used for Application Problems.

NOTES ON MULTIPLE MEANS FOR ACTION AND EXPRESSION:

Learners who have not memorized sixes and sevens facts may not benefit from using the associative property to solve 14 × 3. Adjust the numbers, or encourage students to use a more personally efficient strategy, such as the distribute property.

Student Debrief (10 minutes)

Lesson Objective: Model the associative property as a strategy to multiply.

The Student Debrief is intended to invite reflection and active processing of the total lesson experience. Invite students to review their solutions for the Problem Set. They should check work by comparing answers with a partner before going over answers as a class. Look for misconceptions or misunderstandings that can be addressed in the Debrief. Guide students in a conversation to debrief the Problem Set and process the lesson. You may choose to use any combination of the questions below to lead the discussion.

- In Problem 1, how do the problems on the bottom simplify the problems on the top?
- Invite students to share how they knew where to draw parentheses for the equations in Problem 2.
- In Problem 3, how did Charlotte simplify?

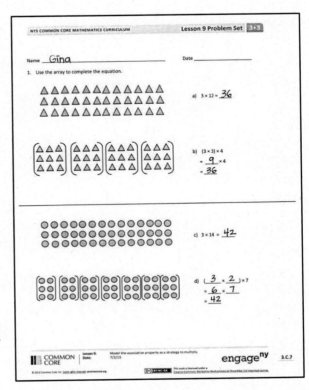

- How are the commutative property and this new strategy helpful for finding unknown, larger facts?

- How did the Application Problems relate to the lesson today?

- In the Application Problems we noticed that it is okay to move the parentheses when every operation is multiplication. Is that true for the other operations too? (Provide examples for subtraction and division; students will quickly see that it is not. Provide addition examples that students can use in conjunction with Application Problem 1 to generalize that it is also true for addition.)

Exit Ticket (3 minutes)

After the Student Debrief, instruct students to complete the Exit Ticket. A review of their work will help you assess the students' understanding of the concepts that were presented in the lesson today and plan more effectively for future lessons. You may read the questions aloud to the students.

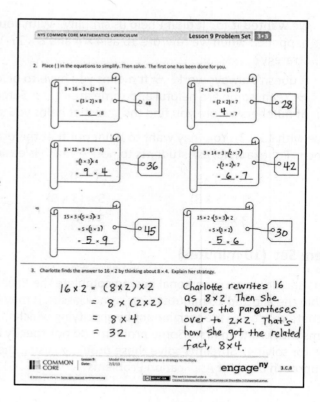

Lesson 9:   Model the associative property as a strategy to multiply.
Date: 7/31/13

3.C.18

Name _____ Date _____

Solve the following pairs of problems. Circle the pairs where both problems have the same answer.

1. a. $7 + (6 + 4)$

   b. $(7 + 6) + 4$

2. a. $(3 \times 2) \times 4$

   b. $3 \times (2 \times 4)$

3. a. $(2 \times 1) \times 5$

   b. $2 \times (1 \times 5)$

4. a. $(4 \times 2) \times 2$

   b. $4 \times (2 \times 2)$

5. a. $(3 + 2) \times 5$

   b. $3 + (2 \times 5)$

6. a. $(8 \div 2) \times 2$

   b. $8 \div (2 \times 2)$

7. a. $(9 - 5) + 3$

   b. $9 - (5 + 3)$

8. a. $(8 \times 5) - 4$

   b. $8 \times (5 - 4)$

COMMON CORE

Lesson 9: Model the associative property as a strategy to multiply.
Date: 7/31/13

3.C.19

Name _____   Date _____

1. Use the array to complete the equation.

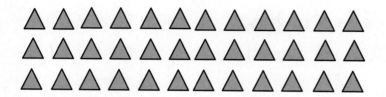

a) 3 × 12 = _____

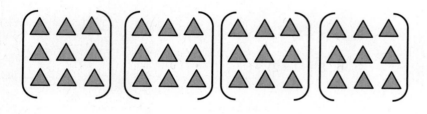

b) (3 × 3) × 4

= _____ × 4

= _____

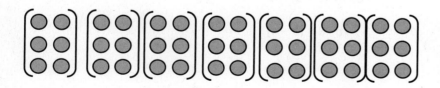

c) 3 × 14 = _____

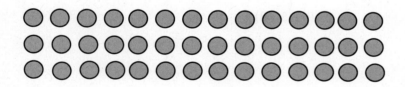

d) (_____ × _____) × 7

= _____ × _____

= _____

COMMON CORE | Lesson 9:   Model the associative property as a strategy to multiply.
Date: 7/31/13

3.C.20

2. Place ( ) in the equations to simplify. Then solve. The first one has been done for you.

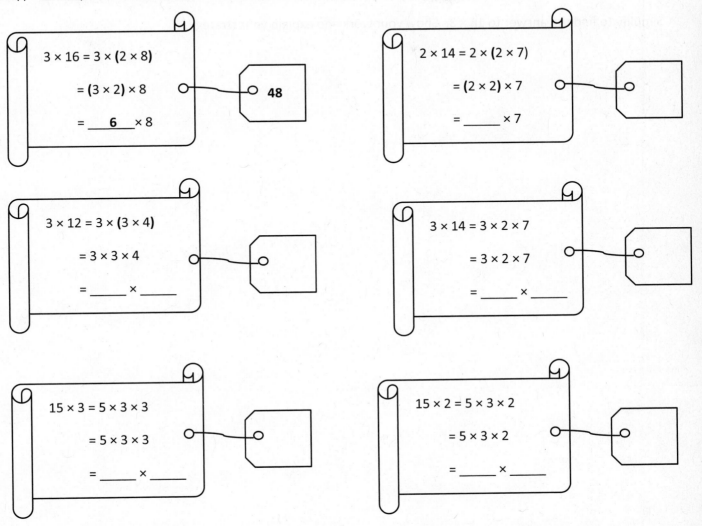

$3 \times 16 = 3 \times (2 \times 8)$

$= (3 \times 2) \times 8$

$= \underline{\quad 6 \quad} \times 8$

48

$2 \times 14 = 2 \times (2 \times 7)$

$= (2 \times 2) \times 7$

$= \underline{\qquad} \times 7$

$3 \times 12 = 3 \times (3 \times 4)$

$= 3 \times 3 \times 4$

$= \underline{\qquad} \times \underline{\qquad}$

$3 \times 14 = 3 \times 2 \times 7$

$= 3 \times 2 \times 7$

$= \underline{\qquad} \times \underline{\qquad}$

$15 \times 3 = 5 \times 3 \times 3$

$= 5 \times 3 \times 3$

$= \underline{\qquad} \times \underline{\qquad}$

$15 \times 2 = 5 \times 3 \times 2$

$= 5 \times 3 \times 2$

$= \underline{\qquad} \times \underline{\qquad}$

3. Charlotte finds the answer to 16×2 by thinking about 8×4. Explain her strategy.

Name _____   Date _____

Simplify to find the answer to 18 × 3. Show your work and explain your strategy.

Name _____　Date _____

1.　Use the array to complete the equation.

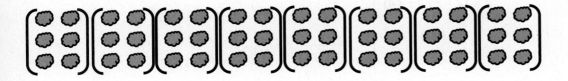

a.　$3 \times 16 =$ _____

b.　$(3 \times$ _____$) \times 8$

　　$=$ _____ $\times$ _____

　　$=$ _____

c.　$4 \times 18 =$ _____

d.　$(4 \times$ _____$) \times 9$

　　$=$ _____ $\times$ _____

　　$=$ _____

2. Place ( ) in the equations to simplify and solve.

$12 \times 4 = (6 \times 2) \times 4$
$= 6 \times (2 \times 4)$ $= \underline{\textbf{48}}$
$= 6 \times \underline{8}$

$3 \times 14 = 3 \times (2 \times 7)$
$= (3 \times 2) \times 7$ $= \underline{\hspace{1cm}}$
$= \underline{\hspace{0.5cm}} \times 7$

$3 \times 12 = 3 \times (3 \times 4)$
$= 3 \times 3 \times 4$ $= \underline{\hspace{1cm}}$
$= \underline{\hspace{0.5cm}} \times 4$

3. Solve. Then match the related facts.

a. $20 \times 2 = \underline{\textbf{40}} =$ $6 \times (5 \times 2)$

b. $30 \times 2 = \underline{\hspace{1cm}} =$ $8 \times (5 \times 2)$

c. $35 \times 2 = \underline{\hspace{1cm}} =$ $4 \times (5 \times 2)$

d. $40 \times 2 = \underline{\hspace{1cm}} =$ $7 \times (5 \times 2)$

COMMON CORE | Lesson 9: | Model the associative property as a strategy to multiply.
Date: | 7/31/13

3.C.24

Lesson 10

Objective: Use the distributive property as a strategy to multiply and divide.

Suggested Lesson Structure

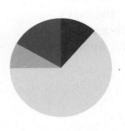

■ Fluency Practice   (7 minutes)
■ Application Problem   (5 minutes)
☐ Concept Development   (38 minutes)
■ Student Debrief   (10 minutes)
Total Time   **(60 minutes)**

Fluency Practice (7 minutes)

- Group Counting **3.OA.1**   (4 minutes)
- Decompose Multiples of 8 **3.OA.5**   (3 minutes)

Group Counting (4 minutes)

Note: Group counting reviews interpreting multiplication as repeated addition. Counting by sixes and sevens reviews multiplication using those units in Topic B. Group counting eights prepares students for multiplication in this topic, and nines anticipates multiplication using those units later in the module.

Direct students to count forward and backward, occasionally changing the direction of the count:

- Sixes to 60
- Sevens to 70
- Eights to 80
- Nines to 90

NOTES ON MULTIPLE MEANS OF ENGAGEMENT:

Students working below grade level may benefit from clear directions as to how to find the missing part of the number bond. Model and instruct students to subtract to find the missing part. You may want to begin with smaller numbers.

Decompose Multiples of 8 (3 minutes)

Materials: (S) Personal white boards

Note: This activity prepares students to use the distributive property in today's lesson.

T: (Project a number bond with a whole of 48 and a part of 16.) On your boards, fill in the missing part in the number bond.

Continue with the following suggested sequence: whole of 56 and 24 as a part, whole of 64 and 40 as a part, whole of 40 and 16 as a part, whole of 72 and 24 as a part.

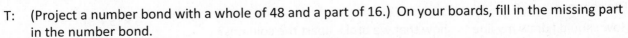

Lesson 10:   Use the distributive property as a strategy to multiply and divide.
Date: 7/31/13

3.C.25

Application Problem (5 minutes)

Use the 5 plus something break apart and distribute strategy to solve 6 × 8. Model with a tape diagram.

Note: This problem reviews modeling the break apart and distribute strategy using a tape diagram from Lesson 6. Until today's lesson students have learned to break apart the first factor and distribute the second factor. Today's Concept Development reverses the order using the fact in this Application Problem.

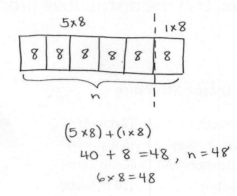

Concept Development (38 minutes)

Materials: (S) Personal white boards

Problem 1: Multiply.

T: When we use the break apart and distribute strategy, which factor do we break apart?

S: We break apart the number of groups.

T: Do you think our strategy would work if we broke apart the size of the groups and distributed the factor representing the number of groups instead? Think about the commutative property. Talk to your partner.

S: I'm not sure. I don't think so. → The commutative property says that you can switch factors around in multiplication, so maybe it would work.

T: Let's try using the break apart and distribute strategy that way to solve 6 × 8. Then we can compare what happens with our work on the Application Problem.

T: Take a look at my array. (Project 6 by 8 array, shown at right.) Which factor will we break apart?

S: The 8! → The size of the groups.

MP.7 T: Breaking it into 5 plus something helps us make 2 smaller facts. We can break 8 into 5 and what?

S: 5 and 3.

T: (Write 6 × (5 + 3) under the array.) Is 8 represented by the number of columns or the number of rows in the array?

S: The columns.

T: How should I draw my line to show that we broke apart the columns?

S: Maybe an up and down line? → You could make a vertical line after 5 columns. Then one part would show 5 columns and the other

NOTES ON
MULTIPLE MEANS FOR
ACTION AND
EXPRESSION:

Support English language learners as they engage in today's discussion. Offer extra time for ELLs to formulate their thoughts and discuss with their partners. If appropriate, preview words such as *factor*. Conduct subtle and frequent checks for understanding. Elaborate, expand, or paraphrase the dialogue as needed.

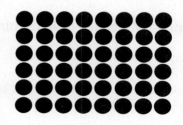

$6 \times (5 + 3)$

COMMON CORE

Lesson 10:   Use the distributive property as a strategy to multiply and divide.
Date: 7/31/13

3.C.26

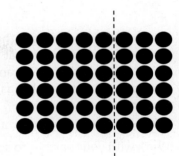

would show 3.

T: (Draw a dotted line after the fifth column.) On your board, write the multiplication facts you would use to label each part of the array.

S: (Write 6 × 5 and 6 × 3.)

T: What did we break our 6 eights into?

S: 6 fives and 6 threes.

T: Talk to your partner about how 6 × (5 + 3) shows 6 fives and 6 threes. Use the array to help you explain.

6 × (5 + 3)

MP.7 T: Solve the problem.

S: (May use 6 × (5 + 3) or (6 × 5) + (6 × 3) to solve.)

T: What does it equal?

S: 48.

T: Look back at your work on the Application Problem. Compare it with this way of solving. Notice what is the same or different. Talk to your partner about what you see.

S: We switched around the factors that we broke apart and distributed. → In the Application Problem, the units never changed. They were always eights. The one we just did had two different units. Fives and threes, but what stayed the same was the number of fives and the number of threes.

T: Does the break apart and distribute strategy work both ways?

S: Yes!

Continue with the following suggested problem: 7 × 8.

Problem 2: Divide.

T: Let's use the break apart and distribute strategy to solve 64 ÷ 8. Draw a number bond with 64 ÷ 8 as the whole. Leave the parts empty. (Allow time for students to draw.)

T: Let's think about how to break apart 64 into two numbers that are easier for us to divide. Make a list with your partner. Remember that when we break apart 64, both numbers need to be divisible by 8, because we originally distributed the 8 in our Application Problem.

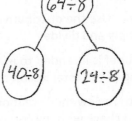

$$64 \div 8 = (40 \div 8) + (24 \div 8)$$
$$64 \div 8 = \quad 5 \quad + \quad 3$$
$$64 \div 8 = \quad 8$$

S: How about 60 and 4? → No, you can't divide those by 8! → Maybe 32 and 32. → Or 40 and 24.

T: Using 32 and 32 works nicely because it's a double. Forty and 24 also work well; 40 ÷ 8 makes 5. Five is easy to add to, so let's try 40 and 24. Write 40 ÷ 8 as one of the parts on your number bond.

T: What division fact goes inside the other circle?

S: 24 ÷ 8.

T: How do you know?

S: 40 plus 24 equals 64. → We started with 40 and we need 24 more to make 64.

COMMON CORE

Lesson 10: Use the distributive property as a strategy to multiply and divide.
Date: 7/31/13

3.C.27

T: Write that division fact as the other part. Our number bond shows us that 64 ÷ 8 has the same value as combining 40 ÷ 8 and 24 ÷ 8. Work with your partner to write that as an addition sentence on your board.

S: (Write 64 ÷ 8 = (40 ÷ 8) + (24 ÷ 8).)

T: Work with your partner to solve.

S: (Write 5 + 3 = 8.)

T: What is 64 ÷ 8?

S: 8!

Continue with the following suggested sequence:

- 96 ÷ 8
- 54 ÷ 6

Problem Set (10 minutes)

Students should do their personal best to complete the Problem Set within the allotted 10 minutes. For some classes, it may be appropriate to modify the assignment by specifying which problems they work on first. Some problems do not specify a method for solving. Students solve these problems using the RDW approach used for Application Problems.

Student Debrief (10 minutes)

Lesson Objective: Use the distributive property as a strategy to multiply and divide.

The Student Debrief is intended to invite reflection and active processing of the total lesson experience.

Invite students to review their solutions for the Problem Set. They should check work by comparing answers with a partner before going over answers as a class. Look for misconceptions or misunderstandings that can be addressed in the Debrief. Guide students in a conversation to debrief the Problem Set and process the lesson.

You may choose to use any combination of the questions below to lead the discussion.

- Describe the steps you took to solve for the missing numbers in Problem 1(a).
- How did you know what division fact to write inside the empty oval in Problem 3?

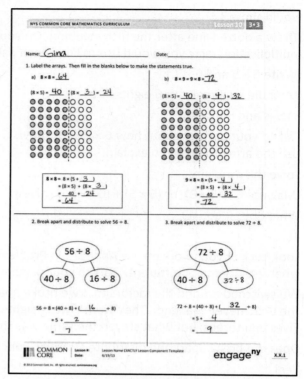

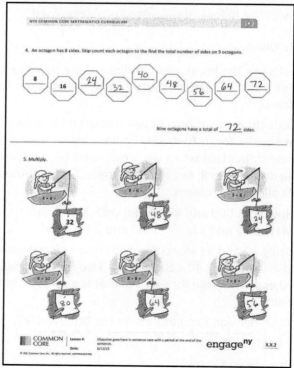

COMMON CORE

Lesson 10:   Use the distributive property as a strategy to multiply and divide.
Date: 7/31/13

3.C.28

- What multiplication sentence is used to solve Problem 4? How did you know?

- Invite students to share how to apply the break apart strategy to any of the expressions in Problem 5.

- In what ways does the break apart and distribute strategy remind you of the simplifying strategy we learned yesterday?

- How did our math work today help make multiplication and division with larger numbers simpler?

Exit Ticket (3 minutes)

After the Student Debrief, instruct students to complete the Exit Ticket. A review of their work will help you assess the students' understanding of the concepts that were presented in the lesson today and plan more effectively for future lessons. You may read the questions aloud to the students.

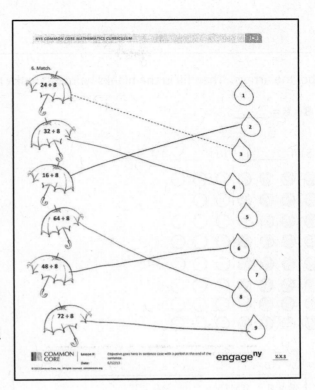

COMMON CORE

Lesson 10: Use the distributive property as a strategy to multiply and divide.
Date: 7/31/13

3.C.29

© 2013 Common Core, Inc. All rights reserved. commoncore.org

Name _____ Date _____

1. Label the arrays. Then fill in the blanks below to make the statements true.

a) **8 × 8 =** _____

(8 × 5) = _____ ¦ (8 × _____) = _____

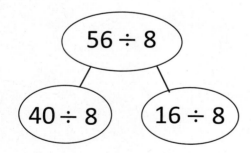

8 × 8 = 8 × (5 + _____)
= (8 × 5) + (8 × _____)
= __40__ + _____
= _____

b) **8 × 9 = 9 × 8 =** _____

(8 × 5) = _____ ¦ (8 × _____) = _____

9 × 8 = 8 × (5 + _____)
= (8 × 5) + (8 × _____)
= __40__ + _____
= _____

2. Break apart and distribute to solve 56 ÷ 8.

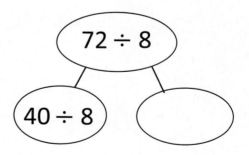

56 ÷ 8 =(40 ÷ 8) + (_____÷ 8)

= 5 + _____

= _____

3. Break apart and distribute to solve 72 ÷ 8.

72 ÷ 8

40 ÷ 8   ( )

72 ÷ 8 = (40 ÷ 8) + (_____÷ 8)

= 5 + _____

= _____

COMMON CORE

Lesson 10:
Date:

7/31/13

Use the distributive property as a strategy to multiply and divide.

3.C.30

4. An octagon has 8 sides. Skip-count to the find the total number of sides on 9 octagons.

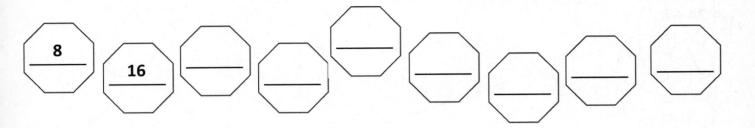

Nine octagons have a total of _____ sides.

5. Multiply.

6. Match.

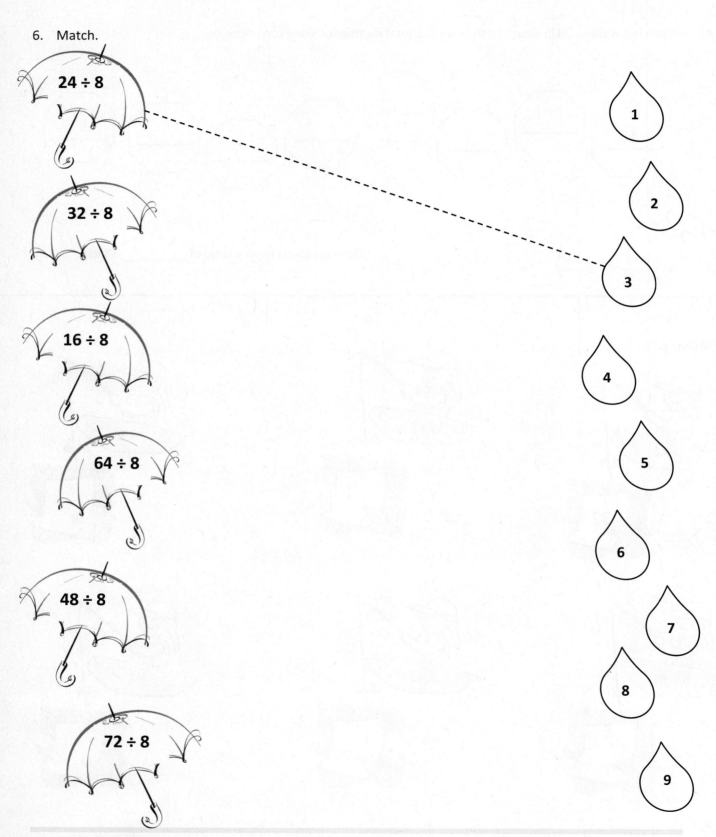

COMMON CORE | **Lesson 10:** | Use the distributive property as a strategy to multiply and divide.
| **Date:** | 7/31/13

© 2013 Common Core, Inc. All rights reserved. **commoncore.org**

3.C.32

Name _____   Date _____

Use the break apart and distribute strategy to solve the following problem. You may or may not choose to draw an array.

7 × 8 =_____

COMMON CORE

Lesson 10:   Use the distributive property as a strategy to multiply and divide.
Date: 7/31/13

3.C.33

Name _____   Date _____

1. Label the array. Then fill in the blanks to make the statements true.

    a)   **8 × 7 = 7 × 8 =** _____

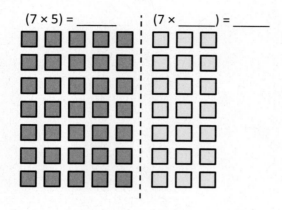

$(7 \times 5) =$ _____ $(7 \times$ _____$) =$ _____

> **8 × 7** $= 7 \times (5 +$ _____$)$
> $= (7 \times 5) + (7 \times$ _____$)$
> $=$ ___35___ $+$ _____
> $=$ _____

2. Break apart and distribute to solve
72 ÷ 8.

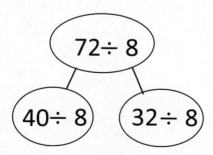

$72 ÷ 8 = (40 ÷ 8) + ($ _____ $÷ 8)$

$= 5 +$ _____

$=$ _____

3. Count by 8. Then match each multiplication problem with its value.

   __8__ ,_____ ,_____ ,_____ ,_____ ,_____ ,_____ ,_____ ,_____ ,_____ ,

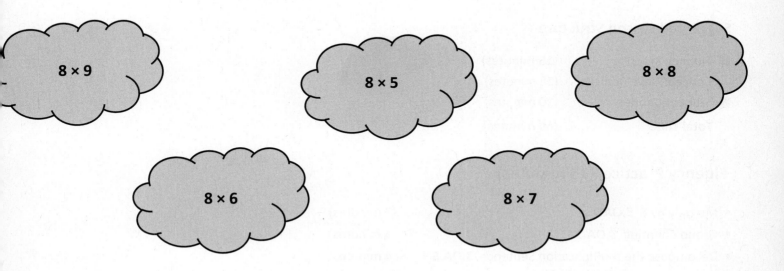

8×9

8×5

8×8

8×6

8×7

4. Divide.

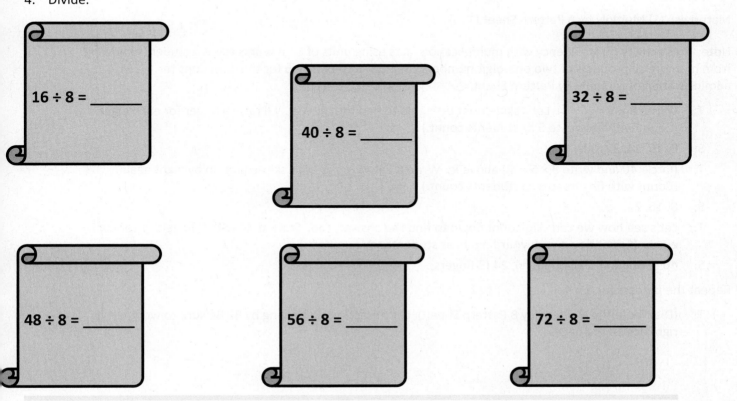

$16 \div 8 = $ _____

$40 \div 8 = $ _____

$32 \div 8 = $ _____

$48 \div 8 = $ _____

$56 \div 8 = $ _____

$72 \div 8 = $ _____

Lesson 11

Objective: Interpret the unknown in multiplication and division to model and solve problems.

Suggested Lesson Structure

■ Fluency Practice   (15 minutes)
  Concept Development   (35 minutes)
■ Student Debrief   (10 minutes)
  Total Time   **(60 minutes)**

Fluency Practice (15 minutes)

- Multiply by 8 **3.OA.7**   (7 minutes)
- Group Counting **3.OA.1**   (4 minutes)
- Decompose the Multiplication Sentence **3.OA.5**   (4 minutes)

Multiply by 8 (7 minutes)

Materials: (S) Multiply by 8 Pattern Sheet (1–5)

Note: This activity builds fluency with multiplication facts using units of 8. It works toward students knowing from memory all products of two one-digit numbers. See G3–M3–Lesson 5 for the directions for administration of Multiply By Pattern Sheet.

    T: (Write 8 × 5 = _____.) Let's skip-count by eights to find the answer. I'll raise a finger for each eight. (Count with fingers to 5 as students count.)

    S: 8, 16, 24, 32, 40.

    T: (Circle 40 and write 8 × 5 = 40 above it. Write 8 × 3 = _____.) Let's skip-count up by eight again. (Count with fingers to 3 as students count.)

    S: 8, 16, 24.

    T: Let's see how we can skip-count down to find the answer, too. Start at 40 with 5 fingers, 1 for each eight. (Count down with your fingers as students say numbers.)

    S: 40 (5 fingers), 32 (4 fingers), 24 (3 fingers).

Repeat the process for 8 × 4.

    T: (Distribute the Multiply by 8 Pattern Sheet.) Let's practice multiplying by 8. Be sure to work left to right across the page.

Group Counting (4 minutes)

Note: Group counting reviews interpreting multiplication as repeated addition. Counting by sixes and sevens reviews multiplication using those units in Topic B. Group counting nines anticipates multiplication in the next topic. Direct students to count forward and backward, occasionally changing the direction of the count.

- Sixes to 60
- Sevens to 70
- Nines to 90

Decompose the Multiplication Sentence (4 minutes)

Materials: (S) Personal white boards

Note: This activity reviews multiplying using the distributive property from G3–M3–Lesson 10.

- T: (Write $8 \times 8 = (5 + \underline{}) \times 8$.) On your boards, write out and complete the equation.
- S: (Write $8 \times 8 = (5 + 3) \times 8$.)
- T: (Write $= (\underline{} \times 8) + (\underline{} \times 8)$.) Write out and complete the equation.
- S: (Write $(5 \times 8) + (3 \times 8)$.)
- T: Solve the multiplication and write an addition sentence. Below it, write your answer.
- S: (Write $40 + 24$ and 64 below it.)

8 × 8	$= (5 + 3) \times 8$
	$= (5 \times 8) + (3 \times 8)$
	$= 40 + 24$
	$= 64$

Continue with the following suggested sequence: 7×8, 6×8, and 9×8.

Concept Development (35 minutes)

Materials: (S) Personal white boards

Problem 1: Interpret the unknown in multiplication.

Write the following problem: Asmir buys 8 boxes of 9 candles for his dad's birthday. After putting some candles on the cake, there are 28 candles left. How many candles does Asmir use?

- T: Model the problem. Then tell your partner the steps you'll need to take to solve.
- S: (Model.) First you have to find out how many candles Asmir has. → After that you could subtract 28 from the total to see how many he used.
- T: Write an equation to find the total number of candles. Instead of using a question mark, use letter c to represent the unknown.
- T: Read your equation out loud.
- S: 8 times 9 equals c.

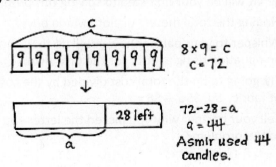

Lesson 11:	Interpret the unknown in multiplication and division to model and solve problems.
Date:	7/31/13

...

T: What does *c* represent?

S: The product. → The total number of candles.

T: Choose a strategy and find the value of *c*. (Possible strategies: known from memory, skip-count, distributive property, associative property.)

T: Use a complete sentence to tell what *c* equals.

S: *c* equals 72. → He bought 72 candles.

T: Did we solve the problem?

S: No, we have to find how many candles Asmir uses.

T: Solve the second step of the problem, this time using letter *a* to represent the unknown.

S: $72 - 28 = a$.

T: Find the value of *a*. This is a good problem to practice your mental math strategies. (Allow time for solving.) What is the value of *a*?

S: 44 candles.

T: Answer the question in a complete sentence.

S: Asmir uses 44 candles.

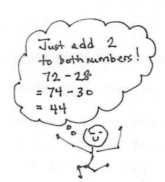

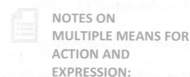

Problem 2: Interpret the unknown in division.

Write the following problem: The fabric store sells 1 meter of cloth for $8. Maria buys some cloth that costs a total of $56. She then uses 3 meters to sew a dress. How many meters of cloth does she have left?

T: Draw a model to represent the problem. Choose letters to represent the unknowns.

T: What is unknown in this problem?

S: The total meters of cloth Maria buys → There's something else too. We don't know how many meters of cloth Maria has left.

T: Tell your partner why you need to know how many meters of cloth Maria buys.

S: First you have to find out how many meters of cloth Maria buys. → After that you could subtract 3 meters from the total to see how many meters she has left.

T: What will be your first step to solving this problem?

S: Finding the total meters of cloth Maria buys.

T: Whisper to your partner how you'll do that, then write an equation using a letter for the unknown.

S: I'm going to do the total cost divided by the cost of 1 meter of fabric. So, $56 ÷ $8 = *t*.

T: Tell your partner why you picked the letter you used to represent the unknown. How does it relate to the problem?

NOTES ON MULTIPLE MEANS FOR ACTION AND EXPRESSION:

Many learners will benefit from this step-by-step guidance from planning a strategy to finding a solution.

Students above grade level and others may be motivated by more choice and autonomy. In addition, welcome various strategies, plans for solving, and modeling.

Lesson 11: Interpret the unknown in multiplication and division to model and solve problems.
Date: 7/31/13

3.C.38

© 2013 Common Core, Inc. All rights reserved. commoncore.org

S: (Possible response: I chose letter *t* to stand for the *total* meters of cloth Maria buys.)

T: Whisper what *t* equals.

S: (Possible response: *t* equals 7 meters.)

T: Tell your partner your next step for solving. Then, write an equation using a letter for the unknown.

S: Now that I know that Maria bought a total of 7 meters, I'll do $7 - 3 = n$. Letter *n* stands for the *number* of meters she has left.

T: Is your letter the same as the one you used for the first step? Why or why not?

S: It's different because it represents something different. → Oh yeah, I need to change mine!

T: Finish solving, and then answer the question using words.

S: (Solve to find *n* is 4 meters. Write: Maria has 4 meters of cloth left.)

T: Does Maria have enough cloth to sew another dress? Why or why not?

S: Yes, she has 4 meters left and she only needs 3 meters. → So, even after making a second dress, she will still have 1 meter of cloth left.

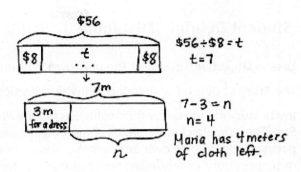

NOTES ON
MULTIPLE MEANS OF
ENGAGEMENT:

Students working above grade level and others may want to omit the tape diagram as they mentally solve the first few problems of the Problem Set. Redirect their focus to the accurate labeling of the unknown. After accurately labeling their tape diagrams, ask students to erase the values and experiment with numbers they choose.

Problem Set (10 minutes)

Students should do their personal best to complete the Problem Set within the allotted 10 minutes. For some classes, it may be appropriate to modify the assignment by specifying which problems they work on first. Some problems do not specify a method for solving. Students solve these problems using the RDW approach used for Application Problems.

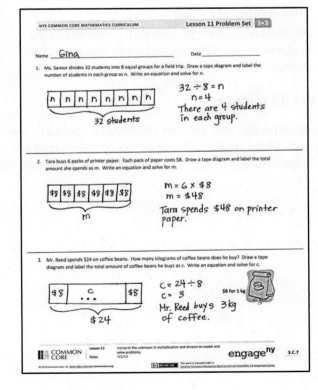

COMMON CORE

Lesson 11:   Interpret the unknown in multiplication and division to model and
Date: solve problems.
              7/31/13

© 2013 Common Core, Inc. All rights reserved. commoncore.org

3.C.39

Student Debrief (10 minutes)

Lesson Objective: Interpret the unknown in multiplication and division to model and solve problems.

The Student Debrief is intended to invite reflection and active processing of the total lesson experience.

Invite students to review their solutions for the Problem Set. They should check work by comparing answers with a partner before going over answers as a class. Look for misconceptions or misunderstandings that can be addressed in the Debrief. Guide students in a conversation to debrief the Problem Set and process the lesson.

You may choose to use any combination of the questions below to lead the discussion.

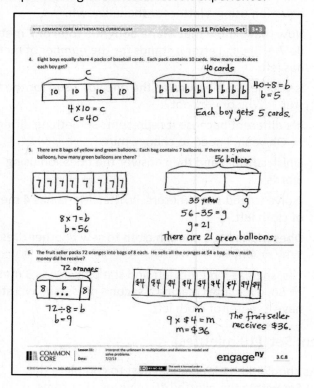

- In Problem 1, did you need to solve to find the number of groups or the number of items in each group?
- What equations can be used to solve Problem 1?
- In Problem 4, how many parts did each pack need to be split into in order for each boy to get 1 part? (Two equal parts.) Could we use that fact to solve the problem without first finding the total number of cards?
- Problems 4–6 are multiple-step problems. Why is it useful to use different letters to represent two unknowns in the same problem?

Exit Ticket (3 minutes)

After the Student Debrief, instruct students to complete the Exit Ticket. A review of their work will help you assess the students' understanding of the concepts that were presented in the lesson today and plan more effectively for future lessons. You may read the questions aloud to the students.

COMMON CORE

Lesson 11:   Interpret the unknown in multiplication and division to model and
Date: solve problems.
               7/31/13

3.C.40

Multiply.

8 x 1 = _____   8 x 2 = _____   8 x 3 = _____   8 x 4 = _____

8 x 5 = _____   8 x 1 = _____   8 x 2 = _____   8 x 1 = _____

8 x 3 = _____   8 x 1 = _____   8 x 4 = _____   8 x 1 = _____

8 x 5 = _____   8 x 1 = _____   8 x 2 = _____   8 x 3 = _____

8 x 2 = _____   8 x 4 = _____   8 x 2 = _____   8 x 5 = _____

8 x 2 = _____   8 x 1 = _____   8 x 2 = _____   8 x 3 = _____

8 x 1 = _____   8 x 3 = _____   8 x 2 = _____   8 x 3 = _____

8 x 4 = _____   8 x 3 = _____   8 x 5 = _____   8 x 3 = _____

8 x 4 = _____   8 x 1 = _____   8 x 4 = _____   8 x 2 = _____

8 x 4 = _____   8 x 3 = _____   8 x 4 = _____   8 x 5 = _____

8 x 4 = _____   8 x 5 = _____   8 x 1 = _____   8 x 5 = _____

8 x 2 = _____   8 x 5 = _____   8 x 3 = _____   8 x 5 = _____

8 x 4 = _____   8 x 2 = _____   8 x 4 = _____   8 x 3 = _____

8 x 5 = _____   8 x 3 = _____   8 x 2 = _____   8 x 4 = _____

8 x 3 = _____   8 x 5 = _____   8 x 2 = _____   8 x 4 = _____

© **Bill Davidson**

COMMON CORE

Lesson 11: Interpret the unknown in multiplication and division to model and solve problems.
Date: 7/31/13

3.C.41

Name _____   Date _____

1. Ms. Santor divides 32 students into 8 equal groups for a field trip. Draw a tape diagram and label the number of students in each group as *n*. Write an equation and solve for *n*.

2. Tara buys 6 packs of printer paper. Each pack of paper costs $8. Draw a tape diagram and label the total amount she spends as *m.* Write an equation and solve for *m*.

3. Mr. Reed spends $24 on coffee beans. How many kilograms of coffee beans does he buy? Draw a tape diagram and label the total amount of coffee beans he buys as *c*. Write an equation and solve for *c*.

$8 for 1 kg

COMMON CORE | **Lesson 11:**   Interpret the unknown in multiplication and division to model and solve problems.
        Date: 7/31/13

3.C.42

4. Eight boys equally share 4 packs of baseball cards. Each pack contains 10 cards. How many cards does each boy get?

5. There are 8 bags of yellow and green balloons. Each bag contains 7 balloons. If there are 35 yellow balloons, how many green balloons are there?

6. The fruit seller packs 72 oranges into bags of 8 each. He sells all the oranges at $4 a bag. How much money did he receive?

COMMON CORE | **Lesson 11:** Interpret the unknown in multiplication and division to model and solve problems.   3.C.43

Date: 7/31/13

Name _____ Date _____

1. Erica buys some packs of rubber bracelets. There are 8 bracelets in each pack.

    a. How many packs of rubber bracelets does she buy if she has a total of 56 bracelets? Draw a tape diagram and label the total number of packages as *p*. Write an equation and solve for *p*.

    b. After giving some bracelets away, Erica has 18 bracelets left. How many did she give away?

Name _____ Date _____

1. Jenny bakes 10 cookies. She puts 7 chocolate chips on each cookie. Draw a tape diagram and label the total of amount of chocolate chips as *c*. Write an equation and solve for *c*.

2. Mr. Lopez arranges 48 dry erase markers into 8 equal groups for his math stations. Draw a tape diagram and label the number of dry erase markers in each group as *v*. Write an equation and solve for *v*.

3. There are 35 computers in the lab. Five students each turn off an equal number of computers. How many computers does each student turn off? Label the unknown as *m*, then solve.

COMMON CORE

Lesson 11:   Interpret the unknown in multiplication and division to model and solve problems.

Date: 7/31/13

3.C.45

4. There are 9 bins of books. Each bin has 6 comic books. How many comic books are there altogether?

5. There are 8 trail mix bags in one box. Clarissa buys 5 boxes. She gives an equal number of bags of trail mix to 4 friends. How many bags of trail mix does each friend receive?

6. Leo earns $8 a week for doing chores. After 7 weeks, he buys a gift and has $38 left. How much does he spend on the gift?

Lesson 11:	Interpret the unknown in multiplication and division to model and solve problems.	3.C.46
Date:	7/31/13	

Topic D
Multiplication and Division Using Units of 9

3.OA.3, 3.OA.4, 3.OA.5, 3.OA.7, 3.OA.9, 3.OA.1, 3.OA.2, 3.OA.6

Focus Standard:	3.OA.3	Use multiplication and division within 100 to solve word problems in situations involving equal groups, arrays, and measurement quantities, e.g., by using drawings and equations with a symbol for the unknown number to represent the problem. (See Glossary, Table 2.)
	3.OA.4	Determine the unknown whole number in a multiplication or division equation relating three whole numbers. *For example, determine the unknown number that makes the equation true in each of the equations 8 × ? = 48, 5 = _ ÷ 3, 6 × 6 = ?*
	3.OA.5	Apply properties of operations as strategies to multiply and divide. (Students need not use formal terms for these properties.) *Examples: If 6 × 4 = 24 is known, then 4 × 6 = 24 is also known. (Commutative property of multiplication.) 3 × 5 × 2 can be found by 3 × 5 = 15, then 15 × 2 = 30, or by 5 × 2 = 10, then 3 × 10 = 30. (Associative property of multiplication.) Knowing that 8 × 5 = 40 and 8 × 2 = 16, one can find 8 × 7 as 8 × (5 + 2) = (8 × 5) + (8 × 2) = 40 + 16 = 56. (Distributive property.)*
	3.OA.7	Fluently multiply and divide within 100, using strategies such as the relationship between multiplication and division (e.g., knowing that 8 × 5 = 40, one knows 40 ÷ 5 = 8) or properties of operations. By the end of Grade 3, know from memory all products of two one-digit numbers.
	3.OA.9	Identify arithmetic patterns (including patterns in the addition table or multiplication table), and explain them using properties of operations. *For example, observe that 4 times a number is always even, and explain why 4 times a number can be decomposed into two equal addends.*
Instructional Days:	4	
Coherence -Links from:	G2–M3	Place Value, Counting, and Comparison of Numbers to 1000
	G2–M6	Foundations of Multiplication and Division
	G3–M1	Properties of Multiplication and Division and Solving Problems with Units of 2–5 and 10
-Links to:	G3–M4	Multiplication and Area
	G4–M3	Multi-Digit Multiplication and Division
	G4–M5	Fraction Equivalence, Ordering, and Operations
	G4–M7	Exploring Multiplication

In Lesson 12, students use the distributive property to establish the $9 = 10 - 1$ pattern for multiplication. Conceptual understanding of the pattern enables students to see this method of multiplication as a tool rather than a trick. This lesson lays the foundation for exploring other patterns that emerge with multiplication using units of 9 in the subsequent lessons.

Lessons 13 and 14 focus on the study of patterns as they relate to the fact $9 = 10 - 1$. Students discover that the tens digit in the product of a nines fact is 1 less than the multiplier, and that the ones digit in the product is 10 minus the multiplier. For example, $9 \times 3 = 27$, $2 = 3 - 1$, and $7 = 10 - 3$. They also see that the digits of nines facts products produce a sum of 9, as in the example above $(2 + 7 = 9)$.

Lesson 15 parallels the final lessons of Topics B and C. Students analyze multiplication and division problems using units of 9, drawing models and writing equations using a letter to represent the unknown. These lessons are intended to provide students with continuous experience relating three numbers to find the unknown, as well as deepen their understanding of the relationship between multiplication and division.

A Teaching Sequence Towards Mastery of Multiplication and Division Using Units of 9
Objective 1: Apply the distributive property and the fact $9 = 10 - 1$ as a strategy to multiply. (Lesson 12)
Objective 2: Identify and use arithmetic patterns to multiply. (Lessons 13–14)
Objective 3: Interpret the unknown in multiplication and division to model and solve problems. (Lesson 15)

Lesson 12

Objective: Apply the distributive property and the fact 9 = 10 – 1 as a strategy to multiply.

Suggested Lesson Structure

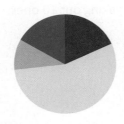

■ Fluency Practice   (11 minutes)
■ Application Problem   (6 minutes)
□ Concept Development   (33 minutes)
■ Student Debrief   (10 minutes)

Total Time   **(60 minutes)**

Fluency Practice (11 minutes)

▪ Multiply by 8 **3.OA.7**   (7 minutes)
▪ Take from the Ten **3.OA.5**   (4 minutes)

Multiply by 8 (7 minutes)

Materials: (S) Multiply by 8 Pattern Sheet (6–10)

Note: This activity builds fluency with multiplication facts using units of 8. It works toward students knowing from memory all products of two one-digit numbers. See G3–M3–Lesson 5 for the directions for administration of a Multiply By Pattern Sheet.

  T: (Write 6 × 8 = _____.) Let's skip-count up by eights to solve. (Count with fingers to 6 as students count.)

  S: 8, 16, 24, 32, 40, 48.

  T: Let's skip-count down to find the answer, too. Start at 80. (Count down from 10 fingers as students count.)

  S: 80, 72, 64, 56, 48.

  T: Let's skip-count up again to find the answer, but this time start at 40. (Count up from 5 fingers as students count.)

  S: 40, 48.

Continue with the following possible sequence: 8 × 8 and 7 × 8, and 9 × 8.

  T: (Distribute the Multiply by 8 Pattern Sheet.) Let's practice multiplying by 8. Be sure to work left to right across the page.

COMMON CORE

Lesson 12: Apply the distributive property and the fact 9 = 10 – 1 as a strategy to multiply.

Date: 7/31/13

3.D.3

Take from the Ten (4 minutes)

Materials: (S) Personal white boards

Note: This fluency prepares students for today's Concept Development.

T: (Write 20 – 2 = _____.) Say the subtraction sentence in unit form.

S: 2 tens – 2 ones.

T: (Point at the 20.) Let's break apart the 20, taking out 10 ones. How many tens will we have left?

S: 1 ten.

T: What's 10 ones – 2 ones?

S: 8 ones.

T: (Write 8.)

T: What's 20 – 2?

S: 18.

T: (Write 20 – 2 = 18.)

T: (Write 30 – 3 = _____.) After writing the equation, break apart the 30, taking out 10 ones.

S: (Break apart the 30 into 20 and 10.)

T: Take 3 ones from 10 ones and complete the equation.

S: (Take 3 from 10 to get 7, 30 – 3 = 27.)

Continue with the following possible sequence: 40 – 4, 50 – 5, 60 – 6, 70 – 7, 80 – 8, 90 – 9.

Application Problem (6 minutes)

A scientist fills 5 test tubes with 9 milliliters of fresh water in each. She fills another 3 test tubes with 9 milliliters of salt water in each. How many milliliters of water does she use in all? Use the break apart and distribute strategy to solve.

$$8 \times 9 = (5+3) \times 9$$
$$= (5 \times 9) + (3 \times 9)$$
$$= 45 + 27$$
$$= 72$$

She used 72 mL of water in all.

Note: The Application Problem is meant to reinforce the 5 + n break apart and distribute strategy to support Problem 1 in the Problem Set, and also to provide a point of comparison between the 5 + n strategy and the 9 = 10 – 1 strategy for multiplying with a factor of 9. Notice that in order to add 45 and 27, the student has taken 3 from 45 to make 30 from 27.

COMMON CORE   Lesson 12:   Apply the distributive property and the fact 9 = 10 – 1 as a strategy
to multiply.   **3.D.4**
             Date: 7/31/13

© 2013 Common Core, Inc. All rights reserved. commoncore.org

Concept Development (33 minutes)

Materials: (S) Personal white boards with tape diagram template

Use the 9 = 10 – 1 strategy to solve 9 × n facts.

Students have tape diagram templates in their personal boards.

**NOTES ON
MULTIPLE MEANS
FOR ACTION AND
EXPRESSION:**

Students who have difficulty
representing 10 × 8 as a tape diagram
may find drawing the familiar
10-square easier.

In addition, adjust your rate of speech
for English language learners and
others as students write equations in
response to your oral prompts. Label
the equations. For example, write
"9 eights" under "9 × 8."

T: We solved 8 × 9 in the Application Problem.
      Does 8 × 9 show 8 units of 9, or 9 units of 8?

S: 8 units of 9.

T: What multiplication fact represents 9 units of 8?

S: 9 × 8.

T: How can our work solving 8 × 9 help us solve 9 × 8?

S: We can use the commutative property to know that if
      8 × 9 = 72, then so does 9 × 8.

T: Sometimes we can't use the commutative property
      because we don't know the product of either fact.
      Let's look at how we can use a tens fact to help solve a
      nines fact when that happens. What's easier to solve,
      9 × 8 or 10 × 8?

S: 10 × 8, because we already know tens facts.

T: How many eights are in 10 × 8?

S: 10 eights!

T: Label them on your tape diagram.

T: How many eights in 9 × 8?

S: 9 eights!

T: Change your tape diagram so it shows 9 eights. (Allow students time to finish their work.)

T: What change did you make?

S: I crossed off an eight. → I took away 1 eight. → I subtracted one unit.

T: 9 eights (point to the tape diagram) equals 10 eights minus…

S: 1 eight!

T: Work with your partner to write a number sentence showing that.

S: (Write 9 × 8 = (10 × 8) – (1 × 8).)

T: Rewrite your equation using the products of 10 × 8 and 1 × 8.

S: (Write 9 × 8 = 80 – 8.)

T: What is 80 – 8?

S: 72!

T: Tell your partner how we used a tens fact to solve a nines fact.

S: We just took the product of 10 × 8 and subtracted 1 eight. → That made the math simple.
      I can do 80 – 8 in my head!

	Lesson 12:	Apply the distributive property and the fact 9 = 10 – 1 as a strategy	
		to multiply.	3.D.5
	Date:	7/31/13	

T: (Write 9 × 8 = (5 + 4) × 8.) One way that we've learned to solve 9 × 8 is by breaking 9 eights up into 5 eights plus 4 eights. Why did it work well to subtract this time instead?

S: Because we only had to subtract 1 eight. → Yeah, 9 is really close to 10, and tens are easy to use. We already know 10 × 8, and besides, it's easy to subtract from a tens fact.

T: Work with your partner to change the equation I just wrote for 9 × 8. Make sure it shows how we used subtraction to solve.

S: (Change the equation to 9 × 8 = (10 − 1) × 8.)

T: What part of the equation did you change?

S: We changed 5 + 4 to 10 − 1.

T: Why?

S: Because we didn't add, we subtracted. We started with 10 eights and then took away 1 eight.

Continue with the following possible suggestions: 9 × 7, 9 × 6.

Problem Set (10 minutes)

Students should do their personal best to complete the Problem Set within the allotted 10 minutes. For some classes, it may be appropriate to modify the assignment by specifying which problems they work on first. Some problems do not specify a method for solving. Students solve these problems using the RDW approach used for Application Problems.

Student Debrief (10 minutes)

Lesson Objective: Apply the distributive property and the fact 9 = 10 − 1 as a strategy to multiply.

The Student Debrief is intended to invite reflection and active processing of the total lesson experience.

Invite students to review their solutions for the Problem Set. They should check work by comparing answers with a partner before going over answers as a class. Look for misconceptions or misunderstandings that can be addressed in the Debrief. Guide students in a conversation to debrief the Problem Set and process the lesson.

You may choose to use any combination of the questions below to lead the discussion.

- What does the nine represent in Problem 1? (It represents the value of each unit.)
  What does the nine represent in Problem 2? (It represents the number of units.)

NOTES ON MULTIPLE MEANS OF ENGAGEMENT:

As students solve the Problem Set, some learners may solve Problem 1 more efficiently using the 9 = 10 − 1 strategy.

Students working above grade level can be encouraged to write equations using parentheses for Problem 2. Challenge students to offer multiple equations. Ask, "How many equations can you write for Problem 2(a)?"

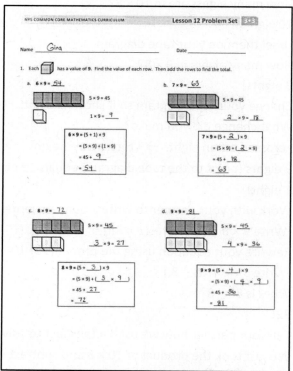

COMMON CORE | Lesson 12:   Apply the distributive property and the fact 9 = 10 − 1 as a strategy to multiply.   **3.D.6**

Date: 7/31/13

- How can multiplication be used to solve the division facts in Problem 4?

- Think about the strategy used to solve 2(a). How could a similar strategy be used to solve 8 × 6 instead of 9 × 6?

- Today we solved 9 × 8 in different ways. How are the strategies we used in the Application Problem and Concept Development similar? How are they different?

Exit Ticket (3 minutes)

After the Student Debrief, instruct students to complete the Exit Ticket. A review of their work will help you assess the students' understanding of the concepts that were presented in the lesson today and plan more effectively for future lessons. You may read the questions aloud to the students.

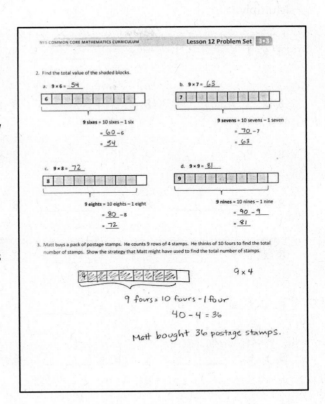

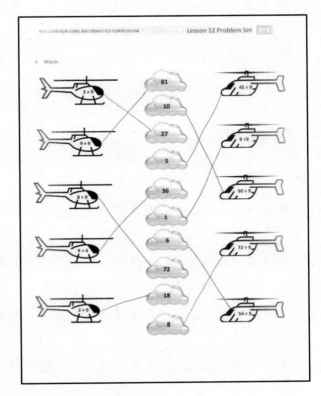

COMMON CORE | Lesson 12:   Apply the distributive property and the fact 9 = 10 − 1 as a strategy to multiply.
Date: 7/31/13

3.D.7

© 2013 Common Core, Inc. All rights reserved. commoncore.org

Multiply.

8 x 1 = _____   8 x 2 = _____   8 x 3 = _____   8 x 4 = _____

8 x 5 = _____   8 x 6 = _____   8 x 7 = _____   8 x 8 = _____

8 x 9 = _____   8 x 10 = _____   8 x 5 = _____   8 x 6 = _____

8 x 5 = _____   8 x 7 = _____   8 x 5 = _____   8 x 8 = _____

8 x 5 = _____   8 x 9 = _____   8 x 5 = _____   8 x 10 = _____

8 x 6 = _____   8 x 5 = _____   8 x 6 = _____   8 x 7 = _____

8 x 6 = _____   8 x 8 = _____   8 x 6 = _____   8 x 9 = _____

8 x 6 = _____   8 x 7 = _____   8 x 6 = _____   8 x 7 = _____

8 x 8 = _____   8 x 7 = _____   8 x 9 = _____   8 x 7 = _____

8 x 8 = _____   8 x 6 = _____   8 x 8 = _____   8 x 7 = _____

8 x 8 = _____   8 x 9 = _____   8 x 9 = _____   8 x 6 = _____

8 x 9 = _____   8 x 7 = _____   8 x 9 = _____   8 x 8 = _____

8 x 9 = _____   8 x 8 = _____   8 x 6 = _____   8 x 9 = _____

8 x 7 = _____   8 x 9 = _____   8 x 6 = _____   8 x 8 = _____

8 x 9 = _____   8 x 7 = _____   8 x 6 = _____   8 x 8 = _____

© Bill Davidson

Lesson 12:   Apply the distributive property and the fact 9 = 10 − 1 as a strategy
               to multiply.
Date: 7/31/13

3.D.8

Name _____   Date _____

1. Each 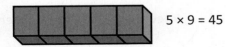 has a value of **9**. Find the value of each row. Then add the rows to find the total.

a. **6 × 9 = _____**

5 × 9 = 45

1 × 9 = _____

6 × 9 = (5 + 1) × 9

= (5 × 9) + (1 × 9)

= 45 + _____

= _____

b. **7 × 9 = _____**

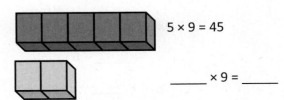

5 × 9 = 45

_____ × 9 = _____

7 × 9 = (5 + _____) × 9

= (5 × 9) + (_____ × 9)

= 45 + _____

= _____

c. **8 × 9 = _____**

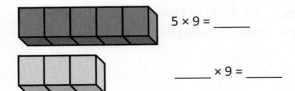

5 × 9 = _____

_____ × 9 = _____

8 × 9 = (5 + _____) × 9

= (5 × 9) + (_____ × _____)

= 45 + _____

= _____

d. **9 × 9 = _____**

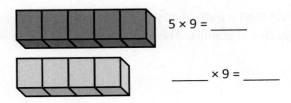

5 × 9 = _____

_____ × 9 = _____

9 × 9 = (5 + _____) × 9

= (5 × 9) + (_____ × _____)

= 45 + _____

= _____

COMMON CORE | Lesson 12: | Apply the distributive property and the fact 9 = 10 − 1 as a strategy to multiply.
Date: | 7/31/13

3.D.9

2. Find the total value of the shaded blocks.

a. **9 × 6 =** _____

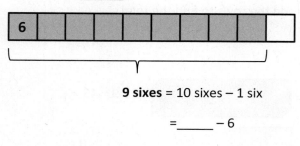

9 sixes = 10 sixes − 1 six

= _____ − 6

= _____

b. **9 × 7 =** _____

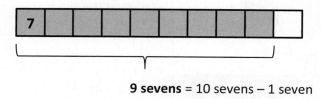

9 sevens = 10 sevens − 1 seven

= _____ − 7

= _____

c. **9 × 8 =** _____

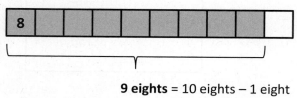

9 eights = 10 eights − 1 eight

= _____ − 8

= _____

d. **9 × 9 =** _____

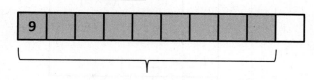

9 nines = 10 nines − 1 nine

= _____ − _____

= _____

3. Matt buys a pack of postage stamps. He counts 9 rows of 4 stamps. He thinks of 10 fours to find the total number of stamps. Show the strategy that Matt might have used to find the total number of stamps.

COMMON CORE

Lesson 12: Apply the distributive property and the fact 9 = 10 − 1 as a strategy to multiply.

Date: 7/31/13

3.D.10

4. Match.

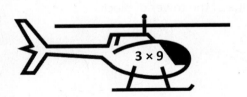

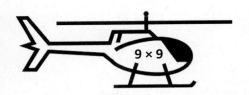

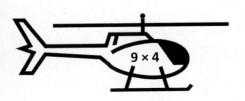

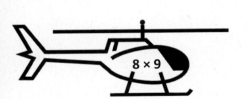

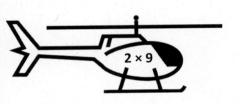

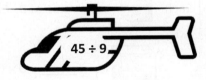

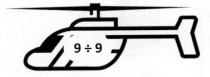

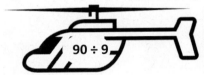

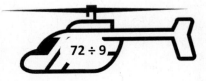

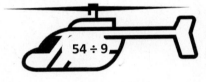

COMMON CORE

Lesson 12:   Apply the distributive property and the fact 9 = 10 − 1 as a strategy to multiply.

Date: 7/31/13

3.D.11

Name _____ Date _____

1. Each 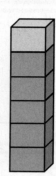 has a value of **9**. Complete the equations to find the total value of the tower of blocks.

 _____ **× 9** = (5 + _____) × 9

 = (5 × _____) + (_____ × _____)

 = 45 + _____

 = _____

2. Hector solves 9 × 8 by subtracting 1 eight from 10 eights. Draw a model and explain Hector's strategy.

COMMON CORE

Lesson 12: Apply the distributive property and the fact 9 = 10 − 1 as a strategy to multiply.

Date: 7/31/13

3.D.12

Name _____   Date _____

1. Find the value of each row. Then add the rows to find the total.

a. Each  has a value of 6.

9 × 6 = _____

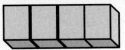   5 × 6 = 30

     4 × 6 = _____

> **9 × 6 = (5 + 4) × 6**
>
> = (5 × 6) + (4 × 6)
>
> = 30 + _____
>
> = _____

b. Each 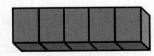 has a value of 7.

9 × 7 = _____

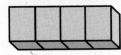   5 × 7 = _____

     _____ × 7 = _____

> **9 × 7 = (5 + _____) × 7**
>
> = (5 × 7) + (_____ × 7)
>
> = 35 + _____
>
> = _____

c. Each 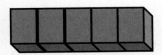 has a value of 8.

9 × 8 = _____

   5 × 8 = _____

_____ × 8 = _____

> **9 × 8 = (5 + _____) × 8**
>
> = (5 × 8) + (_____ × _____)
>
> = 40 + _____
>
> = _____

d. Each 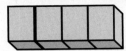 has a value of 9.

9 × 9 = _____

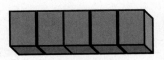   5 × 9 = _____

_____ × 9 = _____

> **9 × 9 = (5 + _____) × 9**
>
> = (5 × 9) + (_____ × _____)
>
> = 45 + _____
>
> = _____

COMMON CORE | Lesson 12: Apply the distributive property and the fact 9 = 10 – 1 as a strategy to multiply.
Date: 7/31/13

3.D.13

2. Match.

a. **9 fives** = 10 fives − 1 five

   = 50 − 5

b. **9 sixes** = 10 sixes − 1 six

   = _____ − 6

c. **9 sevens** = 10 sevens − 1 seven

   = _____ − 7

d. **9 eights** = 10 eights − 1 eight

   = _____ − 8

e. **9 nines** = 10 nines − 1 nine

   = _____ − _____

f. **9 fours** = 10 fours − 1 four

   = _____ − _____

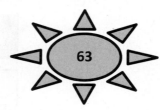

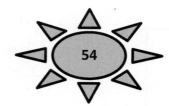

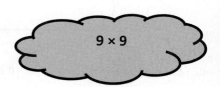

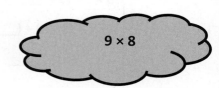

COMMON CORE

Lesson 12: Apply the distributive property and the fact 9 = 10 − 1 as a strategy
to multiply.

Date: 7/31/13

3.D.14

© 2013 Common Core, Inc. All rights reserved. commoncore.org

Lesson 12:   Apply the distributive property and the fact 9 = 10 − 1 as a strategy
to multiply.
Date: 7/31/13

3.D.15

© 2013 Common Core, Inc. All rights reserved. commoncore.org

Lesson 13

Objective: Identify and use arithmetic patterns to multiply.

Suggested Lesson Structure

■ Fluency Practice	(15 minutes)	
■ Concept Development	(20 minutes)	
■ Application Problem	(15 minutes)	
■ Student Debrief	(10 minutes)	
Total Time	**(60 minutes)**	

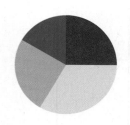

NOTES ON LESSON STRUCTURE:

The Problem Set follows immediately after the Application Problem in this lesson.

The 10 minutes for the Problem Set are included in the time allotted for the Application Problem rather than the Concept Development.

Fluency Practice (15 minutes)

- Sprint: Divide by 8 **3.OA.7**   (8 minutes)
- Group Counting **3.OA.1**   (4 minutes)
- Decompose Multiples of 9 **3.OA.5**   (3 minutes)

Sprint: Divide by 8 (8 minutes)

Materials: (S) Divide by 8 Sprint

Note: This Sprint reviews Lessons 10 and 11, focusing on the relationship between multiplying and dividing using units of 8.

Group Counting (4 minutes)

Note: Group counting reviews interpreting multiplication as repeated addition. Counting by sixes, sevens, and eights reviews multiplication taught earlier in the module. Group counting nines prepares students for multiplication in this lesson. Direct students to count forward and backward, occasionally changing the direction of the count:

- Sixes to 60
- Sevens to 70
- Eights to 80
- Nines to 90

A NOTE ON STANDARDS ALIGNMENT:

Some problems in the Sprint extend beyond Grade 3 multiplication and division standards, because students who have mastered their times tables are likely to otherwise go unchallenged during this activity. By extending to products above 90 and quotients above 10, strong students are provided the stimulus to stretch their conceptual understanding, which will likely keep them engaged and invigorated to improve on Sprint B.

 Lesson 13: Identify and use arithmetic patterns to multiply.
Date: 7/31/13

3.D.16

Decompose Multiples of 9 (3 minutes)

Materials: (S) Personal white boards

Note: This activity prepares students to use the distributive property using units of 9.

> T: (Project a number bond with a whole of 45 and a part of 18.) On your boards, complete the missing
> part in the number bond.
>
> S: (Write 27.)

Continue with the following possible sequence: whole of 90 and 27 as a part, whole of 54 and 36 as a part,
whole of 72 and 27 as a part, whole of 63 and 18 as a part.

Concept Development (20 minutes)

Materials: (S) Personal white boards

Part 1: Identify patterns in multiples of 9.

> T: During the fluency, we group counted nines to say the
> **multiples** of 9. When we skip-count by nines, what are
> we adding each time?
>
> S: 9!
>
> T: Adding nines can be tricky. What's a simplifying strategy
> for adding 9?
>
> S: I can break apart 9 to make the total a ten, then add
> what's left of the 9 to it. → I can add 10, then subtract 1.
>
> T: (Lead students through applying the add 10, subtract 1
> strategy in Problem 2 on the Problem Set. Model the first
> example. Students can then work in pairs to find the rest.
> Allow time for students to finish their work.)
>
> T: Compare the digits in the ones and tens places of the
> multiples. What pattern do you notice?
>
> S: The digit in the tens place increases by 1. → The digit
> in the ones place decreases by 1.
>
> T: Now, with your partner, analyze the sum of the digits
> for each multiple of 9. What pattern do you notice?
>
> S: Every multiple has a sum of the digits equal to 9!
>
> T: How can knowing this help you with nines facts?
>
> S: To check my answer I can add up the digits. If the sum
> isn't equal to 9, I made a mistake.

MP.7

⑨
9 + 10 = 19
⑱ 9 is 1 less than 10 so:
    9 + 9 = 18

18 + 10 = 28
㉗ 9 is 1 less than 10 so:
    18 + 9 = 27

27 + 10 = 37
㊱ 9 is 1 less than 10 so:
    27 + 9 = 36

36 + 10 = 46
㊺ 9 is 1 less than 10 so:
    36 + 9 = 45

45 + 10 = 55
�554 9 is 1 less than 10 so:
    45 + 9 = 54

Etc.

**NOTES ON
MULTIPLE MEANS OF
REPRESENTATION:**

Simplify and clarify "sum of the digits"
for English language learners and
others. Distinguish *some* from *sum*.
Perhaps express the request in another
manner, such as, "Look at the product.
(Point.) Add the number in the ones
place to the number in the tens place.
What's the sum? Now, look at the next
product… "

Part 2: Apply strategies to solve nines facts.

Have students write and solve all facts from 1 × 9 to 10 × 9 in a column on their boards.

T: Let's examine 1 × 9 = 9. Here, what is 9 multiplied by?

S: 9 is multiplied by 1.

T: What number is in the tens place of the product for 1 × 9?

S: Zero.

T: How is the number in the tens place related to 1?

S: It is 1 less. → Zero is one less than 1.

T: Say the product of 2 × 9 at my signal. (Signal.)

S: 18.

T: Which digit is in the tens place of the product?

S: 1.

T: How is the digit in the tens place related to the 2?

S: It's one less again. → 1 is one less than 2!

Repeat the process with 3 × 9 and 4 × 9.

$$1 \times 9 = 9$$
$$2 \times 9 = 18$$
$$3 \times 9 = 27$$
$$4 \times 9 = 36$$
$$5 \times 9 = 45$$
$$6 \times 9 = 54$$
$$7 \times 9 = 63$$
$$8 \times 9 = 72$$
$$9 \times 9 = 81$$
$$10 \times 9 = 90$$

T: What pattern do you notice with the digit in the tens place for each of those products?

S: The number in the tens place is 1 less than the number of groups.

T: With your partner, see if that pattern fits for the rest of the nines facts to ten.

S: It does! The pattern keeps going!

T: Let's see if we can find a pattern involving the ones place. We know that 2 × 9 equals 18. The 2 and 8 are related in some way. We also know that 3 × 9 equals 27. The 3 and 7 are related in the *same* way. Discuss with your partner, how are they related?

S: 2 + 8 = 10 and 3 + 7 = 10! → 10 − 2 = 8 and 10 − 3 = 7!

T: When you take the number of groups and subtract it from 10, what do you get?

S: The ones place in the product!

T: With your partner, see if that pattern fits for the rest of the nines facts on your board. (Allow students time to finish their work.)

T: Did the pattern work for every fact, 1 × 9 through 10 × 9?

S: Yes!

T: Let's try 11 × 9. What is the product?

S: 99!

T: What is the number of groups?

S: 11!

T: Talk to your partner: Does the pattern work for 11 × 9? Why or why not?

S: No, the pattern doesn't make sense. You can't have 10 in the tens place, and we don't know how to solve 10 − 11 to find what digit is in the ones place.

T: The pattern can give you the answer to any nines fact from 1 × 9 to 10 × 9, but it doesn't work for nines facts bigger than 10 × 9.

	Lesson 13:	Identify and use arithmetic patterns to multiply.	
	Date:	7/31/13	3.D.18

Application Problem (15 minutes)

Michaela and Gilda read the same book. It takes Michaela about 8 minutes to read a chapter, and Gilda about 10 minutes. There are 9 chapters in the book. How many fewer minutes does Michaela spend reading than Gilda?

Michaela   8 × 9 = 72 minutes

Gilda   10 × 9 = 90 minutes

90 − 72 = 18 minutes
Michaela spends 18 fewer minutes reading.

Note: This problem comes after the Concept Development so that students have the opportunity to apply some of the strategies they learned in the context of problem solving. Encourage them to check their answers to the nines facts using new learning.

Problem Set (10 minutes)

Students should do their personal best to complete the Problem Set within the allotted 10 minutes. For some classes, it may be appropriate to modify the assignment by specifying which problems they work on first. Some problems do not specify a method for solving. Students solve these problems using the RDW approach used for Application Problems.

NOTES ON MULTIPLE MEANS OF REPRESENTATION:

You may adjust the Problem Set to assist learners with perceptual disabilities. Provide a table for students to record the nine skip-count, and/or highlight the tens or ones. As students solve Problem 2, it may be helpful to write the nines fact for each given product, e.g. in Problem 2(f), have students write 5 × 9 above 45.

Student Debrief (10 minutes)

Lesson Objective: Identify and use arithmetic patterns to multiply.

The Student Debrief is intended to invite reflection and active processing of the total lesson experience.

Invite students to review their solutions for the Problem Set. They should check work by comparing answers with a partner before going over answers as a class. Look for misconceptions or misunderstandings that can be addressed in the Debrief. Guide students in a conversation to debrief the Problem Set and process the lesson.

You may choose to use any combination of the questions below to lead the discussion.

- What patterns did you use to solve Problem 1?
- The add 10, subtract 1 strategy can be used to quickly find **multiples** of 9. How could you change it to quickly find multiples of 8?
- How is the add 10, subtract 1 strategy related to the 9 = 10 − 1 break apart and distribute strategy we learned recently?
- In Problem 3(d) how did you figure out where Kent's strategy stops working? Why doesn't this strategy

work past 10 × 9?

- How can the number of groups in a nines fact help you find the product?

- How did Group Counting during the Fluency help get us ready for today's lesson?

Exit Ticket (3 minutes)

After the Student Debrief, instruct students to complete the Exit Ticket. A review of their work will help you assess the students' understanding of the concepts that were presented in the lesson today and plan more effectively for future lessons. You may read the questions aloud to the students.

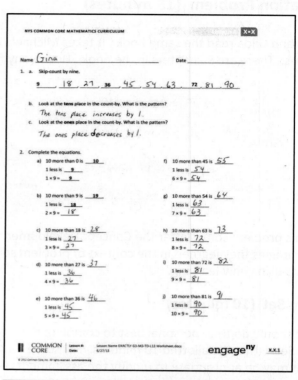

NYS COMMON CORE MATHEMATICS CURRICULUM   X•X

Name __Gina_____   Date _____

1. a. Skip-count by nine.

   9 , __18__ , __27__ , **36** , __45__ , __54__ , __63__ , **72** , __81__ , __90__

   b. Look at the **tens** place in the count-by. What is the pattern?
   The tens place increases by 1.

   c. Look at the **ones** place in the count-by. What is the pattern?
   The ones place decreases by 1.

2. Complete the equations.

   a) 10 more than 0 is __10__   f) 10 more than 45 is __55__
      1 less is __9__   1 less is __54__
      1 × 9 = __9__   6 × 9 = __54__

   b) 10 more than 9 is __19__   g) 10 more than 54 is __64__
      1 less is __18__   1 less is __63__
      2 × 9 = __18__   7 × 9 = __63__

   c) 10 more than 18 is __28__   h) 10 more than 63 is __73__
      1 less is __27__   1 less is __72__
      3 × 9 = __27__   8 × 9 = __72__

   d) 10 more than 27 is __37__   i) 10 more than 72 is __82__
      1 less is __36__   1 less is __81__
      4 × 9 = __36__   9 × 9 = __81__

   e) 10 more than 36 is __46__   j) 10 more than 81 is __91__
      1 less is __45__   1 less is __90__
      5 × 9 = __45__   10 × 9 = __90__

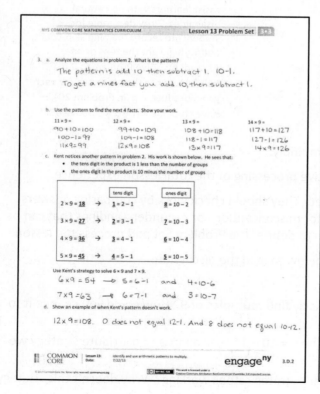

NYS COMMON CORE MATHEMATICS CURRICULUM   Lesson 13 Problem Set 3•3

3. a. Analyze the equations in problem 2. What is the pattern?
   The pattern is add 10 then subtract 1. 10-1.
   To get a nines fact you add 10, then subtract 1.

   b. Use the pattern to find the next 4 facts. Show your work.

   11 × 9 =   12 × 9 =   13 × 9 =   14 × 9 =
   90 + 10 = 100   99 + 10 = 109   108 + 10 = 118   117 + 10 = 127
   100 - 1 = 99   109 - 1 = 108   118 - 1 = 117   127 - 1 = 126
   11 × 9 = 99   12 × 9 = 108   13 × 9 = 117   14 × 9 = 126

   c. Kent notices another pattern in problem 2. His work is shown below. He sees that:
      • the tens digit in the product is 1 less than the number of groups
      • the ones digit in the product is 10 minus the number of groups

	tens digit		ones digit
2 × 9 = **18** →	**1** = 2 - 1		**8** = 10 - 2
3 × 9 = **27** →	**2** = 3 - 1		**7** = 10 - 3
4 × 9 = **36** →	**3** = 4 - 1		**6** = 10 - 4
5 × 9 = **45** →	**4** = 5 - 1		**5** = 10 - 5

   Use Kent's strategy to solve 6 × 9 and 7 × 9.
   6 × 9 = 54 → 5 = 6 - 1   and   4 = 10 - 6
   7 × 9 = 63 → 6 = 7 - 1   and   3 = 10 - 7

   d. Show an example of when Kent's pattern doesn't work.
   12 × 9 = 108. 0 does not equal 12 - 1. And 8 does not equal 10 - 12.

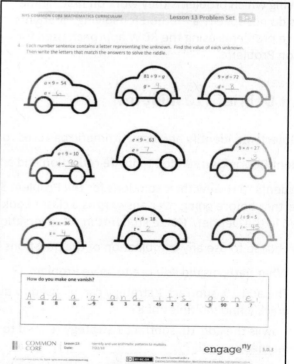

NYS COMMON CORE MATHEMATICS CURRICULUM   Lesson 13 Problem Set 3•3

4. Each number sentence contains a letter representing the unknown. Find the value of each unknown. Then write the letters that match the answers to solve the riddle.

   a × 9 = 54   81 ÷ 9 = g   9 × d = 72
   a = 6   g = 9   d = 8

   a ÷ 9 = 10   e × 9 = 63   9 × n = 27
   a = 90   e = 7   n = 3

   9 × s = 36   t × 9 = 18   i ÷ 9 = 5
   s = 4   t = 2   i = 45

   How do you make one vanish?

A	d	d		a		'g'		a	n	d		i	t	's		g	o	n	e	!
6	8	8		6		9		6	3	8		45	2	4		9	90	3	7	

COMMON CORE

Lesson 13:   Identify and use arithmetic patterns to multiply.
Date: 7/31/13

3.D.20

© 2013 Common Core, Inc. All rights reserved. commoncore.org

A

Correct _____

Multiply or divide.

1	2 x 8 =		23	__ x 8 = 80	
2	3 x 8 =		24	__ x 8 = 32	
3	4 x 8 =		25	__ x 8 = 24	
4	5 x 8 =		26	80 ÷ 8 =	
5	1 x 8 =		27	40 ÷ 8 =	
6	16 ÷ 8 =		28	8 ÷ 1 =	
7	24 ÷ 8 =		29	16 ÷ 8 =	
8	40 ÷ 8 =		30	24 ÷ 8 =	
9	8 ÷ 1 =		31	__ x 8 = 48	
10	32 ÷ 8 =		32	__ x 8 = 56	
11	6 x 8 =		33	__ x 8 = 72	
12	7 x 8 =		34	__ x 8 = 64	
13	8 x 8 =		35	56 ÷ 8 =	
14	9 x 8 =		36	72 ÷ 8 =	
15	10 x 8 =		37	48 ÷ 8 =	
16	64 ÷ 8 =		38	64 ÷ 8 =	
17	56 ÷ 8 =		39	11 x 8 =	
18	72 ÷ 8 =		40	88 ÷ 8 =	
19	48 ÷ 8 =		41	12 x 8 =	
20	80 ÷ 8 =		42	96 ÷ 8 =	
21	__ x 8 = 40		43	14 x 8 =	
22	__ x 8 = 16		44	112 ÷ 8 =	

© Bill Davidson

 **COMMON CORE**   Lesson 13:   Identify and use arithmetic patterns to multiply.   **3.D.21**
Date: 7/31/13

B

Multiply or divide.

Improvement _____   # Correct _____

1	1 x 8 =		23	__ x 8 = 48	
2	2 x 8 =		24	__ x 8 = 80	
3	3 x 8 =		25	__ x 8 = 24	
4	4 x 8 =		26	16 ÷ 8 =	
5	5 x 8 =		27	8 ÷ 1 =	
6	24 ÷ 8 =		28	80 ÷ 8 =	
7	16 ÷ 8 =		29	40 ÷ 8 =	
8	32 ÷ 8 =		30	24 ÷ 8 =	
9	8 ÷ 1 =		31	__ x 8 = 64	
10	40 ÷ 8 =		32	__ x 8 = 32	
11	10 x 8 =		33	__ x 8 = 72	
12	6 x 8 =		34	__ x 8 = 56	
13	7 x 8 =		35	64 ÷ 8 =	
14	8 x 8 =		36	72 ÷8 =	
15	9 x 8 =		37	48 ÷ 8 =	
16	56 ÷ 8 =		38	56 ÷ 8 =	
17	48 ÷ 8 =		39	11 x 8 =	
18	64 ÷ 8 =		40	88 ÷ 8 =	
19	80 ÷ 8 =		41	12 x 8 =	
20	72 ÷8 =		42	96 ÷ 8 =	
21	__ x 8 = 16		43	13 x 8 =	
22	__ x 8 = 40		44	104 ÷ 8 =	

© Bill Davidson

Lesson 13:   Identify and use arithmetic patterns to multiply.
Date: 7/31/13

3.D.22

Name _____   Date _____

1. a.   Skip-count by nine.

   __9__ , _____ , _____ , __36__ , _____ , _____ , _____ , __72__ , _____ , _____

   b.   Look at the **tens** place in the count-by. What is the pattern?

   c.   Look at the **ones** place in the count-by. What is the pattern?

2. Complete to make true statements.

   a.   10 more than 0 is ___10__ ,

       1 less is ___9___ .

       1 × 9 = ___9___

   b.   10 more than 9 is ___19___ ,

       1 less is ___18___ .

       2 × 9 = _____

   c.   10 more than 18 is _____ ,

       1 less is _____ .

       3 × 9 = _____

   d.   10 more than 27 is _____ ,

       1 less is _____ .

       4 × 9 = _____

   e.   10 more than 36 is _____ ,

       1 less is _____ .

       5 × 9 = _____

   f.   10 more than 45 is _____ ,

       1 less is _____ .

       6 × 9 = _____

   g.   10 more than 54 is _____ ,

       1 less is _____ .

       7 × 9 = _____

   h.   10 more than 63 is _____ ,

       1 less is _____ .

       8 × 9 = _____

   i.   10 more than 72 is _____ ,

       1 less is _____ .

       9 × 9 = _____

   j.   10 more than 81 is _____ ,

       1 less is _____ .

       10 × 9 = _____

COMMON CORE

Lesson 13:   Identify and use arithmetic patterns to multiply.
Date: 7/31/13   3.D.23

3. a. Analyze the equations in Problem 2. What is the pattern?

    b. Use the pattern to find the next 4 facts. Show your work.

    $11 \times 9 =$ $12 \times 9 =$ $13 \times 9 =$ $14 \times 9 =$

    c. Kent notices another pattern in Problem 2. His work is shown below. He sees that:
        - the tens digit in the product is 1 less than the number of groups
        - the ones digit in the product is 10 minus the number of groups

		tens digit	ones digit
$2 \times 9 = \underline{\textbf{18}}$	→	$\underline{\textbf{1}} = 2 - 1$	$\underline{\textbf{8}} = 10 - 2$
$3 \times 9 = \underline{\textbf{27}}$	→	$\underline{\textbf{2}} = 3 - 1$	$\underline{\textbf{7}} = 10 - 3$
$4 \times 9 = \underline{\textbf{36}}$	→	$\underline{\textbf{3}} = 4 - 1$	$\underline{\textbf{6}} = 10 - 4$
$5 \times 9 = \underline{\textbf{45}}$	→	$\underline{\textbf{4}} = 5 - 1$	$\underline{\textbf{5}} = 10 - 5$

    Use Kent's strategy to solve 6×9 and 7×9.

    d. Show an example of when Kent's pattern doesn't work.

4. Each number sentence contains a letter representing the unknown. Find the value of each unknown. Then write the letters that match the answers to solve the riddle.

$a \times 9 = 54$

$a =$ _____

$81 \div 9 = g$

$g =$ _____

$9 \times d = 72$

$d =$ _____

$o \div 9 = 10$

$o =$ _____

$e \times 9 = 63$

$e =$ _____

$9 \times n = 27$

$n =$ _____

$9 \times s = 36$

$s =$ _____

$t \times 9 = 18$

$t =$ _____

$i \div 9 = 5$

$i =$ _____

How do you make one vanish?

___ ___ ___ ___ ___ , ___ , ___ ___ ___ ___ ___ , ___ ___ ___ ___ ___ ___ !
6 8 8 6   9   6 3 8 45 2 4   9 90 3 7

COMMON CORE

Lesson 13: Identify and use arithmetic patterns to multiply.
Date: 7/31/13

3.D.25

Name _____   Date _____

1. $6 \times 9 = 54$ $8 \times 9 = 72$

    What is 10 more than 54? _____   What is 10 more than 72? _____

    What is 1 less? _____   What is 1 less? _____

    $7 \times 9 =$ _____ $9 \times 9 =$ _____

2. Explain the pattern used in Problem 1.

COMMON CORE | Lesson 13:   Identify and use arithmetic patterns to multiply.
Date: 7/31/13

3.D.26

Name _____   Date _____

1. a. Skip-count by nines down from 90.

   __**90**__ , _____ , __**72**__ , _____ , _____ , _____ , __**36**__ , _____ , _____ , _____

   b. Look at the **tens** place in the count-by. What is the pattern?

   c. Look at the ones place in the count-by. What is the pattern?

2. Each number sentence contains a letter representing the unknown. Find the value of each unknown.

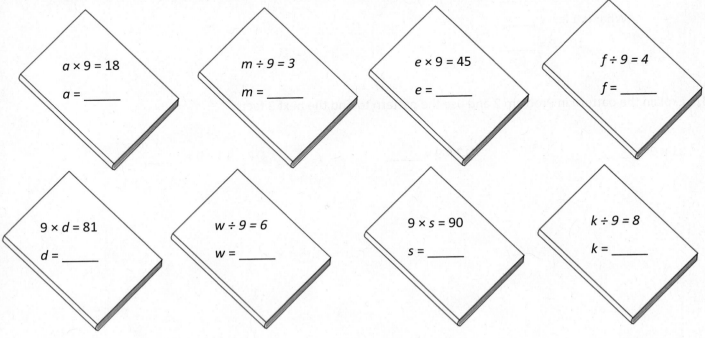

$a \times 9 = 18$

$a =$ _____

$m \div 9 = 3$

$m =$ _____

$e \times 9 = 45$

$e =$ _____

$f \div 9 = 4$

$f =$ _____

$9 \times d = 81$

$d =$ _____

$w \div 9 = 6$

$w =$ _____

$9 \times s = 90$

$s =$ _____

$k \div 9 = 8$

$k =$ _____

COMMON CORE | Lesson 13: | Identify and use arithmetic patterns to multiply.
Date: | 7/31/13

3.D.27

© 2013 Common Core, Inc. All rights reserved. **commoncore.org**

3. Solve.

a. What is 10 more than 0? _____

   What is 1 less? _____

   1 × 9 = _____

b. What is 10 more than 9? _____

   What is 1 less? _____

   2 × 9 = _____

c. What is 10 more than 18? _____

   What is 1 less? _____

   3 × 9 = _____

d. 10 more than 27? _____

   What is 1 less? _____

   4 × 9 = _____

e. What is 10 more than 36? _____

   What is 1 less? _____

   5 × 9 = _____

f. What is 10 more than 45? _____

   What is 1 less? _____

   6 × 9 = _____

g. What is 10 more than 54? _____

   What is 1 less? _____

   7 × 9 = _____

h. What is 10 more than 63? _____

   What is 1 less? _____

   8 × 9 = _____

i. What is 10 more than 72? _____

   What is 1 less? _____

   9 × 9 = _____

j. What is 10 more than 81? _____

   What is 1 less? _____

   10 × 9 = _____

4. Explain the pattern in Problem 2 and use the pattern to find the next 3 facts.

   11 × 9 = _____   12 × 9 = _____   13 × 9 = _____

COMMON CORE

Lesson 13:   Identify and use arithmetic patterns to multiply.
Date: 7/31/13

3.D.28

Lesson 14

Objective: Identify and use arithmetic patterns to multiply.

Suggested Lesson Structure

■ Fluency Practice   (7 minutes)
▨ Concept Development   (43 minutes)
■ Student Debrief   (10 minutes)

  Total Time   **(60 minutes)**

Fluency Practice (7 minutes)

▪ Multiply By 9 **3.OA.7**   (7 minutes)

Multiply by 9 (7 minutes)

Materials: (S) Multiply by 9 Pattern Sheet (1–5)

Note: This activity builds fluency with multiplication facts using units of 9. It works toward students knowing from memory all products of two one-digit numbers. See G3–M3–Lesson 5 for the directions for administration of a Multiply By Pattern Sheet.

  T: (Write $5 \times 9 =$ _____.) Let's skip-count by nines to find the answer. (Count with fingers to 5 as students count.)

  S: 9, 18, 27, 36, 45.

  T: (Circle 45 and write $5 \times 9 = 45$ above it. Write $3 \times 9 =$ _____.) Let's skip-count up by nines again. (Count with fingers to 3 as students count.)

  S: 9, 18, 27.

  T: (Circle 27 and write $3 \times 9 = 27$ above it.) Let's see how we can skip-count down to find the answer, too. Start at 45 with 5 fingers, 1 for each nine. (Count down with your fingers as students say numbers.)

  S: 45 (5 fingers), 36 (4 fingers), 27 (3 fingers).

Repeat the process for 4×9.

  T: (Distribute the Multiply by 9 Pattern Sheet.) Let's practice multiplying by 9. Be sure to work left to right across the page.

	Lesson 14:	Identify and use arithmetic patterns to multiply.
	Date:	7/31/13

3.D.29

Concept Development (43 minutes)

Materials: (S) Personal white boards

Part 1: Extend the 9 = 10 – 1 strategy of multiplying with units of 9.

T: How is the 9 = 10 – 1 strategy—or add ten, subtract 1–from yesterday used to solve 2 × 9?

S: You can do 1 × 9 = 9, then add ten and subtract one like this, (9 + 10) – 1 = 18.

T: Let's use this strategy to find 2 × 9 another way. (Draw a 2 × 10 array.) When we start with 2 × 10, how many tens do we have?

S: 2 tens.

T: In unit form, what is the fact we are finding?

S: 2 nines.

T: To get 1 nine, we subtract 1 from a ten. In our problem there are 2 nines, so we need to subtract 2 from our 2 tens. (Cross off 2 from the array, as shown at right.) When we subtract 2, how many tens are left?

S: 1 ten.

T: What happened to the other ten?

S: We subtracted 2, so now there are 8 left, not ten. → It's not a full ten anymore after we took off 2 ones. → There is just 1 ten and 8 ones.

T: 2 × 9 = 18. Tell your partner how we used the 9 = 10 – 1 strategy with 2 × 10 to find 2 × 9.

S: (Explain.)

T: Let's use the 9 = 10 – 1 strategy to solve 3 × 9. Draw an array for 3 × 10. (Allow time for students to draw.) To solve, how many should we subtract?

S: 3!

T: Tell your partner why it's 3.

S: Because we are trying to find 3 nines. The teacher made 3 tens, and you have to take 1 away from each 10 to make it 3 nines. So you subtract 3.

T: Cross off 3, then talk to your partner: How many tens and ones are left in the array?

S: (Cross off 3.) There are still 2 complete tens, but only 7 ones in the third row.

T: What does our array show is the product of 3 × 9?

S: 27!

T: How is the array related to the strategy of using the number of groups, 3, to help you solve 3 × 9?

S: There are only 2 tens in 27, and 3 – 1 = 2. There are 7 ones in 27, and 10 – 3 = 7.

T: You can use your fingers to quickly solve a nines fact using this strategy. Put your hands out in front of you with all 10 fingers up, like this. (Model, palms facing away.)

COMMON CORE

Lesson 14:
Date:

Identify and use arithmetic patterns to multiply.
7/31/13

3.D.30

T: Imagine your fingers are numbered 1 through 10, with your pinky on the left being number 1, and your pinky on the right being number 10. Let's count from 1 to 10 together, lowering the finger that matches each number. (Count from 1 to 10 with the class.)

T: To solve a nines fact, lower the finger that matches the number of nines. Let's try together with 3 × 9. Hands out, fingers up!

T: For 3 × 9 which finger matches the number of nines?

S: My third finger from the left!

T: Lower that finger. (Model.) How many fingers are to the left of the lowered finger?

S: 2 fingers!

T: 2 is the digit in the tens place. How many fingers are to the right of the lowered finger?

S: 7 fingers!

T: 7 is the digit in the ones place.

T: What is the product of 3 × 9 shown by our fingers?

S: 27!

T: Does it match the product we found using our array?

S: Yes!

NOTES ON
MULTIPLE MEANS OF
ENGAGEMENT:

Display a picture of 10 fingers (numbered) on two hands for English language learners and others. Present a demonstration of the hands strategy yourself, or make an animated video. Make it fun for students with rhythm and/or a song, which you or students compose.

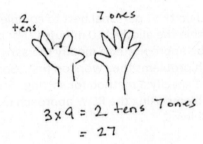

Continue with the following possible suggestions: 7 × 9, 10 × 9, 11 × 9. Use the last example to discuss with students that the finger strategy is limited to facts where the number of groups is between 0 and 10.

T: Talk with your partner. How is the finger strategy we just learned related to the strategy of using the number of groups to help solve a nines fact?

S: (Discuss.)

Part 2: Apply strategies for solving nines facts and reason about their effectiveness.

Part 2 is intended to be a station-based activity where small groups of students rotate through five stations. At each station they use a different strategy to solve nines facts. The suggestions below indicate which recently learned strategy students might use to solve nines facts at each station.

Station 1: Use the add 10, subtract 1 strategy to list facts from 1 × 9 to 10 × 9.

Station 2: Use $9 \times n = (10 \times n) - (1 \times n)$, a distributive strategy, to solve facts from 1 × 9 to 10 × 9.

Station 3: Use the finger strategy to solve facts from 1 × 9 to 10 × 9.

| Lesson 14: | Identify and use arithmetic patterns to multiply. |
| Date: | 7/31/13 |

3.D.31

Station 4: Use the number of groups to find the digits in the tens and ones places of the product to solve facts from 6 × 9 to 9 × 9.

Station 5: Use 9 × n = (5 × n) + (4 × n), a distributive strategy, to solve facts from 6 × 9 to 9 × 9.

After finishing, discuss the effectiveness of the strategies that were used to solve nines facts. Use the following suggested discussion questions:

MP.5

- Is there a strategy that is easiest for you? What makes it easier than the others?
- What strategy helps you solve a nines fact with a large number of groups, such as 12 × 9 = n, the most quickly? Which strategies would not work for such a large fact?
- Which strategies could easily be used to solve a division fact?

NOTES ON
MULTIPLE MEANS OF
ENGAGEMENT:

If appropriate for your class, consider having students complete station work in math journals or reflecting in writing so that they have their work as a reference.

Problem Set (10 minutes)

Students should do their personal best to complete the Problem Set within the allotted 10 minutes. For some classes, it may be appropriate to modify the assignment by specifying which problems they work on first. Some problems do not specify a method for solving. Students solve these problems using the RDW approach used for Application Problems.

Student Debrief (10 minutes)

Lesson Objective: Identify and use arithmetic patterns to multiply.

The Student Debrief is intended to invite reflection and active processing of the total lesson experience.

Invite students to review their solutions for the Problem Set. They should check work by comparing answers with a partner before going over answers as a class. Look for misconceptions or misunderstandings that can be addressed in the Debrief. Guide students in a conversation to debrief the Problem Set and process the lesson.

You may choose to use any combination of the questions below to lead the discussion.

- Invite students to explain the strategy used in each problem.

Lesson 14:   Identify and use arithmetic patterns to multiply.
Date: 7/31/13

3.D.32

© 2013 Common Core, Inc. All rights reserved. commoncore.org

- Encourage students to explain a different strategy that could be used to solve Problem 3.
- Why is it important to know several strategies for solving larger multiplication facts? Which strategies for solving nines facts can be modified to apply to a different set of facts (sixes, sevens, eights, etc.)?

Exit Ticket (3 minutes)

After the Student Debrief, instruct students to complete the Exit Ticket. A review of their work will help you assess the students' understanding of the concepts that were presented in the lesson today and plan more effectively for future lessons. You may read the questions aloud to the students.

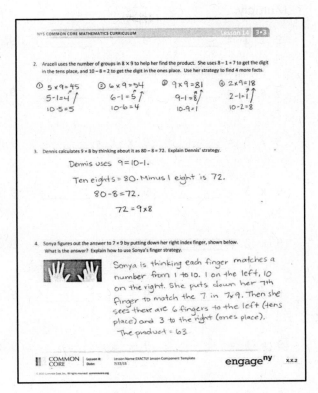

COMMON CORE

Lesson 14:   Identify and use arithmetic patterns to multiply.
Date: 7/31/13

3.D.33

Multiply.

9 x 1 = _____   9 x 2 = _____   9 x 3 = _____   9 x 4 = _____

9 x 5 = _____   9 x 1 = _____   9 x 2 = _____   9 x 1 = _____

9 x 3 = _____   9 x 1 = _____   9 x 4 = _____   9 x 1 = _____

9 x 5 = _____   9 x 1 = _____   9 x 2 = _____   9 x 3 = _____

9 x 2 = _____   9 x 4 = _____   9 x 2 = _____   9 x 5 = _____

9 x 2 = _____   9 x 1 = _____   9 x 2 = _____   9 x 3 = _____

9 x 1 = _____   9 x 3 = _____   9 x 2 = _____   9 x 3 = _____

9 x 4 = _____   9 x 3 = _____   9 x 5 = _____   9 x 3 = _____

9 x 4 = _____   9 x 1 = _____   9 x 4 = _____   9 x 2 = _____

9 x 4 = _____   9 x 3 = _____   9 x 4 = _____   9 x 5 = _____

9 x 4 = _____   9 x 5 = _____   9 x 1 = _____   9 x 5 = _____

9 x 2 = _____   9 x 5 = _____   9 x 3 = _____   9 x 5 = _____

9 x 4 = _____   9 x 2 = _____   9 x 4 = _____   9 x 3 = _____

9 x 5 = _____   9 x 3 = _____   9 x 2 = _____   9 x 4 = _____

9 x 3 = _____   9 x 5 = _____   9 x 2 = _____   9 x 4 = _____

© Bill Davidson

| Lesson 14: | Identify and use arithmetic patterns to multiply. |
| Date: | 7/31/13 |

3.D.34

Name _____   Date _____

1.   a.   Multiply. Then add the tens digit and ones digit of each product.

$1 \times 9 =$ **9**   __**0**__ + __**9**__ = __**9**__

$2 \times 9 =$ **18**   __**1**__ + __**8**__ = _____

$3 \times 9 =$ _____   _____ + _____ = _____

$4 \times 9 =$ _____   _____ + _____ = _____

$5 \times 9 =$ _____   _____ + _____ = _____

$6 \times 9 =$ _____   _____ + _____ = _____

$7 \times 9 =$ _____   _____ + _____ = _____

$8 \times 9 =$ _____   _____ + _____ = _____

$9 \times 9 =$ _____   _____ + _____ = _____

$10 \times 9 =$ _____   _____ + _____ = _____

  b.   What is the sum of the digits in each product? How can this strategy help you check your work with the nines facts?

2. Araceli uses the number of groups in 8 × 9 to help her find the product. She uses 8 − 1 = 7 to get the digit in the tens place, and 10 − 8 = 2 to get the digit in the ones place. Use her strategy to find 4 more facts.

3. Dennis calculates 9 × 8 by thinking about it as 80 − 8 = 72. Explain Dennis' strategy.

4. Sonya figures out the answer to 7 × 9 by putting down her right index finger, shown below. What is the answer? Explain how to use Sonya's finger strategy.

COMMON
CORE

Lesson 14:   Identify and use arithmetic patterns to multiply.
Date: 7/31/13

3.D.36

© 2013 Common Core, Inc. All rights reserved. commoncore.org

Name _____   Date _____

Donald writes 7 × 9 = 63. Explain 2 strategies you could use to check his work.

Name _____ Date _____

1. Multiply. Then add the digits in each product.

$10 \times 9 = $ **90**	__9__ + __0__ = __9__
$9 \times 9 = $ **81**	__8__ + __1__ = __9__
$8 \times 9 = $	_____ + _____ = _____
$7 \times 9 = $	_____ + _____ = _____
$6 \times 9 = $	_____ + _____ = _____
$5 \times 9 = $	_____ + _____ = _____
$4 \times 9 = $	_____ + _____ = _____
$3 \times 9 = $	_____ + _____ = _____
$2 \times 9 = $	_____ + _____ = _____
$1 \times 9 = $	_____ + _____ = _____

What pattern did you notice in the table? How can this strategy help you check your work with nines facts?

COMMON CORE

Lesson 14:   Identify and use arithmetic patterns to multiply.
Date: 7/31/13

3.D.38

2. Thomas calculates 9 × 7 by thinking about it as 70 − 7 = 63. Explain Thomas' strategy.

3. Alexia figures out the answer to 6 × 9 by lowering the thumb on her right hand, shown below. What is the answer? Explain Alexia's strategy.

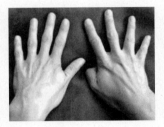

4. Travis writes 72 = 9 × 8. Is he correct? Explain at least 2 strategies Travis can use to help him check his work.

COMMON CORE | Lesson 14: Identify and use arithmetic patterns to multiply.
Date: 7/31/13

3.D.39

Lesson 15

Objective: Interpret the unknown in multiplication and division to model and solve problems.

Suggested Lesson Structure

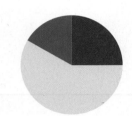

■ Fluency Practice   (15 minutes)
□ Concept Development   (35 minutes)
■ Student Debrief   (10 minutes)
   Total Time   **(60 minutes)**

Fluency Practice (15 minutes)

- Multiply by 9 **3.OA.7**   (7 minutes)
- Group Counting **3.OA.1**   (4 minutes)
- Divide by 9 **3.OA.7**   (4 minutes)

Multiply by 9 (7 minutes)

Materials: (S) Multiply by 9 Pattern Sheet (6–10)

Note: This activity builds fluency with multiplication facts using units of 9. It works toward students knowing from memory all products of two one-digit numbers.   See G3–M3–Lesson 5 for the directions for administration of a Multiply By Pattern Sheet.

   T: (Write $6 \times 9 =$ _____.) Let's skip-count up by nine to solve. (Count with fingers to 6 as students count.)

   S: 9, 18, 27, 36, 45, 54.

   T: Let's skip-count down to find the answer, too. Start at 90. (Starting with 10 fingers, count down as students count.)

   S: 90, 81, 72, 63, 54.

   T: Let's skip-count up again to find the answer, but this time start at 45. (Count up with fingers as students count.)

   S: 45, 54.

Continue with the following possible suggestions: 8×9 and 7×9, and 9×9.

   T: (Distribute the Multiply by 9 Pattern Sheet.) Let's practice multiplying by 9. Be sure to work left to right across the page.

	Lesson 15:	Interpret the unknown in multiplication and division to model and solve problems.	
	Date:	7/31/13	

3.D.40

Group Counting (4 minutes)

Note: Group counting reviews interpreting multiplication as repeated addition. Counting by sixes, sevens, and eights reviews multiplication taught earlier in the module. Direct students to count forward and backward, occasionally changing the direction of the count.

- Sixes to 60
- Sevens to 70
- Eights to 80

Divide by 9 (4 minutes)

Materials: (S) Personal white boards

Note: This fluency reviews using a letter to represent the unknown, first taught in Lesson 3.

T: (Write $a \times 9 = 18$.) On your boards, write the value of a.
S: (Write $a = 2$.)
T: (Write $18 \div 9 =$ ___.) Say the division sentence.
S: $18 \div 9 = 2$.

Continue with the following possible sequence: $b \times 9 = 45, c \times 9 = 36, d \times 9 = 54, e \times 9 = 27, f \times 9 = 90,$ $g \times 9 = 81, h \times 9 = 72$.

Concept Development (35 minutes)

Materials: (S) Personal white boards

Problem 1: Interpret the unknown in multiplication.

Write or project the following problem: Ada buys 9 packs of highlighters with 4 in each pack. After giving 1 highlighter to each classmate, she has 17 left. How many highlighters did Ada give away?

T: Model the problem. Then tell your partner the steps you'll take to solve.

S: (Model.) First you have to find out how many highlighters Ada has. → After that, subtract 17 from the total to see how many she gives away.

T: Write and solve an equation to find the total number of highlighters. Use h to represent the unknown. (Allow students time to finish their work.)

T: What equation did you use?

S: $9 \times 4 = h$.

T: Talk to your partner. What strategy for solving nines facts did you use?

NOTES ON
MULTIPLE MEANS OF
ENGAGEMENT:

Students working above grade level and others may not identify a strategy for solving $9 \times 4 = 36$, instead saying, "It's easy! I just knew it." Challenge students to articulate strategies that work so well they seem automatic. Ask, "Did you count by fours? Did you switch the factors and calculate 4×9 instead? Did you use a pattern to solve? What pattern?"

Lesson 15:	Interpret the unknown in multiplication and division to model and solve problems.
Date:	7/31/13

3.D.41

S: (Discuss.)

T: What is the value of h?

S: The value of h is 36.

T: How many highlighters did Ada have at the start?

S: 36 highlighters.

T: Is the problem complete yet?

S: No, we have to find how many highlighters Ada gives away.

T: Solve the second step of the problem using letter g to represent the unknown.

S: (Write $36 - 17 = g$ and solve.)

T: What is the value of g?

S: The value of g is 19.

T: How many highlighters does Ada give away?

S: Ada gives away 19 highlighters.

T: Can we tell how many classmates Ada has? How do you know?

S: Ada has 19 classmates! I know because she gave 1 highlighter to each classmate, and she gave away 19 highlighters.

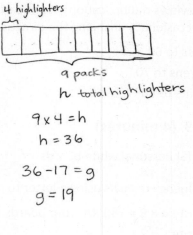

$$9 \times 4 = h$$
$$h = 36$$

$$36 - 17 = g$$
$$g = 19$$

Problem 2: Interpret the unknown in division.

Write the following problem: Eliza finds a bag of 72 marbles and runs to share them with 8 of her friends. She's so excited that she drops the bag and loses 18 marbles. How many marbles will Eliza and each of her friends get?

T: Model the problem.

T: (After finishing.) How many units are in your model?

S: 9 units.

T: What part of the problem tells you that your model needs 9 units?

S: Where it says "Eliza and each of her friends." She has 8 friends, and $8 + 1 = 9$.

T: What should we do first, subtract or divide? Why?

S: We should subtract. → Subtract, because we need to find out how many marbles Eliza has left after she loses some.

T: Write an equation to solve for the first unknown. Use m to represent the number of marbles Eliza has.

S: (Solve $72 - 18 = m$.)

T: What is the value of m?

NOTES ON MULTIPLE MEANS FOR ACTION AND EXPRESSION:

Some students may mistakenly interpret the divisor to be 8 rather than 9. Use this example to highlight the advantages of carefully reading word problems and drawing a picture to solve. Guide students to underline *Eliza and each of her friends* in the final question before attempting an equation.

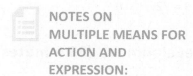

$$72 - 18 = m$$
$$m = 54$$

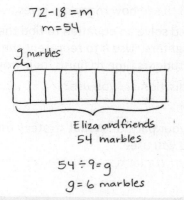

$$54 \div 9 = g$$
$$g = 6 \text{ marbles}$$

Lesson 15:   Interpret the unknown in multiplication and division to model and solve problems.
Date: 7/31/13

3.D.42

S: 54!

T: So, how many marbles does Eliza have to give away?

S: 54 marbles!

T: Is our work on this problem finished?

S: No, now we have to find out how many marbles each friend gets!

T: Complete your model and write an equation to solve for the second unknown. Use *g* to represent the number of marbles each friend gets.

S: (Solve $54 \div 9 = g$.)

T: How many marbles does each friend get? How do you know?

S: Each friend gets 6 marbles. → 6 marbles, because the value of *g* is 6, and *g* represents the number of marbles each friend gets.

Problem Set (10 minutes)

Students should do their personal best to complete the Problem Set within the allotted 10 minutes. For some classes, it may be appropriate to modify the assignment by specifying which problems they work on first. Some problems do not specify a method for solving. Students solve these problems using the RDW approach used for Application Problems.

Student Debrief (10 minutes)

Lesson Objective: Interpret the unknown in multiplication and division to model and solve problems.

The Student Debrief is intended to invite reflection and active processing of the total lesson experience.

Invite students to review their solutions for the Problem Set. They should check work by comparing answers with a partner before going over answers as a class. Look for misconceptions or misunderstandings that can be addressed in the Debrief Guide students in a conversation to debrief the Problem Set and process the lesson.

You may choose to use any combination of the questions below to lead the discussion.

- In your model for Problem 1, is the unknown the number of units or the size of each unit?

- In Problem 3, how did you show what letter you used to represent the unknown and what it stood for?

- How did you solve the large division fact in Problem 5?

- What longer number sentence, including parentheses, can be used to solve Problem 6?

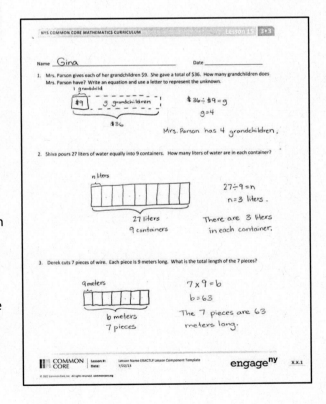

COMMON CORE

Lesson 15: Interpret the unknown in multiplication and division to model and solve problems.

Date: 7/31/13

engage^ny

3.D.43

Exit Ticket (3 minutes)

After the Student Debrief, instruct students to complete the Exit Ticket. A review of their work will help you assess the students' understanding of the concepts that were presented in the lesson today and plan more effectively for future lessons. You may read the questions aloud to the students.

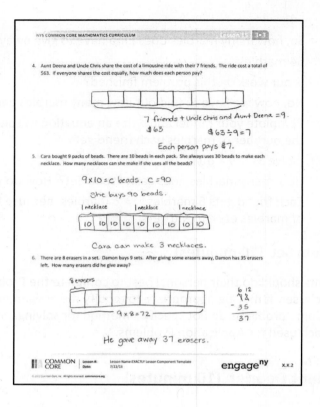

COMMON
CORE

Lesson 15:   Interpret the unknown in multiplication and division to model and
           solve problems.
Date: 7/31/13

3.D.40

Multiply.

9 x 1 = _____	9 x 2 = _____	9 x 3 = _____	9 x 4 = _____
9 x 5 = _____	9 x 6 = _____	9 x 7 = _____	9 x 8 = _____
9 x 9 = _____	9 x 10 = _____	9 x 5 = _____	9 x 6 = _____
9 x 5 = _____	9 x 7 = _____	9 x 5 = _____	9 x 8 = _____
9 x 5 = _____	9 x 9 = _____	9 x 5 = _____	9 x 10 = _____
9 x 6 = _____	9 x 5 = _____	9 x 6 = _____	9 x 7 = _____
9 x 6 = _____	9 x 8 = _____	9 x 6 = _____	9 x 9 = _____
9 x 6 = _____	9 x 7 = _____	9 x 6 = _____	9 x 7 = _____
9 x 8 = _____	9 x 7 = _____	9 x 9 = _____	9 x 7 = _____
9 x 8 = _____	9 x 6 = _____	9 x 8 = _____	9 x 7 = _____
9 x 8 = _____	9 x 9 = _____	9 x 9 = _____	9 x 6 = _____
9 x 9 = _____	9 x 7 = _____	9 x 9 = _____	9 x 8 = _____
9 x 9 = _____	9 x 8 = _____	9 x 6 = _____	9 x 9 = _____
9 x 7 = _____	9 x 9 = _____	9 x 6 = _____	9 x 8 = _____
9 x 9 = _____	9 x 7 = _____	9 x 6 = _____	9 x 8 = _____

© Bill Davidson

Lesson 15: Interpret the unknown in multiplication and division to model and solve problems.
Date: 7/31/13

3.D.41

Name _____   Date _____

1. Mrs. Parson gives each of her grandchildren $9. She gave a total of $36. How many grandchildren does Mrs. Parson have? Write an equation and use a letter to represent the unknown.

2. Shiva pours 27 liters of water equally into 9 containers.   How many liters of water are in each container?

3. Derek cuts 7 pieces of wire. Each piece is 9 meters long. What is the total length of the 7 pieces?

4. Aunt Deena and Uncle Chris share the cost of a limousine ride with their 7 friends. The ride cost a total of $63. If everyone shares the cost equally, how much does each person pay?

5. Cara bought 9 packs of beads. There are 10 beads in each pack. She always uses 30 beads to make each necklace. How many necklaces can she make if she uses all the beads?

6. There are 8 erasers in a set. Damon buys 9 sets. After giving some erasers away, Damon has 35 erasers left. How many erasers did he give away?

COMMON CORE | Lesson 15: | Interpret the unknown in multiplication and division to model and solve problems.
| Date: | 7/31/13

3.D.43

Name _____ Date _____

1. Mrs. Aquino pours 36 liters of water equally into 9 containers. How much water is in each container?
   Use a letter to represent the unknown.

2. Marlon buys 9 packs of hot dogs. There are 6 hot dogs in each pack. After the barbeque, 35 hot dogs are
   left over. How many hot dogs were eaten?

COMMON CORE

Lesson 15:   Interpret the unknown in multiplication and division to model and
             solve problems.
Date: 7/31/13

3.D.44

Name _____   Date _____

1. The store clerk equally divides 36 apples between 9 baskets. Draw a tape diagram and label the number of apples in each basket as *a*. Write an equation and solve for *a*.

2. Elijah gives each of his friends a pack of 9 almonds. He gives away a total of 45 almonds. How many packs of almonds did he give away? Model using a letter to represent the unknown, then solve.

3. Denice buys 7 movies. Each movie costs $9. What is the total cost of 7 movies? Use a letter to represent the unknown. Solve.

COMMON CORE | Lesson 15: | Interpret the unknown in multiplication and division to model and solve problems.
| Date: | 7/31/13

3.D.45

4. Mr. Doyle shares 1 roll of bulletin board paper equally with 8 teachers. The total length of the roll is 72 meters. How much bulletin board paper does each teacher get?

5. There are 9 pens in a pack. Ms. Ochoa buys 9 packs. After giving her students some pens, she has 27 pens left. How many pens did she give away?

6. Allen buys 9 packs of trading cards. There are 10 cards in each pack. He can trade 30 cards for a comic book. How many comic books can he get if he trades all of his cards?

Mathematics Curriculum

Topic E

Analysis of Patterns and Problem Solving Including Units of 0 and 1

3.OA.3, 3.OA.7, 3.OA.8, 3.OA.9, 3.OA.1, 3.OA.2, 3.OA.4, 3.OA.6

Focus Standard:	3.OA.3	Use multiplication and division within 100 to solve word problems in situations involving equal groups, arrays, and measurement quantities, e.g., by using drawings and equations with a symbol for the unknown number to represent the problem. (See Glossary, Table 2.)
	3.OA.7	Fluently multiply and divide within 100, using strategies such as the relationship between multiplication and division (e.g., knowing that $8 \times 5 = 40$, one knows $40 \div 5 = 8$) or properties of operations. By the end of Grade 3, know from memory all products of two one-digit numbers.
	3.OA.8	Solve two-step word problems using the four operations. Represent these problems using equations with a letter standing for the unknown quantity. Assess the reasonableness of answers using mental computation and estimation strategies including rounding. (This standard is limited to problems posed with whole numbers and having whole-number answers; students should know how to perform operations in the conventional order when there are no parentheses to specify a particular order, i.e., Order of Operations.)
	3.OA.9	Identify arithmetic patterns (including patterns in the addition table or multiplication table), and explain them using properties of operations. *For example, observe that 4 times a number is always even, and explain why 4 times a number can be decomposed into two equal addends.*
Instructional Days:	3	
Coherence -Links from:	G2–M6	Foundations of Multiplication and Division
	G3–M1	Properties of Multiplication and Division and Solving Problems with Units of 2–5 and 10
-Links to:	G3–M4	Multiplication and Area
	G4–M3	Multi-Digit Multiplication and Division
	G4–M7	Exploring Multiplication

In Lesson 16 students multiply and divide by 0 and 1. They use patterns to understand that $n \times 0 = 0$, and show why the result of dividing a number by 0 is undefined, but that dividing 0 by another number results in 0. Lesson 17 synthesizes students' knowledge of factors from 0 to 10 in an exploration of patterns using the multiplication table. Students recognize the patterns of particular factors and make connections between

	Topic E:	Analysis of Patterns and Problem Solving Including Units of 0 and 1	**3.E.1**
	Date:	7/31/13	

multiplication and division. In Lesson 18, students apply the tools, representations, and concepts they have learned to solve two-step word problems using all four operations. They call on rounding skills learned in Module 2 to estimate solutions, and use their estimations to assess the reasonableness of answers.

A Teaching Sequence Towards Mastery of Analysis of Patterns and Problem Solving Including Units of 0 and 1
Objective 1: Reason about and explain arithmetic patterns using units of 0 and 1 as they relate to multiplication and division. **(Lesson 16)**
Objective 2: Identify patterns in multiplication and division facts using the multiplication table. **(Lesson 17)**
Objective 3: Solve two-step word problems involving all four operations and assess the reasonableness of solutions. **(Lesson 18)**

Lesson 16

Objective: Reason about and explain arithmetic patterns using units of 0 and 1 as they relate to multiplication and division.

Suggested Lesson Structure

■ Fluency Practice   (9 minutes)
▢ Concept Development   (41 minutes)
■ Student Debrief   (10 minutes)
   Total Time   **(60 minutes)**

Fluency Practice (9 minutes)

- Sprint: Divide by 9 **3.OA.7**   (9 minutes)

Sprint: Divide by 9 (9 minutes)

Materials: (S) Divide by 9 Sprint

Note: This Sprint reviews Lessons 12–15, focusing on the relationship between multiplication and division using units of 9.

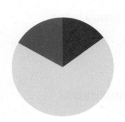
A NOTE ON STANDARDS ALIGNMENT:

The last six problems on the Sprint extend beyond Grade 3 multiplication and division standards because students who have mastered their times tables are likely to otherwise go unchallenged during this activity. By extending to products above 90 and quotients above 10, strong students are provided the stimulus to stretch their conceptual understanding, which will likely keep them engaged and invigorated to improve on Sprint B.

Concept Development (41 minutes)

Materials: (S) Personal white boards

Problem 1: Multiply and divide using units of 1.

T: Draw three large circles on your board. Draw an equal number of dots in each circle. You can draw between 2 and 10 dots in each circle. You choose! How many groups are there?

S: 3!

T: Write a multiplication equation to represent your picture. Read your equation to a partner.

T: Erase one of the circles. How many groups now?

S: 2!

T: Write a multiplication equation to represent your picture. Read your equation to a partner.

NOTES ON MULTIPLE MEANS FOR ACTION AND EXPRESSION:

One group is often harder for students to represent because they tend to interpret it as the number in the set. The opening activity starts with 3 groups and works back to 1 group to avoid this misconception. Stay alert to it as you circulate and support students with their work in Problem 1.

COMMON CORE

Lesson 16: Reason about and explain arithmetic patterns using units of 0 and 1 as they relate to multiplication and division.
Date: 7/31/13

3.E.3

© 2013 Common Core, Inc. All rights reserved. **commoncore.org**

T: Erase one of the circles. How many groups now?

S: 1!

T: Write a multiplication equation to represent your picture. Read your equation to me. (Call on students to read equations and record.)

T: Rewrite your equation. Let *n* equal the number of dots in each group. What is 1 times *n* dots?

S: It's *n*, because the number of dots in each group is the same as the total number of dots.

T: What is 1 times a number equal to?

S: That number!

T: Write the related division fact for your multiplication equation. Read it at my signal. (Signal.)

S: $n \div 1 = n$.

T: Use your picture to discuss with a partner, why is our division equation true?

S: It shows the total number of dots, *n* divided into 1 group. That equals *n* counters in each group.

T: What is a number divided by 1?

S: That number!

Repeat this process, drawing *n* circles with 3 dots in each circle. Students erase 1 dot from each circle and write multiplication equations to represent their pictures, until they are left with *n* circles and 1 dot in each circle. This will demonstrate $n \times 1 = n$ and $n \div n = 1$.

T: What patterns did we discover for multiplying and dividing by units of 1?

S: Any number times 1 equals that number, any number divided by 1 equals that number, and any number divided by itself equals 1.

Problem 2: Multiply and divide using units of 0.

T: (Write $4 \times 0 = b$ on the board.) What does this equation represent?

S: Four groups of 0.

T: Draw a picture of the equation using circles to show the groups and dots to show the number in each group. (Allow students time to draw.) How many dots did you draw in each group?

NOTES ON MULTIPLE MEANS OF REPRESENTATION:

English Language Learners and others may benefit from a scaffolded review of unknowns represented as letters. You may start with a frame using blanks (___ × 1 = ___), then question marks (? × 1 = ?), then *a number* × 1 = *a number,* and finally, $n \times 1 = n$.

$3 \times 4 = 12$

$2 \times 4 = 8$

$1 \times 4 = 4$

$1 \times n = n$

$n \div 1 = n$

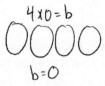

$4 \times 0 = b$

$b = 0$

COMMON CORE

Lesson 16:   Reason about and explain arithmetic patterns using units of 0 and 1 as they relate to multiplication and division.

Date: 7/31/13

3.E.4

S: Zero!

T: There are a total of 0 dots, so 4 times 0 equals?

S: Zero!

T: What is the value of *b* in the equation?

S: *b* equals 0.

$$n \times 0 = 0$$
$$0 \div n = 0$$
$$0 \div 7 = 0$$
$$\bigcirc\bigcirc\bigcirc\bigcirc\bigcirc\bigcirc\bigcirc$$

Continue with the following possible suggestions: 7×0, 6×0, 0×0.

T: What pattern did you notice?

S: Any number times 0 equals 0.

T: Write that equation using *n* to represent a number.

S: $n \times 0 = 0$.

T: Write the related division equation on your board.

S: $0 \div n = 0$.

T: What does this equation represent?

S: Zero divided by a number equals 0.

T: Let's choose a value for *n* and see if we get a true number sentence.   Rewrite the equation letting *n* equal 7.   (After students write $0 \div 7 = 0$.)   What does this equation represent?

S: Zero things divided into 7 groups equals 0.

T: Draw a picture of the equation using circles to show the groups and dots to show the number in each group.   (Allow students time to draw.)   How many dots did you draw in each group?

S: Zero!

T: Zero divided by 7 equals?

S: Zero!

T: Rewrite the equation to show 7 things divided into 0 groups equals *n*.

S: (Write $7 \div 0 = n$.)

$$7 \div 0 = n$$
$$0 \times n = 7$$

T: What is the related multiplication fact?

S: $0 \times n = 7$.

T: What does this equation represent?

S: Zero times a number equals 7!

T: Talk with your partner, is this possible?

S: No, because any number times 0 equals 0, not 7.

T: There's no value for *n* that would make a true multiplication sentence, and the same is true for the division equation.

T: Let's look at a special case of dividing by 0.   Write $0 \div 0 = n$ on your board.   What is the related multiplication fact?

S: $0 \times n = 0$.

T: What does this equation represent?

S: Zero times a number equals 0.

T: Talk with a partner, what is the value of *n*?

$$0 \div 0 = n$$
$$0 \times n = 0$$
$$n = \text{any number}$$

Lesson 16:   Reason about and explain arithmetic patterns using units of 0 and 1   **3.E.5**
              as they relate to multiplication and division.

Date: 7/31/13

S: Any number! → *n* can be any number because when you multiply any number times 0, it equals 0.

T: *n* could be 3, 2, 5, 6, or any other number. *n* can be any number in the multiplication equation, and the same is true for the division equation. Work with your partner to try a few different numbers in the multiplication and division equations.

S: (Plug in a variety of values.)

T: What do you notice?

S: Lots of numbers work!

T: Right, there isn't one single value for *n* in this case. Talk with a partner about what patterns you discovered for dividing by 0.

Problem Set (10 minutes)

Students should do their personal best to complete the Problem Set within the allotted 10 minutes. For some classes, it may be appropriate to modify the assignment by specifying which problems they work on first. Some problems do not specify a method for solving. Students solve these problems using the RDW approach used for Application Problems.

Student Debrief (10 minutes)

Lesson Objective: Reason about and explain arithmetic patterns using units of 0 and 1 as they relate to multiplication and division.

The Student Debrief is intended to invite reflection and active processing of the total lesson experience.

Invite students to review their solutions for the Problem Set. They should check work by comparing answers with a partner before going over answers as a class. Look for misconceptions or misunderstandings that can be addressed in the Debrief. Guide students in a conversation to debrief the Problem Set and process the lesson.

You may choose to use any combination of the questions below to lead the discussion.

- Discuss with a partner, what patterns for multiplying and dividing by 0 and 1 helped you solve Problem 1?

- What pattern for multiplying by 1 does Problem 3 represent?

- Which problems show that we can't define a single, specific value when we divide by 0? Explain your answer to a partner.

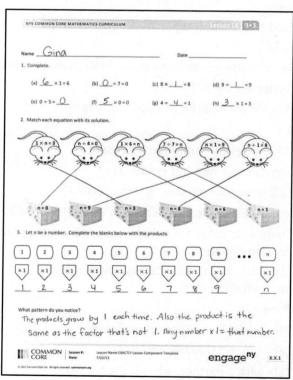

COMMON CORE

Lesson 16:

Date:

Reason about and explain arithmetic patterns using units of 0 and 1 as they relate to multiplication and division.

7/31/13

engage^ny

3.E.6

- How is multiplying by 1 and multiplying units of 1 similar to adding 0 to a number?

MP.7

- How can the patterns for multiplying and dividing by 1 or multiplying and dividing 0 by a number help you solve equations with larger factors (e.g., $346 \times 1 = b$)?

Exit Ticket (3 minutes)

After the Student Debrief, instruct students to complete the Exit Ticket. A review of their work will help you assess the students' understanding of the concepts that were presented in the lesson today and plan more effectively for future lessons. You may read the questions aloud to the students.

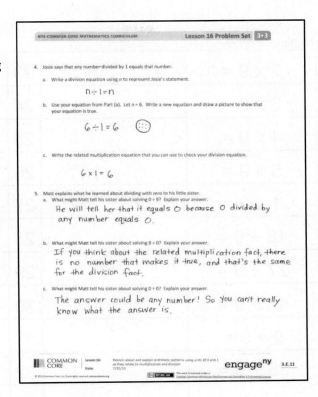

COMMON CORE

Lesson 16:   Reason about and explain arithmetic patterns using units of 0 and 1 as they relate to multiplication and division.

Date: 7/31/13

3.E.7

© 2013 Common Core, Inc. All rights reserved. commoncore.org

A

Correct _____

Multiply or divide.

1	2 x 9 =		23	__ x 9 = 90	
2	3 x 9 =		24	__ x 9 = 18	
3	4 x 9 =		25	__ x 9 = 27	
4	5 x 9 =		26	90 ÷ 9 =	
5	1 x 9 =		27	45 ÷ 9 =	
6	18 ÷ 9 =		28	9 ÷ 9 =	
7	27 ÷ 9 =		29	18 ÷ 9 =	
8	45 ÷ 9 =		30	27 ÷ 9 =	
9	9 ÷ 9 =		31	__ x 9 = 54	
10	36 ÷ 9 =		32	__ x 9 = 63	
11	6 x 9 =		33	__ x 9 = 81	
12	7 x 9 =		34	__ x 9 = 72	
13	8 x 9 =		35	63 ÷ 9 =	
14	9 x 9 =		36	81 ÷ 9 =	
15	10 x 9 =		37	54 ÷ 9 =	
16	72 ÷ 9 =		38	72 ÷ 9 =	
17	63 ÷ 9 =		39	11 x 9 =	
18	81 ÷ 9 =		40	99 ÷ 9 =	
19	54 ÷ 9 =		41	12 x 9 =	
20	90 ÷ 9 =		42	108 ÷ 9 =	
21	__ x 9 = 45		43	14 x 9 =	
22	__ x 9 = 9		44	126 ÷ 9 =	

© Bill Davidson

COMMON CORE

Lesson 16:   Reason about and explain arithmetic patterns using units of 0 and 1 as they relate to multiplication and division.

Date: 7/31/13

3.E.8

© 2013 Common Core, Inc. All rights reserved. commoncore.org

B   Improvement _____   # Correct _____

Multiply or divide.

#	Problem		#	Problem	
1	1 x 9 =		23	__ x 9 = 18	
2	2 x 9 =		24	__ x 9 = 90	
3	3 x 9 =		25	__ x 9 = 27	
4	4 x 9 =		26	18 ÷ 9 =	
5	5 x 9 =		27	9 ÷ 9 =	
6	27 ÷ 9 =		28	90 ÷ 9 =	
7	18 ÷ 9 =		29	45 ÷ 9 =	
8	36 ÷ 9 =		30	27 ÷ 9 =	
9	9 ÷ 9 =		31	__ x 9 = 27	
10	45 ÷ 9 =		32	__ x 9 = 36	
11	10 x 9 =		33	__ x 9 = 81	
12	6 x 9 =		34	__ x 9 = 63	
13	7 x 9 =		35	72 ÷ 9 =	
14	8 x 9 =		36	81 ÷ 9 =	
15	9 x 9 =		37	54 ÷ 9 =	
16	63 ÷ 9 =		38	63 ÷ 9 =	
17	54 ÷ 9 =		39	11 x 9 =	
18	72 ÷ 9 =		40	99 ÷ 9 =	
19	90 ÷ 9 =		41	12 x 9 =	
20	81 ÷ 9 =		42	108 ÷ 9 =	
21	__ x 9 = 9		43	13 x 9 =	
22	__ x 9 = 45		44	117 ÷ 9 =	

© Bill Davidson

Lesson 16: Reason about and explain arithmetic patterns using units of 0 and 1 as they relate to multiplication and division.
Date: 7/31/13

3.E.9

Name _____ Date _____

1. Complete.

(a) _____ × 1 = 6   (b) _____ ÷ 7 = 0   (c) 8 × _____ = 8   (d) 9 ÷ _____ = 9

(e) 0 ÷ 5 = _____   (f) _____ × 0 = 0   (g) 4 ÷ _____ = 1   (h) _____ × 1 = 3

2. Match each equation with its solution.

1 × n = 3   n ÷ 4 = 0   1 × 6 = n   7 ÷ 7 = n   n × 1 = 9   n ÷ 1 = 8

n = 0   n = 9   n = 3   n = 8   n = 6   n = 1

3. Let *n* be a number. Complete the blanks below with the products.

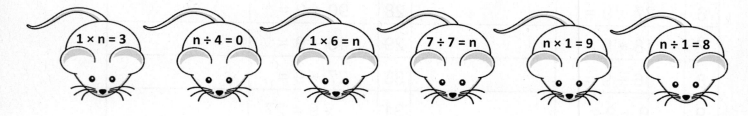

| 1 | 2 | 3 | 4 | 5 | 6 | 7 | 8 | 9 | ••• | n |

× 1   × 1   × 1   × 1   × 1   × 1   × 1   × 1   × 1   × 1

_____ _____ _____ _____ _____ _____ _____ _____ _____   _____

What pattern do you notice?

Lesson 16:   Reason about and explain arithmetic patterns using units of 0 and 1
Date: as they relate to multiplication and division.
               7/31/13

4. Josie says that any number divided by 1 equals that number.

   a. Write a division equation using *n* to represent Josie's statement.

   b. Use your equation from Part (a). Let *n* = 6. Write a new equation and draw a picture to show that your equation is true.

   c. Write the related multiplication equation that you can use to check your division equation.

5. Matt explains what he learned about dividing with zero to his little sister.
   a. What might Matt tell his sister about solving 0 ÷ 9? Explain your answer.

   b. What might Matt tell his sister about solving 8 ÷ 0? Explain your answer.

   c. What might Matt tell his sister about solving 0 ÷ 0? Explain your answer.

COMMON CORE

Lesson 16: Reason about and explain arithmetic patterns using units of 0 and 1 as they relate to multiplication and division.

Date: 7/31/13

3.E.11

Name _____   Date _____

1. Complete the equations.

   a. _____ × 1 = 5   b. 6 × _____ = 6   c. _____ ÷ 7 = 0

   d. 5 × _____ = 0   e. 1 = 9 ÷ _____   f. 8 = 1 × _____

2. Luis divides 8 by 0 and says it equals 0. Is he correct? Explain why or why not.

COMMON CORE

Lesson 16:   Reason about and explain arithmetic patterns using units of 0 and 1 as they relate to multiplication and division.

Date: 7/31/13

3.E.12

Name _____ Date _____

1. Solve.

   a. $4 \times 1 =$ _____

   b. $4 \times 0 =$ _____

   c. _____ $\times 1 = 5$

   d. _____ $\div 5 = 0$

   e. $6 \times$ _____ $= 6$

   f. _____ $\div 6 = 0$

   g. $0 \div 7 =$ _____

   h. $7 \times$ _____ $= 0$

   i. $8 \div$ _____ $= 8$

   j. _____ $\times 8 = 8$

   k. $9 \times$ _____ $= 9$

   l. $9 \div$ _____ $= 1$

2. Match each equation with its solution.

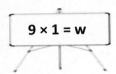

$9 \times 1 = w$

$w \times 1 = 6$

$7 \div w = 1$

$1 \times w = 8$

$w \div 8 = 0$

$9 \div 9 = w$

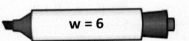

$w = 6$

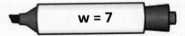

$w = 7$

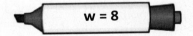

$w = 8$

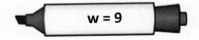

$w = 9$

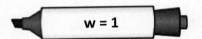

$w = 1$

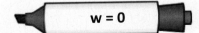

$w = 0$

3. Let $c = 8$. Then determine whether the equations are true or false.

a. $c \times 0 = 8$	Example: False.
b. $0 \times c = 0$	
c. $c \times 1 = 8$	
d. $1 \times c = 8$	
e. $0 \div c = 8$	
f. $8 \div c = 1$	
g. $0 \div c = 0$	
h. $c \div 0 = 8$	

4. Rajan says that any number multiplied by 1 equals that number.

    a. Write a multiplication equation using n to represent Rajan's statement.

    b. Using your equation from Part (a), let $n = 5$ and draw a picture to show that the new equation is true.

COMMON CORE

Lesson 16:   Reason about and explain arithmetic patterns using units of 0 and 1
              as they relate to multiplication and division.

Date: 7/31/13

3.E.14

© 2013 Common Core, Inc. All rights reserved. commoncore.org

Lesson 17

Objective: Identify patterns in multiplication and division facts using the multiplication table.

Suggested Lesson Structure

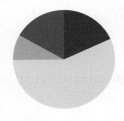

■ Fluency Practice   (11 minutes)
■ Application Problem   (5 minutes)
■ Concept Development   (34 minutes)
■ Student Debrief   (10 minutes)
   Total Time   **(60 minutes)**

Fluency Practice (11 minutes)

- Multiply by 10 **3.NBT.3**   (3 minutes)
- Multiply or Divide **3.OA.7**   (4 minutes)
- Complete the Number Sentence **3.OA.5**   (4 minutes)

Multiply by 10 (3 minutes)

Note: This fluency anticipates Lesson 19, multiplying by multiples of 10.

   T: I'll say a fact. You say the whole equation. 10 × 1.
   S: 10 × 1 = 10.

Continue with the following possible sequence: 10 × 2, 10 × 3, 10 × 8, 10 × 5.

   T: I'll say a product that is a multiple of 10. You say the multiplication fact starting with 10. 20.
   S: 10 × 2 = 20.

Continue with the following possible sequence: 30, 40, 90, 50, 10.

Multiply or Divide (4 minutes)

Materials: (S) Personal white boards

Note: This fluency reviews multiplication and division facts within 100.

   T: (Write 6 × 1 = ___.) Say the multiplication sentence.
   S: 6 × 1 = 6.

Lesson 17:	Identify patterns in multiplication and division facts using the multiplication table.
Date:	7/31/13

3.E.15

Continue with the following possible sequence: 6 × 2 and 6 × 3.

    T: On your personal white boards, show the answer to 6 × 7. If you need to, skip-count.

    S: (Write 42.)

Continue for the following possible sequence, asking students to write answers to the harder problems on their personal white boards, while asking them to orally answer the easier problems: 30 ÷ 6, 24 ÷ 6, 60 ÷ 6, 54 ÷ 6, 7 × 1, 7 × 2, 7 × 3, 7 × 8, 35 ÷ 7, 28 ÷ 7, 70 ÷ 7, 63 ÷ 7, 49 ÷ 7, 8 × 1, 8 × 2, 8 × 3, 8 × 9, 40 ÷ 8, 48 ÷ 8, 32 ÷ 8, 80 ÷ 8, 64 ÷ 8, 9 × 1, 9 × 2, 9 × 3, 9 × 8, 45 ÷ 9, 36 ÷ 9, 54 ÷ 9, 90 ÷ 9, 81 ÷ 9, 63 ÷ 9.

Complete the Number Sentence (4 minutes)

Materials: (S) Personal white boards

Note: This fluency reviews multiplication and division using units of 0 and 1.

    T: (Write ___ × 1 = 6.) On your boards, complete the equation.

    S: (Write 6 × 1 = 6.)

Continue with the following possible sequence: __ × 1 = 7, 9 × __ = 9, 8 × __ = 8, 7 ÷ __ = 7, 9 ÷ __ = 9, 7 ÷ __ = 1, 9 ÷ __ = 1, 8 × __ = 0, 6 × __ = 0, 0 ÷ 7 = __, 0 ÷ 9 = __, __ ÷ 8 = 0, __ ÷ 6 = 0, __ × 1 = 8, 7 × __ = 7, 6 ÷ __ = 6, 9 × __ = 0, 6 ÷ __ = 1, 0 ÷ 6 = __, __ ÷ 9 = 0, and 9 ÷ __ = 1.

Application Problem (5 minutes)

Henry's garden has 9 rows of squash plants. Each row has 8 squash plants. There is also 1 row with 8 watermelon plants. How many squash and watermelon plants does Henry have in all?

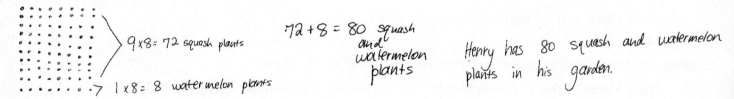

Note: This problem reviews multiplying by units of 9 and 1. Depending on how students choose to solve the problem, it can be used to review multiplying with units of 10, (10 × 8). Be sure to discuss the various strategies that can be used to solve this problem.

COMMON CORE

Lesson 17:   Identify patterns in multiplication and division facts using the multiplication table.

Date: 7/31/13

3.E.16

Concept Development (34 minutes)

Materials: (S) Personal white board, Problem Set, orange crayon

Problems 1(a) and 1(b) from the Problem Set:

T: Write the products to complete the table in Problem 1. Then color all the squares that have even products orange.

T: Let's look at the first orange square in the table. Write the multiplication equation on your board for the product in this square. (Students write.) Are the factors 2 and 1 odd or even?

S: 2 is even and 1 is odd.

T: Look at the orange square below this one. Write the multiplication equation on your board for the product in this square. (Students write.) Are the factors 2 and 2 odd or even?

S: They're both even!

T: Work with a partner to continue to look at the orange squares and tell if the factors are odd or even. (Students finish working.) What did you notice about the factors of even products?

S: The factors are either both even or one is odd and one is even.

T: (Write the following.) Even times even equals even. Odd times even equals even.

T: Work with a partner to find out what kinds of factors are required to produce an odd product. (Students finish working.) What did you notice?

S: Odd times odd equals odd!

T: Answer Problems 1(a) and 1(b) on the Problem Set.

**NOTES ON
MULTIPLE MEANS OF
REPRESENTATION:**

If possible and necessary, transcribe the rapid oral responses of learners who may otherwise work at a slower pace. Use color to outline rows and columns to help learners better discern the content. If you choose to highlight the column of 3 facts, for example, ask students to circle even products (instead of coloring them orange).

Problems 1(c) and 1(d) from the Problem Set:

T: Compare the shaded columns and the shaded rows. Which factors do they have in common?

S: 2, 4, 6, 8.

T: What is 5 × 4?

S: 20!

T: How do these 2 facts help you find 7 × 4? Talk to your partner and answer Problem 1(c) on the Problem Set.

S: 20 and 8 is 28. → 2 fours + 5 fours is 7 fours. → 2 plus 5 is 7, so the products of these 2 facts can be added together to get the product of 7 × 4. (Answer Problem 1(c) on the Problem Set.)

T: Is the product of 7 and 16 on this table?

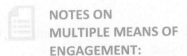

**NOTES ON
MULTIPLE MEANS OF
ENGAGEMENT:**

English language learners may benefit from elaboration on Joe's statement in Problem 2. Read it aloud and check for student understanding. Using multiple ways of expression, for example, *expression* can be simplified as *multiplication fact*. Provide the sentence starter, "I notice a pattern of _____."

Challenge students working above grade level to continue the pattern beyond 9 × 9.

Lesson 17:   Identify patterns in multiplication and division facts using the multiplication table.

Date: 7/31/13

3.E.17

S: No!

T: Talk to a partner, how can we use this table and what we know to solve 7 × 16?

S: 10 sevens and 6 sevens is 16 sevens, 70 + 42. → 8 sevens and 8 sevens, double 56. → 9 sevens and 7 sevens, 63 + 49. → We can think of 16 as 8 + 8 and then the problem is (7 × 8) + (7 × 8). → We could also add 4 sevens four times! 28 + 28 + 28 + 28!

T: Answer Problem 1(d).

Problem 2 from the Problem Set:

T: Complete the chart in Problem 2 by writing the products for each equation. (Students finish working.) Read the products to me.

S: 1, 4, 9, 16, 25, 36.

T: If this chart continued, what would the next equation be?

S: 7 × 7 = 49.

T: And the next equation?

S: 8 × 8 = 64.

T: Draw arrays to match each of these equations in Problem 2. (Students finish working.) Now record the change in the number of squares from one array to the next.

T: (Allow students time to finish.) Talk to a partner, what is the pattern in the number of squares being added?

S: It's 1, 3, 5, 7, like that! → The increase in squares skip-counts by odd numbers, 3, 5, 7, 9, 11, 13, 15.

T: Answer Problem 2(b).

T: What are the first 2 odd numbers when you start counting at 0?

S: 1 and 3.

T: What is their sum?

S: 4!

T: Look at Problem 2. Four is the product of what?

S: 2 × 2.

MP.7   T: The sum of the first 2 odd numbers is the same as the product of 2 × 2.

T: What is the sum of the first 3 odd numbers?

S: 9!

T: Look at Problem 2. Nine is the product of what?

S: 3 × 3.

T: Use the table in Problem 2: What do you think is the sum of the first 5 odd numbers?

S: 25!

T: Check your work: What is 1 + 3 + 5 + 7 + 9?

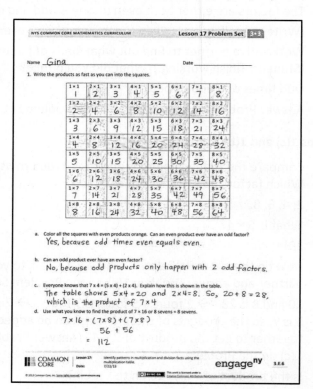

Lesson 17:   Identify patterns in multiplication and division facts using the multiplication table.

Date: 7/31/13   3.E.18

© 2013 Common Core, Inc. All rights reserved. commoncore.org

S: 25!
T: Answer Problem 2(c).

Student Debrief (10 minutes)

Lesson Objective: Identify patterns in multiplication and division facts using the multiplication table.

The Student Debrief is intended to invite reflection and active processing of the total lesson experience.

Invite students to review their solutions for the Problem Set. They should check work by comparing answers with a partner before going over answers as a class. Look for misconceptions or misunderstandings that can be addressed in the Debrief. Guide students in a conversation to debrief the Problem Set and process the lesson.

You may choose to use any combination of the questions below to lead the discussion.

- Talk to a partner: How do the patterns you discovered in Problem 1 for odd and even products help you when multiplying?

- What is the name of the strategy that you used to solve Problem 1(c)? Explain to a partner how this strategy could be used to solve another fact that isn't on the chart, like 6 × 18.

- Look at the arrays you drew for Problem 2. If you drew an array for 7 × 7, how many little squares would you add to the array that you drew for 6 × 6? How do you know?

- In Problem 2(c), you proved that 9 × 9 is the sum of the first 9 odd numbers. Is 10 × 10 the sum of the first 10 odd numbers? Where can you see the odd numbers on the two-colored multiplication table? Can you state a rule that this pattern shows using *n* to represent a number? (Guide students to see that n × n is the sum of the first n odd numbers. These types of problems are included in the homework.)

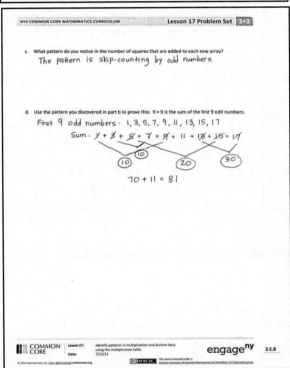

Exit Ticket (3 minutes)

After the Student Debrief, instruct students to complete the Exit Ticket. A review of their work will help you assess the students' understanding of the concepts that were presented in the lesson today and plan more effectively for future lessons. You may read the questions aloud.

Lesson 17:   Identify patterns in multiplication and division facts using the
              multiplication table.
Date: 7/31/13

3.E.19

Name _____   Date _____

1. Write the products as fast as you can into the squares.

1 × 1	2 × 1	3 × 1	4 × 1	5 × 1	6 × 1	7 × 1	8 × 1
1 × 2	2 × 2	3 × 2	4 × 2	5 × 2	6 × 2	7 × 2	8 × 2
1 × 3	2 × 3	3 × 3	4 × 3	5 × 3	6 × 3	7 × 3	8 × 3
1 × 4	2 × 4	3 × 4	4 × 4	5 × 4	6 × 4	7 × 4	8 × 4
1 × 5	2 × 5	3 × 5	4 × 5	5 × 5	6 × 5	7 × 5	8 × 5
1 × 6	2 × 6	3 × 6	4 × 6	5 × 6	6 × 6	7 × 6	8 × 6
1 × 7	2 × 7	3 × 7	4 × 7	5 × 7	6 × 7	7 × 7	8 × 7
1 × 8	2 × 8	3 × 8	4 × 8	5 × 8	6 × 8	7 × 8	8 × 8

a. Color all the squares with even products orange. Can an even product ever have an odd factor?

b. Can an odd product ever have an even factor?

c. Everyone knows that $7 \times 4 = (5 \times 4) + (2 \times 4)$. Explain how this is shown in the table.

d. Use what you know to find the product of 7×16 or 8 sevens + 8 sevens.

COMMON CORE   **Lesson 17:**   Identify patterns in multiplication and division facts using the multiplication table.

Date: 7/31/13   3.E.20

2. In the table, only the products on the diagonal are shown.

a. Label each product on the diagonal.

1 × 1					
	2 × 2				
		3 × 3			
			4 × 4		
				5 × 5	
					6 × 6

b. Draw an array to match each expression in the table below. Then label the number of squares you added to make each new array. The first two arrays have been done for you.

1 × 1	2 × 2	3 × 3	4 × 4	5 × 5	6 × 6
□	▦				

3

Lesson 17: Identify patterns in multiplication and division facts using the multiplication table.

Date: 7/31/13

c.   What pattern do you notice in the number of squares that are added to each new array?

d.   Use the pattern you discovered in Part b to prove this: 9×9 is the sum of the first 9 odd numbers.

COMMON CORE

Lesson 17:   Identify patterns in multiplication and division facts using the
                 multiplication table.
Date: 7/31/13

3.E.22

Name _____   Date _____

1. Use what you know to find the product of 8 × 12 or 6 eights + 6 eights.

2. Luis says 3 × 233 = 626. Use what you learned about odd times odd to prove that Luis is wrong.

Lesson 17:   Identify patterns in multiplication and division facts using the
             multiplication table.
Date: 7/31/13

3.E.23

Name _____   Date _____

1. Write the products as fast as you can into the chart.

×	1	2	3	4	5	6	7	8
1								
2								
3								
4								
5								
6								
7								
8								

a. Color the rows and columns with even factors yellow.

b. What do you notice about the factors and products that are left unshaded?

c. Complete the chart below by filling in each blank and writing an example for the each rule.

Rule	Example
odd times odd equals _____	
even times even equals _____	
even times odd equals _____	

COMMON CORE

Lesson 17: Identify patterns in multiplication and division facts using the multiplication table.
Date: 7/31/13

3.E.24

d. Explain how $7 \times 6 = (5 \times 6) + (2 \times 6)$ is shown in the table.

e. Use what you know to find the product of 4×16 or 8 fours + 8 fours.

2. In the lesson, we found that $n \times n$ is the sum of the first n odd numbers. Use this pattern to find the value of n for each equation below. The first is done for you.

a. $1 + 3 + 5 = n \times n$

   $9 = 3 \times 3$

b. $1 + 3 + 5 + 7 = n \times n$

c. $1 + 3 + 5 + 7 + 9 + 11 = n \times n$

d. $1 + 3 + 5 + 7 + 9 + 11 + 13 + 17 = n \times n$

e. $1 + 3 + 5 + 7 + 9 + 11 + 13 + 15 + 19 + 21 = n \times n$

COMMON CORE | Lesson 17: | Identify patterns in multiplication and division facts using the multiplication table.   3.E.25

Date: | 7/31/13

Lesson 18

Objective: Solve two-step word problems involving all four operations and assess the reasonableness of solutions.

Suggested Lesson Structure

■ Fluency Practice   (15 minutes)
□ Concept Development   (35 minutes)
■ Student Debrief   (10 minutes)
  Total Time   **(60 minutes)**

Fluency Practice (15 minutes)

- Sprint: Multiply and Divide by 1 and 0 **3.OA.5**   (8 minutes)
- Multiply by 10 **3.NBT.3**   (3 minutes)
- Group Counting **3.OA.1**   (4 minutes)

Sprint: Multiply and Divide by 1 and 0 (8 minutes)

Materials: (S) Multiply and Divide by 1 and 0 Sprint

Note: This Sprint reviews Lesson 16, rules and properties when multiplying and dividing by 1 and 0.

Multiply by 10 (3 minutes)

Note: This fluency anticipates Lesson 19, multiplying by multiples of 10.

  T: I'll say a fact. You say the whole equation. 10×1.
  S: $10 \times 1 = 10$.

Continue with the following possible sequence: 10×2, 10×3, 10×9, 10×7.

  T: I'll say a product that is a multiple of 10. You say the multiplication fact starting with 10. 20.
  S: $10 \times 2 = 20$.

Continue with the following possible sequence: 30, 40, 80, 60.

Lesson 18:   Solve two-step word problems involving all four operations and
             assess the reasonableness of solutions.
Date: 7/31/13

3.E.26

Group Counting (4 minutes)

Note: Group counting reviews interpreting multiplication as repeated addition. These counts review multiplication taught earlier in the module. Direct students to count forward and backward, occasionally changing the direction of the count.

- Sixes to 60
- Sevens to 70
- Eights to 80
- Nines to 90

Concept Development (35 minutes)

Materials: (S) Personal white boards

Project: Joe has $173 in the bank. He earns the same amount of money each week for 7 weeks and puts this money in the bank. Now Joe has $208 in the bank. How much money does Joe earn each week?

T: Draw a model to show the total amount of money Joe has in the bank at the end of the 7 weeks. At my signal, show me your board. (Signal.)

T: Do we know the amount of money Joe puts in the bank?

S: No.

T: Label this unknown on your model using the letter *m* for money. Then write what *m* represents. (Students write.) Write an equation to show how to solve for *m*.

S: (Write $208 - 173 = m$.)

T: Solve for *m* and write its value on your model.

S: (Write m = $35.)

T: Is this answer reasonable?

S: Yes, because $173 + $35 equals $208, which is the total amount Joe has in the bank.

T: Did we answer the question in the problem?

S: No, we're trying to figure out how much money he earns each week.

T: Adjust your model to show what you know about the amount of money Joe earns in 7 weeks.

S: (Split $35 into 7 equal pieces.)

T: Label the unknown with the letter *w* to represent how much money Joe earns each week. Then write what *w* represents.

S: (Label. Then write what *w* represents.)

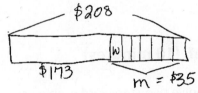

m = number of dollars Joe put in bank

$208 - $173 = m

m = $35

w = number of dollars earned each week

$35 ÷ 7 = w

w = $5

Date: 7/31/13

T: Write an equation on your board and solve for *w*.

S: (Write 35 ÷ 7 = *w*; *w* = $5.)

T: Talk to a partner, is it reasonable that Joe earns $5 a week?

S: Yes, it makes sense because that's how much I earn each week for my allowance! → It's reasonable because $5 a week for 7 weeks is $35 and that's about $40. $173 is about $170 and $40 + $170 is $210, which is close to $208.

T: It's important to make sure the answer makes sense for every part of the problem!

NOTES ON MULTIPLE MEANS OF ENGAGEMENT:

When completing the Problem Set, students working above grade level may enjoy an open-ended extension. Offer students an option to choose one of the models and equations from the Problem Set to write their own word problem.

Problem Set (20 minutes)

Students should do their personal best to complete the Problem Set within the allotted 20 minutes. For some classes, it may be appropriate to modify the assignment by specifying which problems they work on first. Some problems do not specify a method for solving. Students solve these problems using the RDW approach used for Application Problems.

NOTES ON MULTIPLE MEANS OF ENGAGEMENT:

Take advantage of the opportunity in the Student Debrief to review personal and class goals regarding problem solving. Guide students to identify their strengths and weaknesses as problem solvers. Construct new goals for future work.

Student Debrief (10 minutes)

Lesson Objective: Solve two-step word problems involving all four operations and assess the reasonableness of solutions.

The Student Debrief is intended to invite reflection and active processing of the total lesson experience.

Invite students to review their solutions for the Problem Set. They should check work by comparing answers with a partner before going over answers as a class. Look for misconceptions or misunderstandings that can be addressed in the Debrief. Guide students in a conversation to debrief the Problem Set and process the lesson.

You may choose to use any combination of the questions below to lead the discussion.

▪   In Problem 1, you found that Sasha gives Rose a piece of yarn that is 27 centimeters long.

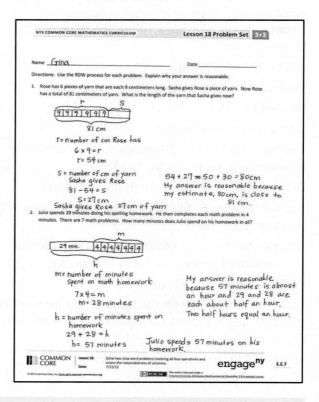

 Lesson 18:   Solve two-step word problems involving all four operations and assess the reasonableness of solutions.
Date: 7/31/13

© 2013 Common Core, Inc. All rights reserved. commoncore.org

3.E.28

How many 9-centimeter pieces can Rose cut this piece into?

- In Problem 2, did Julio spend more time on his spelling homework or his math homework? How do you know?

- Talk to a partner, how are Problems 3 and 4 similar?

- In Problem 5, if Cora weighs 5 pencils, what is the total weight for the pencils and the ruler? How do you know?

- Discuss with a partner the importance of checking the reasonableness of your answer.

Exit Ticket (3 minutes)

After the Student Debrief, instruct students to complete the Exit Ticket. A review of their work will help you assess the students' understanding of the concepts that were presented in the lesson today and plan more effectively for future lessons. You may read the questions aloud to the students.

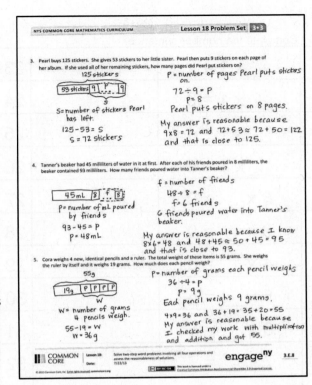

COMMON CORE

Lesson 18:   Solve two-step word problems involving all four operations and
Date: assess the reasonableness of solutions.
             7/31/13

3.E.29

A

Correct _____

Complete the number sentence.

1	__ x 1 = 2		23	9 ÷ __ = 9	
2	__ x 1 = 3		24	8 x __ = 8	
3	__ x 1 = 4		25	__ x 1 = 1	
4	__ x 1 = 9		26	0 ÷ 3 = __	
5	8 x __ = 0		27	__ x 1 = 7	
6	9 x __ = 0		28	6 x __ = 0	
7	4 x __ = 0		29	4 x __ = 4	
8	5 x __ = 5		30	0 ÷ 8 = __	
9	6 x __ = 6		31	0 x __ = 0	
10	7 x __ = 7		32	1 ÷ 1 = __	
11	3 x __ = 3		33	__ x 1 = 24	
12	0 ÷ 1 = __		34	17 x __ = 0	
13	0 ÷ 2 = __		35	32 x __ = 32	
14	0 ÷ 3 = __		36	0 ÷ 19 = __	
15	0 ÷ 6 = __		37	46 x __ = 0	
16	1 x __ = 1		38	0 ÷ 51 = __	
17	4 ÷ __ = 4		39	64 x __ = 64	
18	5 ÷ __ = 5		40	__ x 1 = 79	
19	6 ÷ __ = 6		41	0 ÷ 82 = __	
20	8 ÷ __ = 8		42	__ x 1 = 96	
21	__ x 1 = 5		43	27 x __ = 27	
22	3 x __ = 0		44	43 x __ = 0	

© Bill Davidson

Lesson 18:	Solve two-step word problems involving all four operations and assess the reasonableness of solutions.	3.E.30
Date:	7/31/13	

© 2013 Common Core, Inc. All rights reserved. commoncore.org

B

Improvement _____   # Correct _____

Complete the number sentence.

1	__ x 1 = 3		23	8 ÷ __ = 8	
2	__ x 1 = 4		24	7 x __ = 7	
3	__ x 1 = 5		25	__ x 1 = 1	
4	__ x 1 = 8		26	0 ÷ 5 = __	
5	7 x __ = 0		27	__ x 1 = 9	
6	8 x __ = 0		28	5 x __ = 0	
7	3 x __ = 0		29	9 x __ = 9	
8	4 x __ = 4		30	0 ÷ 6 = __	
9	5 x __ = 5		31	1 ÷ 1 = __	
10	6 x __ = 6		32	0 x __ = 0	
11	2 x __ = 2		33	__ x 1 = 34	
12	0 ÷ 2 = __		34	16 x __ = 0	
13	0 ÷ 3 = __		35	31 x __ = 31	
14	0 ÷ 4 = __		36	0 ÷ 18 = __	
15	0 ÷ 7 = __		37	45 x __ = 0	
16	1 x __ = 1		38	0 ÷ 52 = __	
17	3 ÷ __ = 3		39	63 x __ = 63	
18	4 ÷ __ = 4		40	__ x 1 = 78	
19	5 ÷ __ = 5		41	0 ÷ 81 = __	
20	7 ÷ __ = 7		42	__ x 1 = 97	
21	__ x 1 = 6		43	26 x __ = 26	
22	4 x __ = 0		44	42 x __ = 0	

© Bill Davidson

Lesson 18:   Solve two-step word problems involving all four operations and assess the reasonableness of solutions.
Date: 7/31/13

3.E.31

Name _____   Date _____

Directions: Use the RDW process for each problem. Explain why your answer is reasonable.

1. Rose has 6 pieces of yarn that are each 9 centimeters long. Sasha gives Rose a piece of yarn. Now Rose has a total of 81 centimeters of yarn. What is the length of the yarn that Sasha gives rose?

2. Julio spends 29 minutes doing his spelling homework. He then completes each math problem in 4 minutes. There are 7 math problems. How many minutes does Julio spend on his homework in all?

Lesson 18:   Solve two-step word problems involving all four operations and
assess the reasonableness of solutions.
Date: 7/31/13

3.E.32

3. Pearl buys 125 stickers. She gives 53 stickers to her little sister. Pearl then puts 9 stickers on each page of her album. If she used all of her remaining stickers, how many pages did Pearl put stickers on?

4. Tanner's beaker had 45 milliliters of water in it at first. After each of his friends poured in 8 milliliters, the beaker contained 93 milliliters. How many friends poured water into Tanner's beaker?

5. Cora weighs 4 new, identical pencils and a ruler. The total weight of these items is 55 grams. She weighs the ruler by itself and it weighs 19 grams. How much does each pencil weigh?

Name _____   Date _____

Directions: Use the RDW process to solve. Explain why your answer is reasonable.

On Saturday, Warren swims laps for 45 minutes in the pool. On Sunday, he runs 8 miles. If it takes him 9 minutes to run each mile, how long does Warren spend exercising over the weekend?

Lesson 18:   Solve two-step word problems involving all four operations and
assess the reasonableness of solutions.
Date: 7/31/13   3.E.34

Name _____   Date _____

Directions: Use the RDW process for each problem. Explain why your answer is reasonable.

1. Mrs. Portillo's cat weighs 6 kilograms. Her dog weighs 22 kilograms more than her cat. What is the total weight of her cat and dog?

2. Darren studies for his science test for 39 minutes. He then does 6 chores. Each chore takes him 3 minutes. How many minutes does Darren spend studying and doing chores?

3. Mr. Abbot buys 8 boxes of granola bars for a party. Each box has 9 granola bars. After the party, there are 39 bars left. How many bars were eaten during the party?

COMMON CORE

Lesson 18:   Solve two-step word problems involving all four operations and assess the reasonableness of solutions.

Date: 7/31/13

3.E.35

4. Leslie weighs her marbles in a jar, and the scale reads 474 grams. The empty jar weighs 439 grams. Each marble weighs 5 grams. How many marbles are in the jar?

5. Sharon uses 72 centimeters of ribbon to wrap gifts. Of that total, she uses 24 centimeters to wrap a big gift. She uses the remaining ribbon for 6 small gifts. How much ribbon will she use for each small gift if she uses the same amount on each?

6. Six friends equally share the cost of a gift. They pay $90 and receive $42 in change. How much does each friend pay?

Mathematics Curriculum

Topic F

Multiplication of Single-Digit Factors and Multiples of 10

3.OA.5, 3.OA.8, 3.OA.9, 3.NBT.3, 3.OA.1

Focus Standard:	3.OA.5	Apply properties of operations as strategies to multiply and divide. (Students need not use formal terms for these properties.) *Examples: If 6 × 4 = 24 is known, then 4 × 6 = 24 is also known. (Commutative property of multiplication.) 3 × 5 × 2 can be found by 3 × 5 = 15, then 15 × 2 = 30, or by 5 × 2 = 10, then 3 × 10 = 30. (Associative property of multiplication.) Knowing that 8 × 5 = 40 and 8 × 2 = 16, one can find 8 × 7 as 8 × (5 + 2) = (8 × 5) + (8 × 2) = 40 + 16 = 56. (Distributive property.)*
	3.OA.8	Solve two-step word problems using the four operations. Represent these problems using equations with a letter standing for the unknown quantity. Assess the reasonableness of answers using mental computation and estimation strategies including rounding. (This standard is limited to problems posed with whole numbers and having whole-number answers; students should know how to perform operations in the conventional order when there are no parentheses to specify a particular order, i.e., Order of Operations.)
	3.OA.9	Identify arithmetic patterns (including patterns in the addition table or multiplication table), and explain them using properties of operations. *For example, observe that 4 times a number is always even, and explain why 4 times a number can be decomposed into two equal addends.*
	3.NBT.3	Multiply one-digit whole numbers by multiples of 10 in the range 10–90 (e.g., 9 × 80, 5 × 60) using strategies based on place value and properties of operations.
Instructional Days:	3	
Coherence -Links from:	G2–M3	Place Value, Counting, and Comparison of Numbers to 1000
	G2–M6	Foundations of Multiplication and Division
	G3–M1	Properties of Multiplication and Division and Solving Problems with Units of 2–5 and 10
** -Links to:**	G3–M4	Multiplication and Area
	G4–M3	Multi-Digit Multiplication and Division
	G4–M7	Exploring Multiplication

In Lesson 19, students initially use the place value chart to multiply by multiples of 10. To solve 2 × 40, for example, they begin by modeling 2 × 4 in the ones place. Students relate this to multiplying 2 × 4 tens, locating the same basic fact in the tens column. They see that when multiplied by 10, the product shifts one

place value to the left. Complexities are addressed as regrouping becomes involved with problems like 4×6, where the product has mixed units of tens and ones. However, the same principle applies—the digits shift once to the left.

Lesson 20 carries students' understanding from Lesson 19 to more abstract situations using a wider range of multiples of 10. Students learn to model place value strategies using the associative property. $2 \times 30 = 2 \times (3 \times 10) = (2 \times 3) \times 10$ and $4 \times 60 = 4 \times (6 \times 10) = (4 \times 6) \times 10$. In Lesson 21, students apply learning from Topic F to solving two-step word problems and multiplying single-digit factors and multiples of 10. They use the rounding skills learned in Module 2 to estimate and assess the reasonableness of their solutions.

A Teaching Sequence Towards Mastery of Multiplication of Single-Digit Factors and Multiples of 10

Objective 1: Multiply by multiples of 10 using the place value chart.
(Lesson 19)

Objective 2: Use place value strategies and the associative property $n \times (m \times 10) = (n \times m) \times 10$ (where n and m are less than 10) to multiply by multiples of 10.
(Lesson 20)

Objective 3: Solve two-step word problems involving multiplying single-digit factors and multiples of 10.
(Lesson 21)

Lesson 19

Objective: Multiply by multiples of 10 using the place value chart.

Suggested Lesson Structure

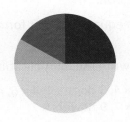

■ Fluency Practice	(15 minutes)
▢ Concept Development	(20 minutes)
▨ Application Problem	(15 minutes)
■ Student Debrief	(10 minutes)
Total Time	**(60 minutes)**

📋 **NOTES ON TIMING:**

Since the Application Problem comes after the Concept Development in this lesson, the 15 minutes allotted for it includes 5 minutes for the Application Problem and 10 minutes for the Problem Set.

Fluency Practice (15 minutes)

- Group Counting **3.OA.1**   (4 minutes)
- Multiply by 10 **3.NBT.3**   (3 minutes)
- Multiply by Different Units **3.NBT.3**   (4 minutes)
- Exchange Number Disks **3.NBT.3**   (4 minutes)

Group Counting (4 minutes)

Note: Group counting reviews interpreting multiplication as repeated addition. These counts review the multiplication taught earlier in the module. Direct students to count forward and backward, occasionally changing the direction of the count:

- Sixes to 60
- Sevens to 70
- Eights to 80
- Nines to 90

Multiply by 10 (3 minutes)

Note: This fluency prepares students for today's lesson.

- T: I'll say a multiplication problem. You say the answer. 10 × 1.
- S: 10 × 1 = 10.

Continue with the following possible sequence: 10 × 2, 10 × 3, 10 × 8, 10 × 6.

- T: I'll say a multiple of 10. You say the multiplication fact starting with 10. 20.
- S: 10 × 2 = 20.

COMMON CORE | Lesson 19: | Multiply by multiples of ten using the place value chart. | 3.F.3
| Date: | 7/31/13 |

Continue with the following possible sequence: 30, 40, 90, 70, 50.

Multiply by Different Units (4 minutes)

Materials: (S) Personal white boards

Note: This fluency prepares students for today's lesson.

- T: (Write 2 × 3 = ___.) Say the multiplication equation in unit form.
- S: 2 ones × 3 = 6 ones.
- T: (Write 2 cats × 3 = ___.) On your boards, write the multiplication equation.

Continue with the following possible sequence: 3 × 4, 3 dogs × 4; 4 × 5, 4 pencils × 5; 5 × 6, 5 books × 6; 6 × 7, 6 cars × 7; 7 × 8, 7 turtles × 8; 8 × 9, 8 chairs × 9; 9 × 7, 9 flowers × 7.

Exchange Number Disks (4 minutes)

Materials: (S) Number disks

Note: This fluency prepares students for today's lesson.

- T: Make an array showing 3 by 2 ones. Say how many ones you have as a multiplication equation.
- S: 3 × 2 ones = 6 ones.

Continue with the following possible sequence: 3 by 3 ones, 4 by 2 ones, and 5 by 2 ones.

- T: 10 ones can be exchanged for 1 of what unit?
- S: 1 ten.
- T: Trade your 10 ones for 1 ten.
- T: Make an array showing 4 by 5 ones.
- T: Say how many ones you have as a multiplication equation.
- S: 4 × 5 ones = 20 ones.
- T: Say the multiplication equation again; this time say the answer in units of 10.
- S: 4 × 5 ones = 2 tens.
- T: Trade your 20 ones for 2 tens.

Concept Development (20 minutes)

Materials: (T/S) Number disks (S) Personal white boards

Problem 1: Multiply by multiples of 10 using place value disks.

- T: Use your disks to show 2 rows of 3 ones.
- S: (Model 2 × 3 ones array.)

NOTES ON MULTIPLE MEANS FOR ACTION AND EXPRESSION:

During the Concept Development, check for understanding as students use concrete number disks. Make sure students are distinguishing between ones disks and tens disks. You may ask students to count out, "1 ten, 2 tens, 3 tens, etc." as they make their array. Alternatively, students may draw the disks.

Lesson 19:   Multiply by multiples of ten using the place value chart.
Date: 7/31/13

3.F.4

T: (Write 2 × 3 ones = _____ ones.) Our array shows this equation, true?

S: True.

T: How many ones do we have in total?

S: 6 ones.

T: Say the multiplication equation in standard form.

S: 2 × 3 = 6.

T: Use your disks to show 2 rows of 3 tens.

S: (Model 2 × 3 tens array.)

T: (Write 2 × 3 tens = _____ tens.) How many tens do we have in total?

S: 6 tens.

T: What is the value of 6 tens?

S: 60.

T: Say the multiplication equation in standard form.

S: 2 × 30 = 60.

Repeat the process with 3 × 4 ones and 3 × 4 tens, 2 × 6 ones and 2 × 6 tens.

2 × 3 ones = 6 ones

2 × 3 = 6

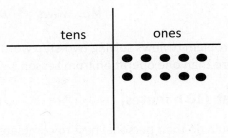

2 × 3 tens = 6 tens

2 × 30 = 60

Problem 2: Multiply by multiples of 10 using a place value chart.

T: (Project or draw the image shown at right.) Use the chart to write an equation in both unit form and standard form.

S: (Write 2 × 5 ones = 10 ones and 2 × 5 = 10.)

T: How many ones do I have in total?

S: 10 ones.

T: (Project or draw the image shown at right.) Compare the two charts. What do you notice about the number of dots?

S: The number of dots is exactly the same in both charts. → The only thing that changes is where they are placed. The dots moved over to the tens place.

T: Since we still have a total of ten dots, what change do you think we will make in our equations?

S: The units will change from ones to tens.

T: Write your equations now.

S: (Write equations.)

T: Say the full equation.

	tens	ones

2 × 5 ones = _____ ones

2 × 5 = _____

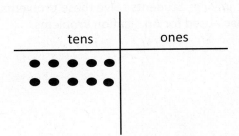

	tens	ones

2 × 5 tens = _____ tens

2 × 50 = _____

S: 2 times 50 equals 100.

Repeat the process with 3 × 6 ones and 3 × 6 tens.

T: (Write 80 × 6 = _____.) How would you use this strategy to solve a more complicated problem like the one on the board?

S: We can first think of the problem as 8 ones × 6, which is 48. We know that fact since we've been practicing our sixes. → Then all we have to do is move the answer over to the tens place, so it becomes 48 tens. → So the answer is 480!

MP.7

Repeat the process with 7 × 90 and 60 × 4 to give the students an opportunity to discuss the unit form strategy with more complex problems.

Application Problem (15 minutes)

Mia has 152 beads. She uses some to make bracelets. Now there are 80 beads. If she uses 8 beads for each bracelet, how many bracelets does she make?

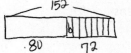
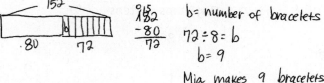

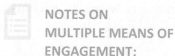

Note: This problem reviews solving two-step word problems involving more than one operation from Lesson 18.

NOTES ON TIMING:

The 15 minutes allotted for the Application Problem includes 5 minutes for the word problem to the left, and 10 minutes for the Problem Set.

Problem Set (10 minutes)

Students should do their personal best to complete the Problem Set within the allotted 10 minutes. For some classes, it may be appropriate to modify the assignment by specifying which problems they work on first. Some problems do not specify a method for solving. Students solve these problems using the RDW approach used for Application Problems.

NOTES ON MULTIPLE MEANS OF ENGAGEMENT:

Instead of completing the Problem Set, give English language learners the option of writing a response to either of the first two Debrief questions. This chance to reflect and prepare their response in English may increase their confidence and participation in the Student Debrief.

Student Debrief (10 minutes)

Lesson Objective: Multiply by multiples of 10 using the place value chart.

The Student Debrief is intended to invite reflection and active processing of the total lesson experience.

Invite students to review their solutions for the Problem Set. They should check work by comparing answers with a partner before going over answers as a class. Look for misconceptions or misunderstandings that can be addressed in the Debrief. Guide students in a conversation to debrief the Problem Set and process the lesson.

You may choose to use any combination of the ideas below to lead the discussion.

- How do the disks in Problem 1 show the strategy we learned today?

- What is the relationship between the charts on the left column and the charts on the right column in Problem 2? How did the left column help you solve the problems on the right column?

- How does knowing your multiplication facts help you easily multiply by multiples of 10?

- Now that we know a strategy for multiplying with multiples of 10, how would we use the same process for multiplying with multiples of 100? What would be the same? (The multiplication facts.) What would change? (The units.)

Exit Ticket (3 minutes)

After the Student Debrief, instruct students to complete the Exit Ticket. A review of their work will help you assess the students' understanding of the concepts that were presented in the lesson today and plan more effectively for future lessons. You may read the questions aloud to the students.

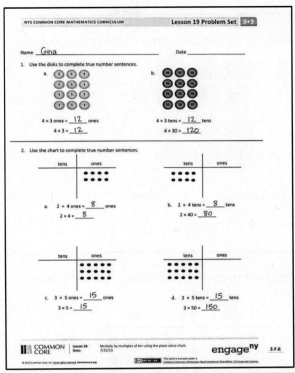

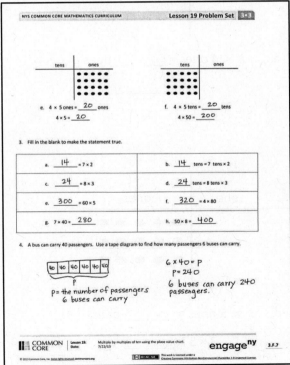

Name _____   Date _____

1. Use the disks to complete true number sentences.

a.
① ① ①
① ① ①
① ① ①
① ① ①

4 × 3 ones = _____ ones

4 × 3 = _____

b.
⑩ ⑩ ⑩
⑩ ⑩ ⑩
⑩ ⑩ ⑩
⑩ ⑩ ⑩

4 × 3 tens = _____ tens

4 × 30 = _____

2. Use the chart to complete true number sentences.

tens	ones
	● ● ● ●
	● ● ● ●

a.   2 × 4 ones = _____ ones

2 × 4 = _____

tens	ones
● ● ● ●	
● ● ● ●	

b.   2 × 4 tens = _____ tens

2 × 40 = _____

tens	ones
	● ● ● ● ●
	● ● ● ● ●
	● ● ● ● ●

c.   3 × 5 ones = _____ ones

3 × 5 = _____

tens	ones
● ● ● ● ●	
● ● ● ● ●	
● ● ● ● ●	

d.   3 × 5 tens = _____ tens

3 × 50 = _____

tens	ones
	● ● ● ● ●
	● ● ● ● ●
	● ● ● ● ●
	● ● ● ● ●

e.   4 × 5 ones = _____ ones

   4 × 5 = _____

tens	ones
● ● ● ● ●	
● ● ● ● ●	
● ● ● ● ●	
● ● ● ● ●	

f.   4 × 5 tens = _____ tens

   4 × 50 = _____

3.   Fill in the blank to make the statement true.

a. _____ = 7 × 2	b. _____ tens = 7 tens × 2
c. _____ = 8 × 3	d. _____ tens = 8 tens × 3
e. _____ = 60 × 5	f. _____ = 4 × 80
g. 7 × 40 = _____	h. 50 × 8 = _____

4.   A bus can carry 40 passengers. Use a tape diagram to find how many passengers 6 buses can carry.

Name _____ Date _____

1. Use the chart to complete true number sentences.

tens	ones
	• • • • •
	• • • • •
	• • • • •
	• • • • •
	• • • • •
	• • • • •

tens	ones
• • • • •	
• • • • •	
• • • • •	
• • • • •	
• • • • •	
• • • • •	

6 × 5 ones = _____ ones   6 × 5 tens = _____ tens

6 × 5 = _____   6 × 50 = _____

---

2. A small plane has 20 rows of seats. Each row has 4 seats.

   a. Find the total number of seats on the plane.

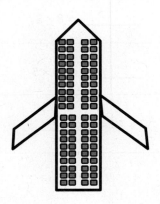

   b. How many seats are on 3 small planes?

COMMON CORE

Lesson 19:   Multiply by multiples of ten using the place value chart.
Date: 7/31/13

3.F.10

Name _____   Date _____

1. Use the disks to complete true number sentences.

a.

3 ones × 3 = _____ ones

3 × 3 = _____

b.

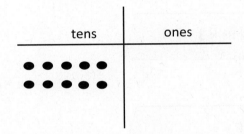

3 tens × 3 = _____ tens

30 × 3 = _____

2. Use the chart to complete true number sentences.

tens	ones
	● ● ● ● ● ● ● ● ● ●

a.   2 × 5 ones = _____ ones

2 × 5 = _____

tens	ones
● ● ● ● ● ● ● ● ● ●	

b.   2 × 5 tens = _____ tens

2 × 50 = _____

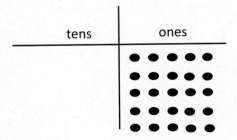

tens	ones
	● ● ● ● ●

c. 5 × 5 ones = _____ ones

5 × 5 = _____

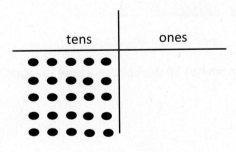

tens	ones

d. 5 × 5 tens = _____ tens

5 × 50 = _____

3. Match.

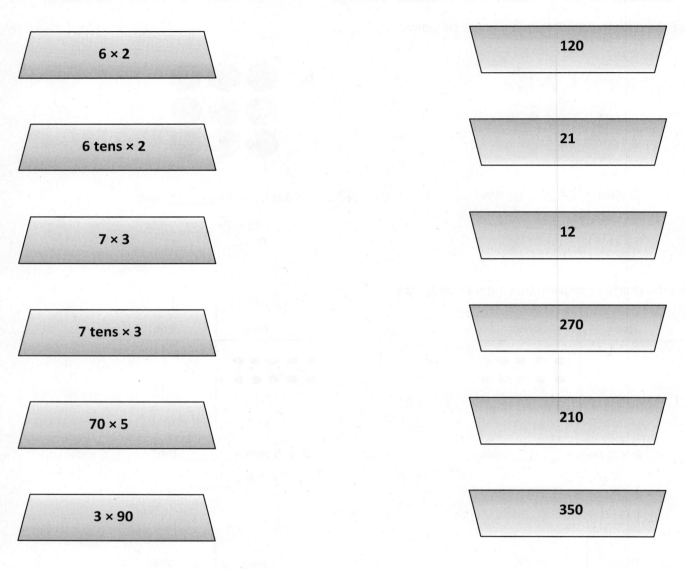

6 × 2	120
6 tens × 2	21
7 × 3	12
7 tens × 3	270
70 × 5	210
3 × 90	350

4. Each classroom has 30 desks. Use a tape diagram to find the total number of desks in 8 classrooms.

COMMON CORE

Lesson 19:
Date:

Multiply by multiples of ten using the place value chart.
7/31/13

3.F.12

Lesson 20

Objective: Use place value strategies and the associative property $n \times (m \times 10) = (n \times m) \times 10$ (where n and m are less than 10) to multiply multiples of 10.

Suggested Lesson Structure

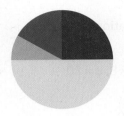

■ Fluency Practice	(15 minutes)
■ Application Problem	(5 minutes)
▫ Concept Development	(30 minutes)
■ Student Debrief	(10 minutes)
Total Time	**(60 minutes)**

Fluency Practice (15 minutes)

- Group Counting **3.OA.1**   (3 minutes)
- Multiply by Different Units **3.NBT.3**   (6 minutes)
- Write In the Parentheses **3.OA.7**   (6 minutes)

Group Counting (3 minutes)

Note: Group counting reviews interpreting multiplication as repeated addition. The counts in these lessons review the multiplication taught earlier in the module. Direct students to count forward and backward, occasionally changing the direction of the count:

- Sixes to 60
- Sevens to 70
- Eights to 80
- Nines to 90

Multiply by Different Units (6 minutes)

Materials: (S) Personal white boards

Note: This fluency reviews Lesson 19.

- T: (Write $2 \times 3 =$ ____.) Say the multiplication equation in unit form.
- S: 2 ones × 3 = 6 ones.
- T: Say it in standard form.

Lesson 20: Use place value strategies and the associative property $n \times (m \times 10) = (n \times m) \times 10$ (where n and m are less than 10) to multiply multiples of 10.
Date: 7/31/13

3.F.13

S: 2 × 3 = 6.

T: (Write 2 tens × 3 = _____.) On your boards, write the multiplication equation.

S: (Write 2 tens × 3 = 6 tens.)

T: Below your equation, write a second multiplication equation in standard form.

S: (Write 20 × 3 = 60.)

Continue with the following possible sequence: 4 × 2, 4 tens × 2, 5 × 3, 5 × 3 tens, 6 × 4, 6 × 4 tens.

T: (Write 7 × 6 = _____.) Say the multiplication equation.

S: 7 × 6 = 42.

T: (Write 70 × 6 = _____.) Write the multiplication equation.

S: (Write 70 × 6 = 420.)

Continue with the following possible sequence: 8 × 8, 8 × 80; 9 × 8, 90 × 8; 6 × 6, 60 × 6; 8 × 7, 8 × 70; 4 × 9, 40 × 9; 9 × 6, 90 × 6.

Write In the Parentheses (6 minutes)

Materials: (S) Personal white boards

Note: This fluency reviews the use of parentheses and prepares students for today's lesson.

T: (Write 4 × 5 = 2 × 2 × 5.) What's 4 × 5?

S: 20.

T: On your boards, copy the equation. Then write in parentheses and solve.

S: (Write 4 × 5 = 2 × 2 × 5. Beneath it, write 20 = (2 × 2) × 5.)

4 × 5 = 2 × 2 × 5
20 = (2 × 2) × 5

Continue with the following possible sequence: 6 × 4 = 6 × 2 × 2, 6 × 6 = 6 × 2 × 3, 4 × 7 = 2 × 2 × 7, 7 × 8 = 7 × 4 × 2, 8 × 4 = 8 × 2 × 2, 8 × 6 = 8 × 3 × 2, 9 × 6 = 9 × 3 × 2, 9 × 8 = 9 × 4 × 2.

COMMON CORE

Lesson 20:   Use place value strategies and the associative property
$n × (m × 10) = (n × m) × 10$ (where n and m are less than 10)
to multiply multiples of 10.
Date: 7/31/13

3.F.14

Application Problem (5 minutes)

Model 3 × 4 on a place value chart. Then explain how the array can help you solve 30 × 4.

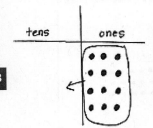

This array shows 3 ones × 4 = 12 ones. 30 × 4 is just 3 tens × 4 which is equal to 12 tens, or 120. We can move the dots over to the tens place to show this, because the only thing that changes is the unit.

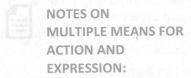

NOTES ON MULTIPLE MEANS FOR ACTION AND EXPRESSION:

Allow English language learners more time to compose their explanation, access to a math picture dictionary, an example of a well written response, and an opportunity to share their response (perhaps during the Debrief).

Note: This problem reviews multiplying by multiples of 10 from Lesson 19. In today's Concept Development, students will build on their understanding from Lesson 19 to multiply by multiples of 10 using the associative property.

Concept Development (30 minutes)

Materials: (S) Personal white boards

NOTES ON MULTIPLE MEANS OF ENGAGEMENT:

Allow students who are working above grade level more autonomy to experiment in the manner and with numbers they choose. Example prompts are given below:

- Write a multiplication fact that you think is best solved using the associative property.

- Write another three-factor multiplication equation with a product of 40. Compare the two equations. What do you notice?

- In the equation 10 × (4 × 2), what would happen if you changed the factors inside the parentheses to numbers greater than 10?

T: (Write 40 × 2.) Which tens fact gives us a product of 40?

S: 10 × 4.

T: Let's rewrite our equation. (Write (10 × 4) × 2.) Why do you think I put 10 × 4 in parentheses?

S: The parentheses show that when you group those numbers together and multiply, you get 40. → The parentheses remind us that we put 10 × 4 where 40 used to be.

T: Let's move the parentheses to change the way the numbers are grouped.

T: On your board, use the parentheses to group the numbers differently.

S: (Write 10 × (4 × 2).)

T: Is this problem friendlier than 40 × 2?

S: Oh, it's just 10 × 8! That's the same as 80! That was a little easier than multiplying by 40.

Repeat the process with 20 × 3, 30 × 3, and 50 × 2.

T: (Project or draw Image A shown below.) Use the chart to write a multiplication equation in unit form.

S: (Write 3 × 6 ones = 18 ones.)

Lesson 20:   Use place value strategies and the associative property
              $n \times (m \times 10) = (n \times m) \times 10$ (where n and m are less than 10)
              to multiply multiples of 10.
Date: 7/31/13

3.F.15

T: Now I want to multiply my 18 ones by ten. Watch as I show this on the chart. I redraw my dots into the tens place and draw an arrow (draw arrow) to remind myself that they move to the next unit. Let's multiply our 3 groups of 6 ones by 10.

T: (Write (3 × 6 ones) × 10 = _____.) What is the answer to 18 ones × 10 in unit form?

S: 18 tens!

T: What is the value of 18 tens?

S: 180.

T: (Project or draw Image B shown at right.) This time I already moved my 6 ones to make them 6 tens. Use the chart to write a multiplication equation in unit form.

S: (Write 6 ones × 10 = 6 tens.)

T: Now I want to multiply my 6 tens by 3. How many rows do I need to add to show 3 rows of 6 tens?

S: 2 rows.

T: (Add 2 rows of 6 tens and write 3 × (6 × 10).) How does my array show this expression? Tell your partner.

S: There are 3 rows of 6 tens. → Six tens is the same as 6 × 10. It has the parentheses around it because we did that first on the chart. → Then we multiplied the 6 × 10 by 3.

T: What is the answer to 3 × 6 tens in unit form?

S: 18 tens! → 180.

T: Compare the equations (3 × 6 ones) × 10 and 3 × (6 × 10). What do you notice about the factors we used?

S: The factors are the same! 3, 6, and 10. The units are different, and so is the order of what you multiply first.

T: In both charts we saw how multiplying the ten, even at different times, made it easier to solve.

Repeat the process with (4 × 5) × 10 and 4 × (5 × 10).

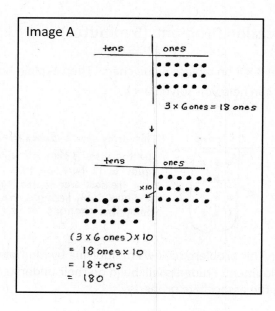

Image A

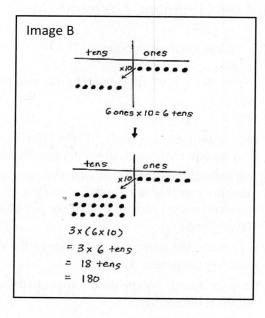

Image B

Problem Set (10 minutes)

Students should do their personal best to complete the Problem Set within the allotted 10 minutes. For some classes, it may be appropriate to modify the assignment by specifying which problems they work on first. Some problems do not specify a method for solving. Students solve these problems using the RDW approach used for Application Problems.

Lesson 20:	Use place value strategies and the associative property $n \times (m \times 10) = (n \times m) \times 10$ (where n and m are less than 10) to multiply multiples of 10.
Date:	7/31/13

3.F.16

Student Debrief (10 minutes)

Lesson Objective: Use place value strategies and the associative property $n \times (m \times 10) = (n \times m) \times 10$ (where n and m are less than 10) to multiply by multiples of 10.

The Student Debrief is intended to invite reflection and active processing of the total lesson experience.

Invite students to review their solutions for the Problem Set. They should check work by comparing answers with a partner before going over answers as a class. Look for misconceptions or misunderstandings that can be addressed in the Debrief. Guide students in a conversation to debrief the Problem Set and process the lesson.

You may choose to use any combination of the questions below to lead the discussion.

- In Problem 1, which grouping is easier for you to solve? Why?
- How do you see the parentheses move in the place value charts in Problem 1?
- Invite students to share how they knew where to draw parentheses for the equations in Problem 2.
- In Problem 3, how did Gabriella simplify the problem?
- Why didn't we have to have a hundreds column in our place value charts?
- How is this new strategy helpful in finding unknown, larger facts?

Exit Ticket (3 minutes)

After the Student Debrief, instruct students to complete the Exit Ticket. A review of their work will help you assess the students' understanding of the concepts that were presented in the lesson today and plan more effectively for future lessons. You may read the questions aloud to the students.

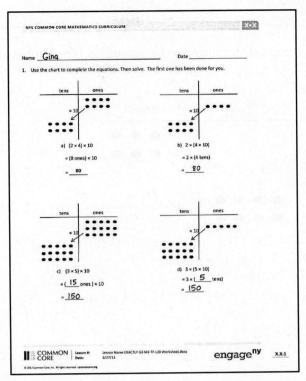

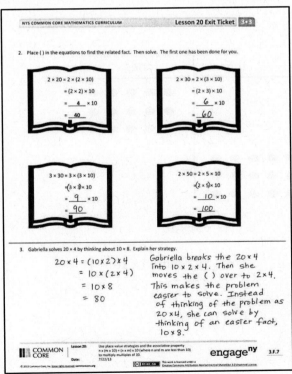

COMMON CORE

Lesson 20:   Use place value strategies and the associative property
$n \times (m \times 10) = (n \times m) \times 10$ (where n and m are less than 10)
to multiply multiples of 10.

Date: 7/31/13

3.F.17

Name _____   Date _____

1. Use the chart to complete the equations. Then solve. The first one has been done for you.

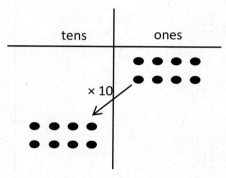

a.   (2 × 4) × 10

= (8 ones) × 10

= ___**80**___

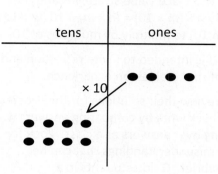

b.   2 × (4 × 10)

= 2 × (4 tens)

= _____

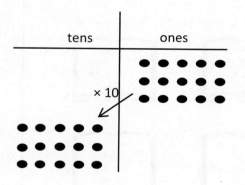

c.   (3 × 5) × 10

= (_____ ones) × 10

= _____

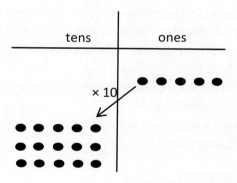

d.   3 × (5 × 10)

= 3 × (_____ tens)

= _____

COMMON CORE

Lesson 20:   Use place value strategies and the associative property
$n × (m × 10) = (n × m) × 10$ (where n and m are less than 10)
to multiply multiples of 10.

Date: 7/31/13

3.F.18

2. Place ( ) in the equations to find the related fact. Then solve. The first one has been done for you.

$2 \times 20 = 2 \times (2 \times 10)$

$= (2 \times 2) \times 10$

$= \underline{\textbf{4}} \times 10$

$= \underline{\textbf{40}}$

$2 \times 30 = 2 \times (3 \times 10)$

$= (2 \times 3) \times 10$

$= \underline{\hspace{1cm}} \times 10$

$= \underline{\hspace{1cm}}$

$3 \times 30 = 3 \times (3 \times 10)$

$= 3 \times 3 \times 10$

$= \underline{\hspace{1cm}} \times 10$

$= \underline{\hspace{1cm}}$

$2 \times 50 = 2 \times 5 \times 10$

$= 2 \times 5 \times 10$

$= \underline{\hspace{1cm}} \times 10$

$= \underline{\hspace{1cm}}$

3. Gabriella solves 20×4 by thinking about 10×8. Explain her strategy.

COMMON CORE

Lesson 20:   Use place value strategies and the associative property
$n \times (m \times 10) = (n \times m) \times 10$ (where n and m are less than 10)
to multiply multiples of 10.

Date: 7/31/13

3.F.19

Name _____ Date _____

1. Place ( ) in the equations to show how to use the associative property to find the related fact. Then solve.

   a. $4 \times 20 = 4 \times 2 \times 10$

   $= 4 \times 2 \times 10$

   $= \underline{\hspace{1cm}} \times 10$

   $= \underline{\hspace{1cm}}$

   b. $3 \times 30 = 3 \times 3 \times 10$

   $= 3 \times 3 \times 10$

   $= \underline{\hspace{1cm}} \times 10$

   $= \underline{\hspace{1cm}}$

2. Jamila solves 20×5 by thinking about 10 tens. Explain her strategy.

Name _____   Date _____

1. Use the chart to complete the equations. Then solve.

tens	ones
	●●●●●
	●●●●●

× 10 ↓

●●●●●
●●●●●

   a. (2 × 5) × 10

   = (10 ones) × 10

   = _____

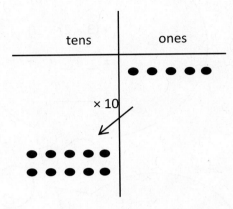

   b. 2 × (5 × 10)

   = 2 × (5 tens)

   = _____

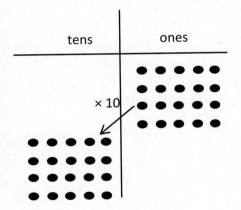

   c. (4 × 5) × 10

   = (_____ ones) × 10

   = _____

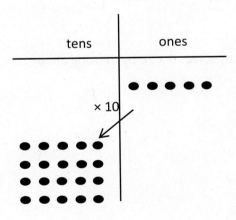

   d. 4 × (5 × 10)

   = 4 × (_____ tens)

   = _____

2. Solve. Place ( ) in (c) and (d) as needed to find the related fact.

a. $3 \times 20 = 3 \times (2 \times 10)$

   $= (3 \times 2) \times 10$

   $= \underline{\ 6\ } \times 10$

   $= \underline{\ \ \ \ \ }$

b. $3 \times 30 = 3 \times (3 \times 10)$

   $= (3 \times 3) \times 10$

   $= \underline{\ \ \ \ \ } \times 10$

   $= \underline{\ \ \ \ \ }$

c. $3 \times 40 = 3 \times (4 \times 10)$

   $= 3 \times 4 \times 10$

   $= \underline{\ \ \ \ \ } \times 10$

   $= \underline{\ \ \ \ \ }$

d. $3 \times 50 = 3 \times 5 \times 10$

   $= 3 \times 5 \times 10$

   $= \underline{\ \ \ \ \ } \times 10$

   $= \underline{\ \ \ \ \ }$

3. Danny solves 5×20 by thinking about 10×10. Explain his strategy.

Lesson 20: Use place value strategies and the associative property
$n \times (m \times 10) = (n \times m) \times 10$ (where n and m are less than 10)
to multiply multiples of 10.

Date: 7/31/13

3.F.22

Lesson 21

Objective: Solve two-step word problems involving multiplying single-digit factors and multiples of 10.

Suggested Lesson Structure

A NOTE ON STANDARDS ALIGNMENT:

This lesson incorporates the use of seconds in both the Concept Development and in the Problem Set. Students are familiar with seconds from G3–M2–Lesson 1, although they are included in the Grade 4 standard (**4.MD.1**). In this lesson the conversion between minutes and seconds is always provided when needed.

■ Fluency Practice   (15 minutes)
■ Concept Development   (35 minutes)
■ Student Debrief   (10 minutes)
   Total Time   **(60 minutes)**

Fluency Practice (15 minutes)

- Sprint: Multiply by Multiples of 10 **3.NBT.3** (9 minutes)
- Group Counting **3.OA.1**   (3 minutes)
- Write In the Parentheses **3.OA.7**   (3 minutes)

Sprint: Multiply by Multiples of 10 (9 minutes)

Materials: (S) Multiply by Multiples of 10 Sprint

Note: This Sprint reviews Lesson 19, multiplying single-digit numbers by multiples of 10.

Group Counting (3 minutes)

Note: Group counting reviews interpreting multiplication as repeated addition. These counts review multiplication taught earlier in the module. Direct students to count forward and backward, occasionally changing the direction of the count:

- Sixes to 60
- Sevens to 70
- Eights to 80
- Nines to 90

Write In the Parentheses (3 minutes)

Materials: (S) Personal white boards

Note: This fluency reviews Lesson 20.

T: (Write $2 \times 40 = 2 \times 4 \times 10$.) What's 2×40?

S: 80.

T: On your boards, copy the number sentence. Then write in parentheses and solve.

S: (Write $2 \times 40 = 2 \times 4 \times 10$. Beneath it, write $2 \times 40 = (2 \times 4) \times 10$). Beneath it, write $2 \times 40 = 8 \times 10$. Beneath it, write $2 \times 40 = 80$.

$2 \times 40 = 2 \times 4 \times 10$
$2 \times 40 = (2 \times 4) \times 10$
$2 \times 40 = 8 \times 10$
$2 \times 40 = 80$

Continue with the following possible sequence: $3 \times 30 = 3 \times 3 \times 10$ and $2 \times 50 = 2 \times 5 \times 10$.

Concept Development (35 minutes)

Materials: (T) Stopwatch, Multiples of 10 multiplication cards (S) Personal white boards

Place one card face down on each student's desk. When you say, "Go," each student solves his problem and then lines up with the entire class, ordering products from least to greatest. Instruct students to complete these tasks silently and quickly. Let them know that you will time them and that extra time will be added as a penalty if they are too noisy.

T: It took you *4* minutes and *13* seconds to find the products and order them from least to greatest. How do we find the total number of seconds it took to complete this activity?

S: Add the total seconds in 4 minutes to 13 seconds. → We need to know how many seconds are in 1 minute first.

T: There are 60 seconds in 1 minute. Draw and label a tape diagram to show the total number of seconds in 4 minutes. Label the unknown as *n*. Then check with a partner.

S: (Draw and label. Then check with a partner.)

T: Write an equation. Then solve.

S: (Write $4 \times 60 = n$, $n = 240$.)

T: Discuss with a partner the strategy you used to solve 4×60.

T: (After discussion, call on some to share.)

S: I thought of it as 4×6 tens, which equals 24 tens. And 24 tens is 240. → I thought of it as $(4 \times 6) \times 10$, which is 24×10, which equals 240. → It's like 24 tens is 10 tens + 10 tens + 4 tens or 100 + 100 + 40 = 240.

T: Four minutes is equal to how many seconds?

S: 240 seconds.

T: Whisper the next step to your partner.

S: (Add 13 seconds to 240 seconds.)

![A NOTE ON STANDARDS ALIGNMENT:]
A NOTE ON STANDARDS ALIGNMENT:

The time used in this problem, 4 minutes and 13 seconds, is an arbitrary time used to demonstrate how to solve this problem. Be sure to use the actual time it takes the class to complete the activity. Seconds are part of the Grade 4 standard **4.MD.1.**

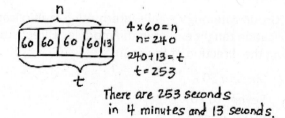

$4 \times 60 = n$
$n = 240$
$240 + 13 = t$
$t = 253$

There are 253 seconds in 4 minutes and 13 seconds.

COMMON CORE

Lesson 21:   Solve two-step word problems involving multiplying single-digit factors and multiples of 10.

Date: 7/31/13

3.F.24

T: Add that to your diagram and label the total number of seconds using a letter for the unknown. Then solve for *t*. How many seconds did it take you to complete the activity?

S: 253 seconds!

Project the following problems on the board and invite students to problem solve independently or in pairs using the RDW process:

MP.1

- Each day Andrea does 25 squats to warm up for gymnastics practice and 15 squats to cool down after practice. How many squats does she do in all when she practices Monday through Friday?

- Benny gets $5 a week for allowance. After saving his money for 20 weeks, how much more does Benny need to buy a bike that costs $108?

- Genevieve makes 43 bracelets. She gives 13 bracelets away as gifts and sells the rest for $4 each. How much money does Genevieve make in all?

The above problems represent a variety of two-step word problems and will provide varied practice for the students.

Problem Set (15 minutes)

Students should do their personal best to complete the Problem Set within the allotted 10 minutes. For some classes, it may be appropriate to modify the assignment by specifying which problems they work on first. Some problems do not specify a method for solving. Students solve these problems using the RDW approach used for Application Problems.

NOTES ON MULTIPLE MEANS OF ENGAGEMENT:

Give English language learners and others practice reading aloud the word problems on the Problem Set. Have students read the problems to their partners and paraphrase what the question asks them to find to help with understanding.

Student Debrief (10 minutes)

Lesson Objective: Solve two-step word problems involving multiplying single-digit factors and multiples of 10.

The Student Debrief is intended to invite reflection and active processing of the total lesson experience.

Invite students to review their solutions for the Problem Set. They should check work by comparing answers with a partner before going over answers as a class. Look for misconceptions or misunderstandings that can be addressed in the Debrief. Guide students in a conversation to debrief the Problem Set and process the lesson.

You may choose to use any combination of the questions below to lead the discussion.

- In Problem 2, how many more months will Lupe

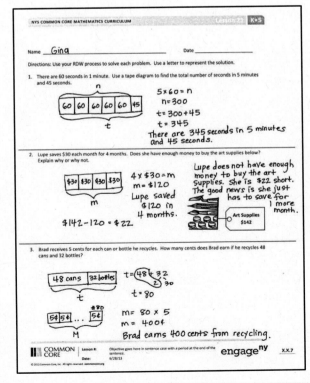

| Lesson 21: | Solve two-step word problems involving multiplying single-digit factors and multiples of 10. |
| Date: | 7/31/13 |

3.F.25

© 2013 Common Core, Inc. All rights reserved. commoncore.org

need to save so she has enough to buy the art supplies? How do you know?

- In Problem 3, how many dollars does Brad earn? You may want prompt students by asking how many cents are in 1 dollar.

- Discuss the second step of Problem 4 with a partner. How was this different than the other problems? Explain how you could you solve it with multiplication.

- Explain how you needed to find three unknowns to complete Problem 5.

- Explain to a partner how you solved Problem 6. Explain how you could have used the multiplying by 10 strategy to help you solve this problem.

Exit Ticket (3 minutes)

After the Student Debrief, instruct students to complete the Exit Ticket. A review of their work will help you assess the students' understanding of the concepts that were presented in the lesson today and plan more effectively for future lessons. You may read the questions aloud to the students.

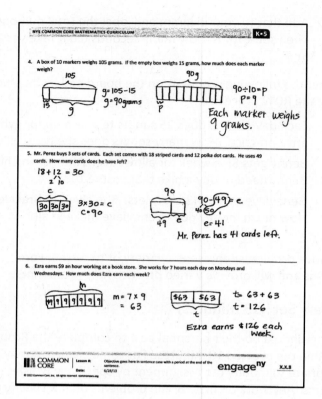

A

Correct _____

Multiply.

1	2 x 3 =		23	8 x 40 =	
2	2 x 30 =		24	80 x 4 =	
3	20 x 3 =		25	9 x 6 =	
4	2 x 2 =		26	90 x 6 =	
5	2 x 20 =		27	2 x 5 =	
6	20 x 2 =		28	2 x 50 =	
7	4 x 2 =		29	3 x 90 =	
8	4 x 20 =		30	40 x 7 =	
9	40 x 2 =		31	5 x 40 =	
10	5 x 3 =		32	6 x 60 =	
11	50 x 3 =		33	70 x 6 =	
12	3 x 50 =		34	8 x 70 =	
13	4 x 4 =		35	80 x 6 =	
14	40 x 4 =		36	9 x 70 =	
15	4 x 40 =		37	50 x 6 =	
16	6 x 3 =		38	8 x 80 =	
17	6 x 30 =		39	9 x 80 =	
18	60 x 3 =		40	60 x 8 =	
19	7 x 5 =		41	70 x 7 =	
20	70 x 5 =		42	5 x 80 =	
21	7 x 50 =		43	60 x 9 =	
22	8 x 4 =		44	9 x 90 =	

© Bill Davidson

Lesson 21:	Solve two-step word problems involving multiplying single-digit factors and multiples of 10.
Date:	7/31/13

3.F.27

B

Improvement _____   # Correct _____

Multiply.

1	4 x 2 =		23	9 x 40 =	
2	4 x 20 =		24	90 x 4 =	
3	40 x 2 =		25	8 x 6 =	
4	3 x 3 =		26	80 x 6 =	
5	3 x 30 =		27	5 x 2 =	
6	30 x 3 =		28	5 x 20 =	
7	3 x 2 =		29	3 x 80 =	
8	3 x 20 =		30	40 x 8 =	
9	30 x 2 =		31	4 x 50 =	
10	5 x 5 =		32	8 x 80 =	
11	50 x 5 =		33	90 x 6 =	
12	5 x 50 =		34	6 x 70 =	
13	4 x 3 =		35	60 x 6 =	
14	40 x 3 =		36	7 x 70 =	
15	4 x 30 =		37	60 x 5 =	
16	7 x 3 =		38	6 x 80 =	
17	7 x 30 =		39	7 x 80 =	
18	70 x 3 =		40	80 x 6 =	
19	6 x 4 =		41	90 x 7 =	
20	60 x 4 =		42	8 x 50 =	
21	6 x 40 =		43	80 x 9 =	
22	9 x 4 =		44	7 x 90 =	

© Bill Davidson

Lesson 21: Solve two-step word problems involving multiplying single-digit factors and multiples of 10.

Date: 7/31/13

3.F.28

30 × 6 =	9 × 60 =	40 × 2 =	10 × 6 =
70 × 3 =	50 × 6 =	80 × 9 =	20 × 5 =
8 × 30 =	3 × 30 =	5 × 50 =	4 × 40 =
6 × 80 =	70 × 7 =	20 × 7 =	10 × 7 =
90 × 7 =	2 × 60 =	50 × 7 =	80 × 5 =
60 × 6 =	9 × 50 =	30 × 9 =	4 × 80 =

COMMON CORE

Lesson 21:   Solve two-step word problems involving multiplying single-digit factors and multiples of 10.

Date: 7/31/13

3.F.29

Name _____ Date _____

Directions: Use the RDW process to solve each problem. Use a letter to represent the solution.

1. There are 60 seconds in 1 minute. Use a tape diagram to find the total number of seconds in 5 minutes and 45 seconds.

2. Lupe saves $30 each month for 4 months. Does she have enough money to buy the art supplies below? Explain why or why not.

Art Supplies
$142

3. Brad receives 5 cents for each can or bottle he recycles. How many cents does Brad earn if he recycles 48 cans and 32 bottles?

COMMON CORE | Lesson 21: | Solve two-step word problems involving multiplying single-digit factors and multiples of 10.
Date: | 7/31/13

3.F.30

4. A box of 10 markers weighs 105 grams. If the empty box weighs 15 grams, how much does each marker weigh?

5. Mr. Perez buys 3 sets of cards. Each set comes with 18 striped cards and 12 polka dot cards. He uses 49 cards. How many cards does he have left?

6. Ezra earns $9 an hour working at a book store. She works for 7 hours each day on Mondays and Wednesdays. How much does Ezra earn each week?

COMMON CORE

| Lesson 21: | Solve two-step word problems involving multiplying single-digit factors and multiples of 10. |
| Date: | 7/31/13 |

3.F.31

Name _____ Date _____

Directions: Use the RDW process to solve. Use a letter to represent the unknown.

Frederick buys a can of 3 tennis balls. The empty can weighs 20 grams and each tennis ball weighs 60 grams. What is the total weight of the can with 3 tennis balls?

Lesson 21:	Solve two-step word problems involving multiplying single-digit factors and multiples of 10.
Date:	7/31/13

3.F.32

Name _____   Date _____

Directions: Use the RDW process for each problem. Use a letter to represent the solution.

1. There are 60 minutes in 1 hour. Use a tape diagram to find the total number of minutes in 6 hours and 15 minutes.

2. Ms. Lemus buys 7 boxes of snacks. Each box has 12 packets of fruit snacks and 18 packets of cashews. How many snacks did she buy altogether?

3. Tamara wants to buy a tablet that costs $437. She saves $50 a month for 9 months. Does she have enough money to buy the tablet? Explain why or why not.

Lesson 21:	Solve two-step word problems involving multiplying single-digit factors and multiples of 10.
Date:	7/31/13

3.F.33

4. Mr. Ramirez receives 4 sets of books. Each set has 16 fiction books and 14 non-fiction books. He puts 97 books in his library and donates the rest of his books. How many books does he donate?

---

5. Celia sells calendars for a fundraiser. Each calendar costs $9. She sells 16 calendars to her family members and 14 calendars to the people in her neighborhood. Her goal is to earn $300. Does Celia reach her goal? Explain your answer.

---

6. The video store sells science and history movies for $5 each. How much money does the video store make if it sells 33 science movies and 57 history movies?

| Lesson 21: | Solve two-step word problems involving multiplying single-digit factors and multiples of 10. |
| Date: | 7/31/13 |

3.F.34

Name _____   Date _____

1. The carnival is in town for 21 days. How many weeks is the carnival in town? (There are 7 days in 1 week). Write an equation and solve.

2. There are 48 liters needed to finish filling the dunk tank at the carnival. Each container holds 8 liters. How many containers are needed to finish filling the dunk tank? Represent the problem using multiplication and division sentences and a letter for the unknown. Solve.

    _____ × _____ = _____

    _____ ÷ _____ = _____

3. There are 4 rows of 7 chairs setup for the Magic Show. A worker sees the large number of people lined up and doubles the number of rows of chairs. They are shown below.

    Explain and label to show how the array represents both 8 × 7 and 2 × (4 × 7).

    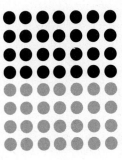

4.

a. Fabrizio wins a bumble-bee doll with 6 stripes. He notices that 5 other children in line for the Magic Show won the same doll. How many stripes are on 6 bumble-bee dolls? Write an equation using a letter to represent the unknown. Solve.

b. The magician uses a magic box. Every time he puts an object in, it gets multiplied. Fabrizio writes down what happens to try and find a pattern. Look at his notes to the right.

- Use the pattern to fill in the number of bean bags.
- What does the magic box do? Explain how you know.

In	Out
2 Feathers	14 Feathers
3 Marbles	21 Marbles
4 Dice	28 Dice
5 Wands	35 Wands
6 Bean bags	____ Bean bags

c. The magician puts 12 rings into the magic box. Fabrizio draws a number bond to find the total number of rings that come out. Use the number bond to show how Fabrizio solved the problem.

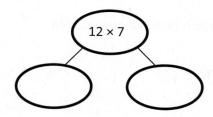

d. After the show, Fabrizio and 5 friends equally share the cost of a $54 magic set. They use the equation $6 \times n = \$54$ to figure out how much each person pays. How much does Fabrizio pay?

Mid- Module Assessment Task	Topics A–C
Standards Addressed	

Represent and solve problems involving multiplication and division.

3.OA.3   Use multiplication and division within 100 to solve word problems in situations involving equal groups, arrays, and measurement quantities, e.g., by using drawings and equations with a symbol for the unknown number to represent the problem. (See Glossary, Table 2.)

3.OA.4   Determine the unknown whole number in a multiplication or division equation relating three whole numbers. *For example, determine the unknown number that makes the equation true in each of the equations 8 × ? = 48, 5 = _ ÷ 3, 6 × 6 = ?.*

Understand properties of multiplication and the relationship between multiplication and division.

3.OA.5   Apply properties of operations as strategies to multiply and divide. (Students need not use formal terms for these properties.) *Examples: If 6 × 4 = 24 is known, then 4 × 6 = 24 is also known. (Commutative property of multiplication.) 3 × 5 × 2 can be found by 3 × 5 = 15, then 15 × 2 = 30, or by 5 × 2 = 10, then 3 × 10 = 30. (Associative property of multiplication.) Knowing that 8 × 5 = 40 and 8 × 2 = 16, one can find 8 × 7 as 8 × (5 + 2) = (8 × 5) + (8 × 2) = 40 + 16 = 56. (Distributive property.)*

Multiply and divide within 100.

3.OA.7   Fluently multiply and divide within 100, using strategies such as the relationship between multiplication and division (e.g., knowing that 8 × 5 = 40, one knows 40 ÷ 5 = 8) or properties of operations. By the end of Grade 3, know from memory all products of two one-digit numbers.

Solve problems involving the four operations, and identify and explain patterns in arithmetic.

3.OA.9   Identify arithmetic patterns (including patterns in the addition table or multiplication table), and explain them using properties of operations. *For example, observe that 4 times a number is always even, and explain why 4 times a number can be decomposed into two equal addends.*

Evaluating Student Learning Outcomes

A Progression Toward Mastery is provided to describe steps that illuminate the gradually increasing understandings that students develop *on their way to proficiency.* In this chart, this progress is presented from left (Step 1) to right (Step 4). The learning goal for each student is to achieve Step 4 mastery. These steps are meant to help teachers and students identify and celebrate what the student CAN do now and what they need to work on next.

Module 3:	Multiplication and Division with Units of 0, 1, 6–9, and Multiples of 10	
Date:	7/31/13	**3.S.3**

A Progression Toward Mastery

Assessment Task Item and Standards Assessed	STEP 1 Little evidence of reasoning without a correct answer. (1 Point)	STEP 2 Evidence of some reasoning without a correct answer. (2 Points)	STEP 3 Evidence of some reasoning with a correct answer or evidence of solid reasoning with an incorrect answer. (3 Points)	STEP 4 Evidence of solid reasoning with a correct answer. (4 Points)
1 **3.OA.3** **3.OA.4**	Student is unable to write an equation for the problem. The attempt shows the student may not understand the meaning of the question.	The student mixes up the order of numbers in the division sentence (e.g., $21 \div 3 = ?$).	The student writes the correct equation, but divides incorrectly (e.g., $21 \div 7$ = wrong answer).	The student correctly: • Writes $21 \div 7 = 3$ • Identifies that the answer represents the number of weeks.
2 **3.OA.3** **3.OA.4**	Student is unable to answer any part of the question correctly. The attempt shows the student may not understand the meaning of the questions.	The student gives an incorrect answer with reasonable attempt that must include: • Attempt to represent the problem with multiplication and division equations. • Use of a letter to represent the unknown.	Student provides partially correct answer. Student must: • Write $n \times 8$ liters = 48 liters. • Write 48 liters $\div$ 8 liters = n.	The student correctly: • Writes $n \times 8$ liters = 48 liters. • Writes 48 liters $\div$ 8 liters = n. • Solves to find 6 containers.
3 **3.OA.5**	Student is unable to explain and label how the array represents both expressions.	Student attempts to explain and label how the array represents one of the expressions.	Student accurately labels how the array represents both expressions, but explanation lacks clarity.	Student accurately explains and labels how the array represents both expressions, showing understanding of the associative property of multiplication.

A Progression Toward Mastery

4 3.OA.3 3.OA.4 3.OA.5 3.OA.9	Student answers one question correctly.	Student answers two questions correctly.	Student answers three questions correctly. Mistakes may include: ■ Completing the number sentence in Part (a) incorrectly (e.g. $6 \times 6 = n$; $n =$ wrong answer). ■ Providing inaccurate explanation in Part (b). ■ Providing incorrect total in Part (c) (e.g., $12 \times 7 =$ wrong total).	The student correctly: ■ Writes and solves an equation using a letter to represent the total number of stripes in Part (a) ($6 \times 6 = b$; $b = 36$). ■ Accurately explains how the magic box multiplies objects by 7 in Part (b). ■ Fills in 42 bean bags in the chart in Part (b). ■ Uses a number bond to break apart the 12×7 and distribute to find the total number of rings, 84 in Part (c). ■ Writes $n =$ \$9 in Part (d).

Name _____Gina_____   Date _____

1. The carnival is in town for 21 days. How many weeks is the carnival in town? (There are 7 days in 1 week). Write an equation and solve.

   7, 14, 21 $21 \div 7 = 3$
   ① ② ③

   The carnival is in town for 3 weeks.

2. There are 48 liters needed to finish filling the dunk tank at the carnival. Each container holds 8 liters. How many containers are needed to finish filling the dunk tank? Represent the problem using multiplication and division sentences and a letter for the unknown. Solve.

   $\underline{n} \times \underline{8} = \underline{48}$
   $\underline{48} \div \underline{8} = \underline{n}$

   n = the number of containers
   n = 6
   6 containers are needed to finish filling the dunk tank.

3. There are 4 rows of 7 chairs setup for the Magic Show. A worker sees the large number of people lined up and doubles the number of rows of chairs. They are shown below.

   Explain and label to show how the array represents both 8 × 7 and 2 × (4 × 7).

   8×7   4 × 7   4 × 7

   You can see the array 2 ways. You can see the total array as 8 rows of 7, or you can see 4 rows of 7 two times (the black rows and gray rows.) They both have the same total of 56 chairs.

4.

a. Fabrizio wins a bumble-bee doll with 6 stripes. He notices that 5 other children in line for the Magic Show won the same doll. How many stripes are on 6 bumble-bee dolls? Write an equation using a letter to represent the unknown. Solve.

$6 \times 6 = b$ b = the total number of stripes.
$b = 36$
There are 36 stripes on 6 bumble-bee dolls.

b. The magician uses a magic box. Every time he puts an object in, it gets multiplied. Fabrizio writes down what happens to try and find a pattern. Look at his notes to the right.

- Use the pattern to fill in the number of bean bags.
- What does the magic box do? Explain how you know.

In	Out	
2 Feathers	14 Feathers	+7
3 Marbles	21 Marbles	+7
4 Dice	28 Dice	+7
5 Wands	35 Wands	+7
6 Bean bags	_42_ Bean bags	

The objects that come out are multiplied by 7. Any time you put in an object, it grows by 7 times. That's how we know 6 bean bags will come out as 42 bean bags.

c. The magician puts 12 rings into the magic box. Fabrizio draws a number bond to find the total number of rings that come out. Use the number bond to show how Fabrizio solved the problem.

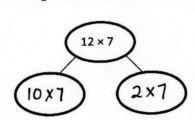

$(10 \times 7) + (2 \times 7) = 12 \times 7$
$70 + 14 = 84$
When the magician puts 12 rings into the magic box, 84 rings will come out.

d. After the show, Fabrizio and 5 friends equally share the cost of a $54 magic set. They use the equation $6 \times n = \$54$ to figure out how much each person pays. How much does Fabrizio pay?

$6 \times n = \$54$ is the same as $54 \div 6 = n$,
where n = the amount each person pays.
$n = \$9$

Fabrizio pays $9.

COMMON CORE | Module 3: | Multiplication and Division with Units of 0, 1, 6–9, and Multiples of 10   3.S.7
Date: | 7/31/13

© 2013 Common Core, Inc. All rights reserved. commoncore.org

Name _____   Date _____

1. Aunt Korina and her 3 friends decide to share a cab and go to the mall. If they each spent $6, how much did the cab ride cost altogether? Write an equation using a letter to represent the unknown. Solve.

2. Aunt Korina's 3 friends each order pasta and a lemonade for lunch. Aunt Korina orders only chicken salad.

   a. Use the menu to find how much they spend altogether. Write equations using letters to represent the unknown. Solve.

Lunch Menu	
Pasta	$7
Chicken Salad	$9
Lemonade	$2

   b. Aunt Korina mentally checks the total using $9 × 4. Explain her strategy.

3. After lunch the friends notice a sale. Compare the crossed out prices to the new sale prices. If all sale prices are calculated in the same way, what would the sale price be on an item that originally cost $24? Use words and equations to explain how you know.

  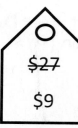 

$12 $21 $27 $3

$4 $7 $9 $1